The Arab States of the Gulf and BRICS: New Strategic Partnerships in Politics and Economics

The Gulf Research Center Book Series at Gerlach Press

The GCC in the Global Economy
Ed. by Richard Youngs
ISBN 9783940924018, 2012

Resources Blessed:Diversification and the Gulf Development Model
Ed. by Giacomo Luciani
ISBN 9783940924025, 2012

GCC Financial Markets:The World's New Money Centers
Ed. by Eckart Woertz
ISBN 9783940924032, 2012

National Employment, Migration and Education in the GCC
Ed. by Steffen Hertog
ISBN 9783940924049, 2012

Asia-Gulf Economic Relations in the 21st Century: The Local to Global Transformation
Ed. by Tim Niblock with Monica Malik
ISBN 9783940924100, 2013

A New Gulf Security Architecture: Prospects and Challenges for an Asian Role
Ed. by Ranjit Gupta, Abubaker Bagader, Talmiz Ahmad and N. Janardhan
ISBN 9783940924360, 2014

Gulf Charities and Islamic Philanthropy in the 'Age of Terror' and Beyond
Ed. by Robert Lacey and Jonathan Benthall
ISBN 9783940924322, 2014

State-Society Relations in the Arab Gulf States
Ed. by Mazhar Al-Zoby and Birol Baskan
ISBN 9783940924384, 2014

Political Economy of Energy Reform:The Clean Energy-Fossil Fuel Balance in the Gulf
Ed. by Giacomo Luciani and Rabia Ferroukhi
ISBN 9783940924407, 2014

The Silent Revolution: The Arab Spring and the Gulf States
Ed. by May Seikaly and Khawla Mattar
ISBN 9783940924346, 2014

Security Dynamics of East Asia in the Gulf Region
Ed. by Tim Niblock with Yang Guang
ISBN 9783940924483, 2014

Islamic Finance: Political Economy, Performance and Risk
Ed. by Mehmet Asutay and Abdullah Turkistani
ISBN 9783940924124, 3 vols set, 2015

Gulf Research Centre Cambridge
Knowledge for All

Employment and Career Motivation in the Arab Gulf States: The Rentier Mentality Revisited
Ed. by Annika Kropf and Mohamed Ramady
ISBN 9783940924605, 2015

The Changing Energy Landscape in the Gulf:Strategic Implications
Ed. by Gawdat Bahgat
ISBN 9783940924643, 2015

Sustainable Development Challenges in the Arab States of the Gulf
Ed. by David Bryde, Yusra Mouzughi and Turki Al Rasheed
ISBN 9783940924629, 2015

The United States and the Gulf:Shifting Pressures, Strategies and Alignments
Ed. by Steven W. Hook and Tim Niblock
ISBN 9783940924667, 2015

Africa and the Gulf Region:Blurred Boundaries and Shifting Ties
Ed. by Rogaia Mustafa Abusharaf and Dale F. Eickelman
ISBN 9783940924704, 2015

Rebuilding Yemen: Political, Economic and Social Challenges
Ed. by Noel Brehony and Saud Al-Sarhan
ISBN 9783940924681, 2015

Science and Technology Development in the Gulf States:Economic Diversification through Regional Collaboration
Ed. by Afreen Siddiqi and Laura Diaz Anadon
ISBN 9783959940023, 2016

Higher Education in the Arab States of the Gulf:Linkages and Interdependence
Ed. by Dale Eickelman and Rogaia Mustafa Abusharaf
ISBN 9783959940122, 2016

Iran's Relations with the Arab States of the Gulf: Common Interests over Historic Rivalry
Ed. by Maaike Warnaar, Luciano Zaccara and Paul Aarts
ISBN 9783959940047, 2016

Egypt and the Gulf: A Renewed Regional Policy Alliance
Ed. by Robert Mason
ISBN 9783959940061, 2016

Intellectual Property Rights:Development and Enforcement in the Arab States of the Gulf
Ed. by David Price
ISBN 9783959940108, 2016

The Arab States of the Gulf and BRICS:New Strategic Partnerships in Geopolitcs and Economics
Ed. by Tim Niblock, Alejandra Galindo and Degang Sun
ISBN 9783959940085, 2016

The Arms Trade, Military Services and the Security Market in the Gulf States: Trends and Implications
Ed. by David B. Des Roches and Dania Thafer
ISBN 9783959940160, 2016

The Arab States of the Gulf and BRICS: New Strategic Partnerships in Politics and Economics

Edited by Tim Niblock
with Degang Sun and Alejandra Galindo

GerlachPress

First published 2016
by Gerlach Press Berlin, Germany
www.gerlach-press.de

Cover Design: www.brandnewdesign.de, Hamburg
Printed and bound in Germany by Hubert & Co, Göttingen
www.hubertundco.de

British Library Cataloguing in Publication Data.
A catalogue record for this book is available from the British Library.

Bibliographic data available from Deutsche Nationalbibliothek
http://d-nb.info/1104276267

ISBN: 978-3-95994-008-5 (hardcover)
ISBN: 978-3-95994-009-2 (ebook)

Contents

List of Tables

Introduction

Tim Niblock

All of the BRICS countries have undergone setbacks, economic or political, since the time when the term "BRIC" was first coined. The latter date was 2001 and, as is well known, it was introduced by the Goldman Sachs economist Jim O'Neill in a paper entitled "Building Better Global BRICS".[1] The term covered the major emerging economies whose growth had been particularly impressive in the late 1990s and at the turn of the century and which, it was confidently predicted, would take a growing proportion of global trade in the early years of the 21st century.

While the economies maintained high rates of growth through the first decade of the 21st century, and into the second, the confident predictions of continued exponential expansion have looked less well-based in recent years. Indeed, in two of the BRICS countries (Russia and Brazil) GDP actually declined in 2015, and is expected to decline further in 2016.[2] The South African economy has, over the period since the late 1990s, generally registered more modest rates of growth than those of the other BRICS countries, and the current rate of growth (while positive) is nonetheless low.[3] The major part of BRICS growth over the past 10 years has come from China and India. India's record of economic expansion has generally been less consistent than China's, although in 2015 its growth rate exceeded China's by a narrow margin. It is expected to retain that small marginal lead over the next few years.[4] China's rapid growth rate has been relatively consistent over the past 25 years, but it is clear that this – albeit remaining very high by international comparison – will be rather more modest in the years ahead.[5]

Issues of governance and international conflict have also caused some (primarily Western) observers to re-assess the earlier optimistic projections of the future of the BRICS countries. Without political stability, neither the political nor the economic future looks so assured. The sanctions imposed on Russia following its occupation of Crimea, the impeachment proceedings against President Roussef in Brazil, the possibility of conflict over territorial claims in the China seas, the weaknesses in governance structures in India, and the deep social and economic divisions in South Africa, are all cited as possible threats to future stability.

Contrary to what some observers have asserted, however, these economic and political developments (whether or not they constitute realistic grounds for revising earlier projections, which may be doubted) do not impinge negatively on the future BRICS as an organisation. Indeed, it could be argued that the reverse is true. The global and domestic pressures facing the BRICS governments may give them added incentive to work together, reinforcing both their global positions and their domestic support. This, indeed, is what has occurred in practice. Since 2012 BRICS as an organisation has steadily become stronger. At each of the annual summit meetings, a new range of coordinating measures is agreed, new institutions for financial cooperation and coordination are agreed, and new dimensions of cross-BRICS social interaction (academic, business, trade union, professional etc) are initiated. The scope of the international issues on which common positions are taken, furthermore, expands steadily.[6]

BRICS has never been simply a gathering of states which have a high rate of growth. From the outset, and increasingly over the years which have followed, BRICS's activities and objectives have interwoven political and economic dimensions. Political means, in the form of intergovernmental coordination and common action in international fora, are needed so as to achieve even "purely economic" objectives. Ensuring that the international economy caters for the interests of emerging markets and developing countries requires, in other words, a coordinated campaign – together with the organisational structures at every level which make such a campaign possible. This is what BRICS has been steadily developing since its formation.

A further aspect of BRICS's increasing significance and vitality has been the growing linkages between BRICS and other organisations or groupings which are similarly committed to promoting cooperation among some of the BRICS members. BRICS's formation, indeed, owed much to two pre-existing (and continuing) groupings: the Shanghai Cooperation Organisation (with primarily security concerns) and the India Brazil South Africa Dialogue Forum (with its strong commitment to South-South cooperation). The inclusion of India and Pakistan in the Shanghai Cooperation Organisation (from 2016), creates a new area of overlap between BRICS and the SCO. China's One Belt One Road initiative is also engendering a new dynamic to relations among at least some of the BRICS countries. The prospective injection of massive financial backing for the construction of a transport and communications network which will shape a new

Eurasian entity – with the maritime dimension stretching down into Africa – is of global significance.

How the Gulf Cooperation Council (GCC) relates to BRICS is, in the light of the growing strength and importance of this organisation and the countries which comprise it, of critical importance. The GCC countries have fast-growing economies, and they share some of the attributes and concerns of BRICS countries. The issue is not simply how the GCC countries handle their relations with the individual BRICS countries, but more importantly how they relate to what is emerging as an alternative structure of coordination and perhaps power in the global order. Their established links and alliances may no longer be enough to satisfy either their economic needs or their security concerns.

This, then, is the objective of this book: to examine the commonalities and the differences in economic and political interest between the BRICS countries and the GCC countries, so as to assess the potential for cooperation and collective action. Whether the GCC could itself become a part of BRICS is also worth consideration. The title of the book refers to the Gulf as a whole rather than the GCC specifically, and this is deliberate. While the focus is on the GCC, the GCC's relations with BRICS countries have been, and will continue to be, closely affected by the wider Gulf dimension – the state of their relations with Iran and Iraq, and the manner in which BRICS countries relate to those two countries.

Chapter One, "The Dynamics of the BRICS Grouping: Convergences and Disparities with the GCC's Global Posture and Stance", by the editor, sets out the background and analytical framework relevant to the chapters which follow. It first examines the dynamics of the BRICS grouping, the factors which created it, and the range of activities and concerns which it has developed. Then the overlap with the GCC is considered: the extent to which the GCC countries share the BRICS countries' characteristics and concerns. The chapter concludes that BRICS and the GCC have strong reason to engage with each other, although neither side could viably envisage GCC membership of BRICS.

Chapter Two, "GCC-BRICS Strategic Cooperation in the New Era: The Dual Implications of Geoeconomics and Geopolitics", by Degang Sun, locates the rationale of BRICS-GCC cooperation within the wider context of changes in the global economic and political orders. The extent to which the two sides share common interests within this changing global environment is given emphasis, as also are the far-reaching cooperative links which already exist between them. He concludes that GCC-BRICS cooperation could help to transform the century-long western global governance to a more balanced and multi-faceted "East-West co-governance".

Chapter Three, "Taking BRICS to the GCC: Shaping an Indian Initiative to Promote a BRICS Role in the Gulf Security Scenario", by Talmiz Ahmad, is also set within the context of the changing global order, focusing in this case on how this impinges on the security needs of the GCC states. All the BRICS countries – but particularly China and India - have an abiding stake in West Asian security, due not only to their substantial energy and economic ties, but also in wider strategic concerns linked to their nationals' presence in the region, terrorism, extremism, sectarianism, drugs and arms trafficking and piracy. Rather than compete for position, the interests of BRICS countries are best served by a collective BRICS diplomatic initiative aimed at finding solutions to divisions within the Gulf region – especially those between Iran and Saudi Arabia. India could take the lead in bringing the BRICS countries together for such an initiative.

Chapter Four, "GCC and BRICS: Exploring the Nuclear Energy Cooperation Route", by Stuti Bannerjee, looks at another field of GCC-BRICS interaction where BRICS countries have a choice between competition and cooperation: civil nuclear energy. The GCC countries do not at present have the human expertise or the technical knowledge to build or operate nuclear plants, but most of them have a clear intention of developing civil nuclear energy. The BRICS countries all have suitable expertise, at least for enabling parts of such a development to come to fruition. Rather than compete against each other, they have a collective interest in working together to aid the development of the GCC programmes in civil nuclear energy, within a cooperative framework where there is transparency and adequate safeguards to prevent civil nuclear energy being transferred to military uses.

Chapter Five, "United Arab Emirates and Brazil: Ideas, Perceptions and Perspectives of Unlikely Allies", by Vania Carvalho Pinto and Danielly Ramos Becard, examines an area of perhaps-unexpected and little publicised commonality between a GCC country and a BRICS country: that of humanitarian discourse. The UAE and Brazil both seek to project themselves internationally as law abiding, trustworthy and ethical countries, where engagement in humanitarian undertakings regionally and sometimes internationally forms an important part in how they situate themselves in global politics. The writers examine and compare Brazilian engagement in Haiti, and UAE engagement in Afghanistan, showing that the two countries have adopted similar approaches and promoted similar ideas – even though the elements they emphasise are derived from different cultural worlds.

Chapter Six, "Russia and the GCC Countries: Hard to be Friends but Impossible to Remain Foes", by Nikolay Kozhanov, focuses on Russia as a key BRICS country whose relations with GCC have followed an uneven path, where periods of developing amity are followed by quasi-confrontational phases arising mainly from different policies and approaches in the regional and wider global contexts. What is, at first sight, surprising is the speed with which apparently sharp divisions can lead back to attempts to create a closer relationship – even when the policy differences in the regional and international spheres continue. The reality is that, despite there being relatively little trade between Russia and the GCC, they are brought together by a complex of economic, strategic and international concerns. In spite of the contradictions between them on a variety of issues, neither side intends to "cross red lines which would deprive them of rapprochement".

Chapter Seven, "India in BRICS and Indo-GCC Relations: Assessing Conflicts and Complementarities", by Shanthie Dsouza and Bibhu Prasad Routray, brings out the specific individuality of India's position in BRICS, characterised by a strong and increasing commitment to remain engagement with the West while at the same time maintaining its strategic autonomy. BRICS, in fact, serves India as a balancing association, providing for cooperative relations with Russia and China at the same time as new engagements with the United States are explored. With regard to the GCC, India needs to engage with its extended neighbourhood more productively if it is to play the role of a major world power. It can work together with other BRICS countries in this regard, or it could pursue a more competitive strategy. Which approach is chosen will have a big impact on the Gulf region, as also on India's economic and political standing in the world.

Chapter Eight, "China's One Belt One Road Initiative and its Strategic Connections with Arab Countries in the Gulf", by Tingyi Wang, provides an up-to-date and detailed account of the OBOR initiative, bringing out clearly the impact which the Silk Road Economic Belt and the 21st Century Maritime Silk Road will have on the restructuring of a major portion of global trade, with critical effects on the development of countries across Central Asia and around the Indian Ocean. The strong links which already exist between China and the GCC states provide a basis for the latter to engage with, and perhaps work, with China in developing and implementing the initiative – in collaboration perhaps with other Asian countries with strong interests in the Gulf such as India and Pakistan. Whether the GCC will respond to the opportunities available remains to be seen.

Chapter Nine, "In Search of a Strategic Partnership: China-Qatar Energy Cooperation, from 1988 to 2015", by Gafar K. Ahmed, looks at how the relationship between one BRICS country, China, and one GCC country, Qatar, developed over a period where the two countries gradually worked towards a strategic partnership – facing considerable difficulties along the way. The importance of the chapter comes in part from the position of the writer as an "insider" – serving as an adviser to the Qatar Embassy in Beijing over the crucial periods of disagreement and finally agreement with the Chinese side. He makes use of documentary sources which were available to him in that capacity. His conclusion for the wider BRICS-GCC context is important: that GCC countries should focus on the value of building long-term strategic relations in those fields which are significant to both sides, and then use these as a basis for creating a wider strategic relationship encompassing full-going political, economic and perhaps military relations.

Chapter Ten, "A GCC-China Security 'Strategic Partnership': Its Potential and Contours", by Imad Mansour, focuses primarily on how closer strategic relations with China are seen from the perspective of GCC countries. He brings out clearly the shared interests which the two sides have but at the same time recognises the extent to which GCC security interests are critically dependent on the existing links with the United States. He also examines other issues where the approaches taken by the Chinese and GCC governments are markedly different. His conclusion is that while there is no lack of opportunities to explore and exploit in GCC-China cooperation, there is a gap between their approaches to, and understandings of, their strategic interests vis-à-vis each other. The gap needs time to attend to, and perhaps will never be closed.

Chapter Eleven, "The GCC and the BRICS in Sub-Saharan Africa. Is China the main driver?", by Gladys Lechini and Maria Noel Dussort, takes an approach to understanding Sub-Saharan African relations with the GCC which is both distinctive and significant. The focus is on the possibility of creating a triangular relationship between Sub-Saharan African countries, GCC countries and BRICS countries. The GCC countries and BRICS countries have both been developing their relations with Sub-Saharan Africa, sometimes in fields where they are competitors and sometimes where their roles are complementary. The GCC countries are in a strong position to facilitate the relations between BRICS countries and Africa. This could be positive if they are part of a scenario where all-round cooperation is being promoted. But it could also be negative if the GCC countries are adversely affected by China's dominant position in trade with Africa. It remains to be seen whether an effective triangular relationship can be created.

Notes

1 Jim O'Neill, "Building Better Global Economic BRICs", Global Economics Paper No: 66 (New York: Goldman Sachs, November 2001).

2 Russia's GDP in 2015 shrank by 3.7%, while Brazil's shrank by 3.8%. Data from International Monetary Fund, *World Economic Outlook April 2016* (Washington: IMF, 2016), Table A1. Accessed April 2016, at <http://www.imf.org/external/pubs/ft/weo/2016/01/pdf/tblparta.pdf>.

3 *Ibid.* The South African economy grew by 1.3% in 2015, and is expected to grow by 0.6% in 2016.

4 *Ibid.* India's economy in 2015 grew by 7.3%, while China's grew by 6.9%.

5 *Ibid.* Between 1998 and 2011, China's growth maintained a rate of between 9% and 10%, with slightly lower figures between 2012 and 2014. In 2015 the economy registered a 6.9% increase, and current IMF projections are that this will gradually decline to 6.0% in 2021.

6 This is documented in Chapter One. A practical indication of how the range of coordination has expanded is found in the length of the statements/declarations which follow the summit meetings. Following the first summit, held in Yekaterinburg (Russia) in 2009, the final statement covered less than two pages. Following the seventh summit, held in Ufa (Russia), the declaration which was issued ran to 43 pages.

1

The Dynamics of the BRICS[1] Grouping: Convergences and Disparities with the GCC's Global Posture and Stances

Tim Niblock

1. Introduction

This chapter will begin by defining the aims, interests and objectives around which the BRICS grouping has developed. Use will be made of the joint statements, declarations and action plans issued at the end of the summit meetings of BRICS countries. These documents have become more detailed over time, so it is the most recent declarations (especially the Fortaleza Declaration following the July 2014 6th BRICS Summit in Brazil) which will be given most attention. Nonetheless, it is also important to take note of how concerns and positions have developed over time, as reflected in all 7 of the joint statements and declarations. The chapter will then examine the extent to which the GCC's political economy, structure and its international posture converge with the interests and objectives of the existing BRICS countries.

The trajectory through which the BRICS grouping has developed must first be documented. The organisation's existence is sometimes linked to the development of the term "BRIC", in a 2001 paper by the Goldman Sachs economist Jim O'Neill entitled "Building Better Global BRICs".[2] In practice, though, this is of limited relevance to the emergence of the BRICS grouping.[3] The beginnings of cooperation among the states concerned had occurred before then, and the main organisational structure (in the form of the annual BRICS Summits) did not come into being until 8 years after O'Neill's article – in 2009. The setting for the initial cooperation was the G-20 grouping, established in

September 1999. There was a natural tendency for the leading emerging markets and developing countries in this grouping to adopt common positions (given that they related to the global economy in similar ways), and on occasion to act collaboratively.

The countries which were to form the BRICS grouping began to establish formal links of consultation and cooperation among themselves in the late 1990s and early 2000s. China and Russia had come together in the Shanghai Five grouping in 1996 (together with the Kazakhstan, Kyrgyzstan and Tajikistan), and in 2001 this was transformed into the Shanghai Cooperation Organisation (SCO) with the addition of Uzbekistan. In the latter year, China and Russia also signed a Treaty of Good Neighbourliness and Friendly Cooperation. The SCO Charter was adopted at a summit meeting in June 2002. It covered the purposes, principles, structures and form of organisation of the SCO. Some of these were later echoed in BRICS documents. The SCO, however, has an added focus on military and security cooperation, and the economic dimension is more focused on practical cooperation among the countries concerned. At an important SCO Summit in Astana, in July 2005, observer countries were included for the first time, and among these was India (together with Iran, Pakistan and Mongolia). Both India and Pakistan will be admitted into full membership from 2016.

India, Brazil, and South Africa, for their part, formed the IBSA Dialogue Forum in June 2003. This envisaged regular summit meetings among the leaders of the three countries, and consultations among senior officials, academics, intellectuals and other members of civil society. The Brazilia Declaration, which followed the initial summit (as also similar declarations which have followed the subsequent annual summits), covered many of the topics which were to appear later in BRICS statements and declarations: the reform of the United Nations (specifically including expanding the Security Council membership); making the operation of the global economy more inclusive, integrative and equitable; changing the quota system underlying IMF governance; promoting South-South cooperation, etc.[4] There has in practice been more carry-over of ideas and principles from IBSA to BRICS than from the SCO to BRICS.

The first formal move towards the formation of BRICS as an organised grouping took place in September 2006 when BRIC foreign ministers met together on the margins of the opening of the 61st UN General Assembly. The objective was to explore commonalities in their external policies, and possibilities for coordinated action. Similar meetings were held in September 2007 and September 2008. Some other meetings of BRICS ministers and officials were held in 2008, most significantly a heads of state/government in July 2008, and a meeting of Finance Ministers in November 2008 (held in the shadow of the global economic and financial crisis, which powerfully underlined the need for the BRICS countries to defend their interests by acting collectively). These gatherings formed the basis for the key BRICS development: the initiation of Summit Meetings, the first of which was held in June 2009. At the time of writing seven such summits have been held. The conferences have been the following:

First Summit, Yekaterinburg (Russia), June 2009
Second Summit, Brasilia (Brazil), April 2010
Third Summit, Sanya (China), April 2011. The first to include South Africa
Fourth Summit, New Delhi (India), March 2012
Fifth Summit, Durban (South Africa), March 2013
Sixth Summit, Fortaleza (Brazil), July 2014
Seventh Summit, Ufa (Russia), July 2015

Some observers have suggested that economic developments have undermined the coherence and rationale of the BRICS grouping. In 2015 the GDPs of Russia and Brazil not only failed to achieve the high rates of economic growth which all BRICS countries shared in the first decade of the 2000s, but actually declined. Questions have also been raised about whether the Chinese economy can sustain the high rate of growth which has characterised its economy over the past 30 years. Such observations, however, misunderstand the nature of the BRICS grouping. Its primary dynamic does not rest on high rates of growth but on the political commitment of these countries to create a bigger stake for themselves in the global political and economic orders.

2. The Aims, Interests and Commonalities Underpinning the BRICS Grouping

While there are many statements, declarations and action plans which are issued during and after BRICS summits, these do not directly explain the rationale for the existence of the organisation – i.e. what it is which has drawn this particular group of countries together, and what they hope to achieve by working together.[5] The contention made here is that four key elements have drawn them together. These are:

1. <u>Similarity of economic status in the global economy</u>. The economies of the BRICS countries have all become significant to the global economy, as a

result of the high rates of growth they have achieved in recent times and the nature of their resource-bases. The size and significance of their GDPs is reflected in their membership of the G20 grouping.

2. Belief that this group of countries can gain economically by working together. The economic gains envisaged by the governments would flow from three processes:
   - *Gaining a more significant role in global economic management.* The perception here is that global financial and political-economic institutions need to be re-structured. The operations of the latter institutions are perceived as serving the interests of the countries which manage them – largely the established leading global economic powers. By acting collectively to re-structure these institutions, with a more broadly-based representation in the management, the BRICS countries can benefit their own economies and those of the developing world in general. They will be better-equipped to safeguard their interests in the global economy, and to block the adoption of measures and policies which are harmful to their economies.
   - *Enhancing economic exchange between them, covering the full range of sectoral activity: trade, investment and finance.* While substantial economic exchange already exists (to varying degrees, depending on the country), there is clearly a belief that there is further room for expansion and that this should be proactively promoted. This is necessary in order to ensure that the BRICS economies are not overly-dependent on their relations with Western economies. Such over-dependence must be avoided, so as to ensure that BRICS economies are not damaged by a recurrence of economic instability in the West. Close economic relations among BRICS countries, therefore, will act as a stabilising force underpinning their further economic development, and requires deliberate planning collectively.
   - *Sharing experience of best practice*, given that they face some of the same problems in developing their economies and in managing their relations with the global economy.

3. Commitment to preventing global institutions (in particular the United Nations) from being used to further the interests and objectives of the Western powers – especially on matters which relate to the sovereignty of UN member states. This not only involves seeking to establish common

positions when such issues arise, but also acting collectively in demanding the re-structuring of the Security Council of the UN so as to ensure that the views of BRICS countries carry more weight and influence. The significance of the United Nations in representing global opinion is emphasised.

4. Pronounced alignment with the global South, with a commitment to promoting South-South cooperation generally, and to defending the interests of Less Developed Countries in the global economy.

Governmental perceptions of commonality, whether in economic or political realms, do not necessarily equate to actual commonality. It is important, therefore, to examine the aspects covered in the previous section and consider the realities of commonality. Do the BRICS countries actually share a common position relative to the global order (economically and politically), and does this provide a coherent basis for collective action and activity?

3. The Realities of Convergence and Difference: Similarity of Economic Status in the Global Economy.

The BRICS organisation publishes statistics which compare the economies of the five countries, and the data does indicate both their collective importance and also a significant level of commonality among them. With regard to their collective importance, the 2012 BRICS Report portrays their collective significance to the global economy as follows:

> Together, the BRICS account for more than 40 per cent of the global population, nearly 30 per cent of the land mass, and a share in world GDP (in PPP terms) that increased from 16 per cent in 2000 to nearly 25 per cent in 2010, and is expected to rise significantly in the near future. If one compares the GDP in PPP terms for 2010, four economies figure among the G-20 top ten, with China, India, Russia, Brazil, and South Africa in 2nd, 4th, 6th, 8th, and 26th place, respectively. In terms of contribution to growth of PPP-adjusted global GDP of the world, these five economies accounted for 55 per cent during 2000–8, and their contribution is expected to rise in the coming years. However, as per the criterion of GDP at market prices, among the members of the G-20, China holds the 2nd position while Brazil, India, Russia, and South

Africa hold the 7th, 9th, 11th, and 19th positions, respectively.[6]

The most recent figures from the IMF put the position yet more favourably for three of the BRICS countries. In the figures for 2014, China for the first time emerged as the largest global economy in terms of GDP at PPP, with India in 3rd position, Brazil moving up to 7th, Russia retaining the 6thposition, and South Africa falling to 34th.[7] When the relevant figures are put in overall non-PPP GDP terms, they do not sound quite so impressive, but they remain substantial. IMF 2013 figures show BRICS combined GDP as making up 21% of global GDP. Even in GDP at market prices, however, the BRICS countries have accounted for more than half of global economic growth over the period since 2008. Population figures for 2013 give the BRICS a slightly higher share of global population than appeared in the 2012 BRICS Report: 43% rather than 40%. Intra-BRICS trade flows reached $282 billion in 2012 and the target was for these to have reached $500 billion by 2015. The actual figures for 2015, however, have not been published at the time of writing. [8] In 2002, the trade stood at only $27.3 billion.

While the BRICS countries are collectively a highly important component of the global economy, they differ substantially in their economic weight – so much so that they may appear not to cohere well as an economic grouping. The GDPs of the five states in 2013 came to $8.25 trillion for China, $2.43 trillion for Brazil, $1.95 trillion for each of Russia and India, and $390.9 billion for South Africa.[9] China's GDP, it can be seen, came to more than half of that of the BRICS total. A very large gap, therefore, separates China at the top from South Africa at the bottom. In 2013 China became the second largest economy in the world, and calculated by PPP was the largest. China's foreign reserves, moreover, made up about three-quarters of the $4.4 billion held by the BRICS grouping collectively.

Nonetheless, some other measures create a more balanced picture of the comparative strengths of the economies. Per capita GDP for 2012 was estimated for the five countries as follows: Russia $13,765, Brazil $12,340, South Africa $7,636, China $6,094, and India $1,592.[10] South Africa's inclusion in BRICS, moreover, reflects the South African economy's significance within the African continent[11], and the need for the BRICS grouping to have an African member. The BRICS grouping is therefore strengthened by the inclusion of South Africa in its membership, and South Africa's membership gains weight and significance through that. As for India, Russia and Brazil, while their economies are substantially smaller than China's, they are nonetheless of considerable global importance (as noted above ranked respectively at 3rd, 6th and 7th in terms of PPP).

4. Collective Concern to Obtain for BRICS Countries a Significant Role in Global Economic Management

The consistency and strength of the BRICS campaign to obtain a more significant role in global economic management will now be examined, with some analysis of the measure of success achieved.

The topic has in fact been a significant concern of all BRICS Summits since the organisation was established. In the first Summit, in 2010, much of the concluding Joint Statement revolved around the issue, directly or indirectly. The third paragraph states:

> We are committed to advance the reform of international financial institutions, so as to reflect changes in the world economy. The emerging and developing economies must have greater voice and representation in international financial institutions, and their heads and senior leadership should be appointed through an open, transparent, and merit-based selection process. We also believe that there is a strong need for a stable, predictable and more diversified international monetary system.[12]

Similar statements were made in a prominent position in all subsequent Summit Joint Statements and Joint Declarations. The eThekwini Declaration, which followed the 2013 Summit, was particularly explicit as to the measures which needed to be taken. It projected the BRICS role, furthermore, in terms of the demands of developing countries generally:

> We call for the reform of International Financial Institutions to make them more representative and to reflect the growing weight of BRICS and other developing countries. We remain concerned with the slow pace of the reform of the IMF. We see an urgent need to implement, as agreed, the 2010 International Monetary Fund (IMF) Governance and Quota Reform. We urge all members to take all necessary steps to achieve an agreement on the quota formula and complete the next general quota review by January 2014. The reform of the IMF should strengthen the voice and representation of the poorest members of the IMF, including Sub-Saharan Africa. All options should be explored, with an open mind, to achieve this. We support the reform and improvement of the international monetary system, with a broad-based international

> reserve currency system providing stability and certainty. We welcome the discussion about the role of the SDR in the existing international monetary system including the composition of SDR's basket of currencies. We support the IMF to make its surveillance framework more integrated and even-handed. The leadership selection of IFIs should be through an open, transparent and merit-based process and truly open to candidates from the emerging market economies and developing countries.[13]

The BRICS governments have pursued these aims, especially as they relate to the IMF, with considerable determination. The main vehicle for exerting pressure for change has been through G20 meetings, where they meet together with the governments and central bank governors of the G7 "major advanced economies" and of some other significant economies (Argentina, Australia, Indonesia, Mexico, Saudi Arabia, South Korea and Turkey).[14] Their campaign to amend the IMF's Articles of Agreement, creating an all-elected executive board and granting larger quota shares to emerging market and developing countries, has now been adopted by the IMF and put into effect. Brazil, Russia, India and China are now among the 10 largest members of the IMF. The process whereby these changes were finally adopted, however, was a very slow one. The G20's initial agreement to review IMF quotas and governance was taken in October 2010, but the ensuing proposals were only accepted by the leading powers in the IMF in January 2016.[15] In order to be accepted, the proposals had to be supported by 85% of the "voting power" in the IMF (weighted according to the size of the economies), and the crucial support of the United States was not forthcoming until the beginning of 2016.[16] The reality, moreover, is that the leadership of the IMF remains heavily dominated by the major advanced economies.[17] The frustration of BRICS at the slow pace of change was stated clearly in the 2014 Fortaleza Declaration: "We remain disappointed and seriously concerned with the current non-implementation of the 2010 International Monetary Fund (IMF) reforms, which negatively impacts on the IMF's legitimacy, credibility and effectiveness".[18]

A separate approach to lessening Western influence/control of the global financial system has been the creation of alternative channels for economic and financial organisation. Of key importance here were three agreements which were signed in 2014 – all of which sprang from ideas and decisions which had been mooted and supported in Summit meetings since 2012. These agreements involved the establishment of the New Development Bank (NDB), with an initial authorised capital of $100 billion (with headquarters in Shanghai, and an associated NDB Africa Regional Centre in South Africa); a BRICS Contingent Reserve Arrangement (CRA), with an initial size of US$100 billion; and a Memorandum of Understanding on Cooperation among BRICS Export Credit and Guarantee Agencies.[19] Currently under discussion are a BRICS Economic Cooperation Strategy and a Framework of BRICS Closer Economic Partnership.[20]

The creation of alternative BRICS channels for economic and financial organisation, moreover, complements (and indeed dovetails with) the other measures which individual BRICS countries are taking to establish new institutions and networks outside of those dominated by the major advanced economies. Notable among these are the Shanghai Cooperation Organisation, the Asian Infrastructural Investment Bank, and China's One Belt, One Road policy initiative. The linkage between the BRICS grouping and the SCO is given substance by the overlapping of some of their meetings: an SCO summit coincided with the first BRICS summit in 2009, and this was repeated in 2015 at Ufa.[21] The admission of India and Pakistan into the SCO's membership in 2016 will mean that 3 out of the 5 BRICS countries are SCO members. The support which BRICS countries have consistently given to UNCTAD, which provides an alternative scenario to that of the international financial institutions for developing countries, is also significant. The Fortaleza Declaration describes UNCTAD as "the focal point in the UN system dedicated to consider the interrelated issues of trade, investment, finance and technology from a development perspective".[22]

The recommendations for change in the global economic order, which are present in Summit statements and declarations, are generally projected in terms of initiatives which will benefit poorer and developing countries generally. In the First Summit Joint Statement, clause 6 states:

> The poorest countries have been hit hardest by the financial crisis. The international community needs to step up efforts to provide liquidity for these countries. The international community should also strive to minimize the impact of the crisis on development and ensure the achievement of the Millennium Development Goals.[23]

This concern found its strongest articulation in the eThekwini Declaration which followed the Fifth Summit, held in South Africa. The Declaration, in clause 3, stressed the BRICS' openness to "increasing our engagement and cooperation with non-BRICS countries, in particular Emerging Market and Developing Countries", with an immediate initiative on Africa:

> We will hold a Retreat together with African leaders after this Summit, under the theme, "Unlocking Africa's potential: BRICS and Africa Cooperation on Infrastructure". The Retreat is an opportunity for BRICS and African leaders to discuss how to strengthen cooperation between the BRICS countries and the African Continent.[24]

Further research would be required to establish the extent to which BRICS' self-perception as a vehicle for improving the conditions of developing countries is shared by non-BRICS developing countries themselves.

5. Creating Practical Cooperation Between BRICS States

As to practical cooperation among the BRICS states, there is now a wide range of councils, committees, ministerial meetings, for a and contact groups which bring representatives of the member states together, with a view to developing fields of cooperation – in addition to the summit meetings themselves. The concerns are mainly economic, although health and security also figure. BRICS documents[25] mention the following fields where there is ongoing cooperation and dialogue:

i. <u>Finance and Central Banks.</u> The BRICS finance ministers have been meeting since November 2008. Their initial meeting occurred in response to the global financial crisis, and was shaped by their collective needs in that crisis. The objective was to ensure that their economies were not damaged by the mismanagement of the major Western governments which had caused the crisis. The BRICS finance ministers meet "at the margins of G-20 meetings and of the annual and of the biennual IMF and World Bank meetings, as well as the margins of BRICS Summits, together with the Governors of Central Banks".[26] There is also a Financial Forum, bringing together the presidents of the major development banks of the BRICS countries. They meet in parallel with the BRICS Summits and, as of 2014, had concluded a total of eight agreements on financial cooperation.
ii. <u>Trade.</u> The BRICS trade ministers meet on the eve of the annual Summit meetings, and also at the margins of WTO ministerial

meetings. Reporting to the ministers there is a Contact Group for Economic and Trade Issues (CGETI), whose responsibility it is to propose "an institutional framework and concrete measures to expand cooperation on economic and trade issues amongst the BRICS".[27] At the July 2015 meeting of trade ministers prior to the 7th BRICS Summit in Ufa, the ministers agreed a joint cooperation strategy to promote trade between the 5 countries. The Russian trade minister reported that trade among them had already increased by 70% over the 2008-14 period, rising from an annual $168 billion to $291 billion.[28]

iii. Business Forum and Council. The Business Forum first met in 2010, and has since then met on the eve of the Summit meetings. Its objective is to expand and diversify "trade and mutual investments, including through the identification of new business opportunities".[29] It consists of governmental representatives. The Business Council, on the other hand, is composed of CEOs of major companies based in the 5 countries. Its role is to make recommendations on issues of trade and investment to the BRICS Summits.

iv. Academic Forum and Think Tanks Council. The Academic Forum (established in 2010) brings together leading academics from the 5 countries and meets annually, while the Think Tanks Council (established in 2013) is composed of 5 think tanks - one from each of the countries. They play similar roles: sharing and disseminating information and producing ideas and recommendations for the further development of the BRICS grouping.

v. Health. The BRICS health ministers have been meeting regularly since 2011, usually at the margins of World Health Organisation meetings. They have a commitment to creating a Technological Cooperation Network, which would "promote the transfer of, and access to, technologies that would allow increased availability and lower prices of medicines in developing countries".[30] A BRICS Framework for Collaboration in Strategic Health Projects was adopted in 2013.

vi. Science and Technology. Senior government officials in this field had been meeting since 2011, and in 2014 the first meeting of the BRICS Ministers of Science and Technology took place. They are currently working towards signing a memorandum covering their joint commitment to promoting "partnerships with other stakeholders in the developing world, based on the experiences and complementarities of the BRICS".[31]

vii. Security. This formed part of BRICS activity from an early stage – 2009. The BRICS "high representatives responsible for security" meet on a regular basis, exchanging views on "cyber security, counterterrorism, transportation security, and regional crises".[32]

viii. Agriculture. The BRICS Ministers of Agriculture have been meeting annually since 2010, aided by a Working Group of Agricultural Experts. They currently work within the framework of an "Action Plan 2012-2016" which was adopted at their 2011 meeting. The plan sets out guidelines for their cooperation in this field.

ix. Statistics. Maintaining and publishing statistical information covering and comparing the economic performance of the 5 BRICS countries is seen as important. At the annual BRICS Summits a BRICS joint statistical publication is issued, compiled from information supplied by the 5 national statistical offices banks.[33]

It may, of course, be questioned whether the holding of meetings and the signing of agreements lead to actual and significant cooperation, or how it compares with cooperation in the wider global environment. It is perhaps too early for this to be assessed, but for the moment it can simply be affirmed that a fairly-intense framework of contact is in place – at least in the economic field.

The scope for the countries to learn from each other in terms of best practice is also there, although again the actual impact needs a longer-term assessment. One theme which is strongly stated in the declarations following the fifth and sixth Summits has been the positive role which State-Owned Companies (SOCs) can play in economic development, and the benefits to BRICS countries of exchanging information and best practices in this field. At the same time the important role of small and medium-sized enterprises (SMEs) is stressed. The Fortaleza Declaration, issued after the sixth Summit, is most explicit on this:

> We acknowledge the important role that State Owned Companies (SOCs) play in the economy and encourage our SOCs to continue to

> explore ways of cooperation, exchange of information and best practices. We also recognize the fundamental role played by small and medium-sized enterprises in the economies of our countries as major creators of jobs and wealth. We will enhance cooperation and recognize the need for strengthening intra-BRICS dialogue with a view to promote international exchange and cooperation and to foster innovation, research and development.[34]

The insistence on recognising the importance of these two dimensions of economic development is clearly intended to counter the neo-liberal ideas espoused by some Western governments and the IMF. The BRICS countries are, in this statement, asserting their continuing commitment to a strong role for the state in economic development – protecting the economies from damage which might ensue if multinational corporations are given unfettered and uncontrolled access. SOCs can ensure that key sectors of the economy are given protection, while SMEs need a level of state support and protection if they are to compete against globally-dominant corporations. It is significant that none of the BRICS countries have formed part of the negotiations for the Transatlantic Trade and Investment Pact (TTIP) or Trans Pacific Partnership (TPP), both of which would strengthen the relative position of business interests against governmental interests – and particularly big business interests which would have the resources to take legal action against governments.[35] The United States government has been taking the lead in both initiatives.

6. Activities Aimed at Preventing Global Institution from Being Used to Further the Interests and Objectives of the Western Powers

Non-economic global concerns have been part of BRICS discussions from the outset. Three aspects of BRICS activities in this field, however, need to be noted. First, the central and continued focus have been on the need to ensure that global institutions are "democratised", with an underlying ethos which is protective of the sovereign rights of governments. Second, each successive Summit has broadened the scope of the international relations issues mentioned in the final statements or declarations. Third, the existence of common positions on some issues, and coordination on these, should not be interpreted in terms of anything resembling an alliance. Riding alongside the commonality there are important elements of political difference and even confrontation between individual BRICS countries.

The emphasis on the need to prevent international institutions being dominated by Western governments is, of course, not articulated in those terms (i.e. the specification of "Western governments") – but rather within the context of broadening the basis on which global decision-making functions. In the Joint Statement following the First Summit, this is first expressed in the context of the need for a change in the world order – towards one which is "more democratic" and is based on globally-accepted principles:

> We underline our support for a more democratic and just multi-polar world order based on the rule of international law, equality, mutual respect, cooperation, coordinated action and collective decision-making of all states. We reiterate our support for political and diplomatic efforts to peacefully resolve disputes in international relations.[36]

This is then linked, in a subsequent clause, to support for the United Nations and an allied demand for the reform of that institution:

> We express our strong commitment to multilateral diplomacy with the United Nations playing the central role in dealing with global challenges and threats. In this respect, we reaffirm the need for a comprehensive reform of the UN with a view to making it more efficient so that it can deal with today's global challenges more effectively. We reiterate the importance we attach to the status of India and Brazil in international affairs, and understand and support their aspirations to play a greater role in the United Nations[37]

All subsequent final BRICS Summits statements and declarations have repeated the same overall points, although becoming more elaborate and forthright over time. Increasingly there is an explicit condemnation of unilateral actions conducted outside of the UN framework, and the need to respect the sovereignty of UN member states. The Ufa Declaration (2015) states:

> We note the global character of current security challenges and threats and express our support for international efforts to address these challenges in a way that provides equal and indivisible security for all states, through respect for international law and principles of the UN Charter. We stress our commitment to the sustainable and peaceful settlement of disputes,

> according to principles and purposes of the UN Charter.
>
> We condemn unilateral military interventions and economic sanctions in violation of international law and universally recognized norms of international relations. Bearing this in mind, we emphasize the unique importance of the indivisible nature of security, and that no State should strengthen its security at the expense of the security of others.[38]

All Summits since the 3rd have specified that the reform which BRICS countries seek of the UN includes that of the Security Council, which clearly relates to its composition as well as its mode of operation. Reference is made to making the UN and its Security Council "more representative, effective and efficient", and to China and Russia's appreciation of "the importance they attach to Brazil, India and South Africa's status and role in international affairs and support their aspiration to play a greater role in the UN".[39] Whether they are calling for those states to be brought in to the Security Council is not made specific, although perhaps it is implied.

The emphasis on the United Nations role in international relations, often with comments on the need to avoid unilateral actions by outside powers, also finds expression in the clauses of the statements/declaration relating to ongoing crises in different parts of the world. As noted above, the range of global conflicts figuring in final statements/declarations has increased over time. The First Summit Joint Statement in fact makes no reference to any country-specific crises. The Fortaleza Declaration, on the other hand, expresses support for UN bodies in resolving conflicts in a variety of different geographical contexts: Mali, South Sudan, the Central African Republic, the Democratic Republic of the Congo, Syria, Palestine/Israel and Afghanistan. In most of the other conflicts mentioned there is reference to the role which regional institutions could play. With regard to the crisis in Ukraine, there is a call for a "comprehensive dialogue, the de-escalation of the conflict and restraint from all the actors involved with a view to finding a peaceful political solution, in full compliance with the UN Charter and universally recognised human rights and fundamental freedoms".[40]

Assessing whether the resolutions have led to the BRICS countries pursuing concerted common lines in UN voting, and how much coordination there is between their representatives in the UN, would require further research. Clearly there can be a wide gap between conference pronouncements and practical action, but the attempt to frame common positions (even at the level of pronouncement) itself carries some significance.

One other issue which has figured in all BRICS Summits final statements and declarations has been terrorism. Besides the condemnation of "any forms of terrorism, whether based upon ideological, religious, racial, ethnic or any other justification", there is an increasing insistence that the United Nations is the appropriate vehicle for orchestrating the global struggle against terrorism. The Ufa Declaration states:

> We stress that the UN has a central role in coordinating international action against terrorism, which must be conducted in accordance with international law, including the UN Charter, and with respect to human rights and fundamental freedoms. We believe that terrorist threats can be effectively addressed through a comprehensive implementation by states and the international community of all relevant resolutions of the UN Security Council and the UN Global Counter-Terrorism Strategy.[41]

The existence of commonalities in the approach which BRICS countries have to the global system does not imply that their foreign policies are in unison (or perhaps even compatible) in some key fields. The relationship between China and India, for example, contains elements of confrontation as well as cooperation, with issues ranging from borders to contests over regional strategic influence. China's most constant and consistent regional partner over recent decades has been Pakistan – a country which India views as potentially threatening to both its security interests and its territorial unity.[42] The relationship between Russia and China contains a similar mix of cooperative intention and hesitant suspicion which is found in the China-India relationship.[43]

7. Putting the GCC in the Perspective of BRICS

An analysis will now be given of whether and how the GCC countries could fit into the BRICS grouping. The relevant issues to be covered are:

i. Whether the structure and weight of the GCC economy (with all GCC countries taken collectively) makes it comparable to those of the BRICS countries.
ii. Whether the existing economic links between the BRICS countries and the GCC countries are indicative of a strong long-term economic relationship.

iii. Whether the economic benefits which the two sides could draw from GCC membership of BRICS are significant enough to warrant membership.

iv. Whether the global political orientation which BRICS countries currently share is ones which GCC countries also share.

v. Whether there are institutional or geopolitical reasons which would either facilitate or complicate GCC inclusion.

7.1 Comparing the Structure and Weight of the GCC Economy with that of the BRICS

The overall size of the GCC economy (taking all of the GCC countries together) puts GCC GDP at a level comparable to that of some of the BRICS countries – lower than the four largest economies, but substantially higher than that of South Africa. In PPP terms, the GCC ranking relative to the Brazilian and Russian economies is very similar and significantly higher than that of South Africa, while remaining much lower than those of China and India. The relevant statistics can be found in Table 1.1 below.

Table 1.1: GDP Comparisons, BRICS and the GCC

Country	GDP 2014 $billion	PPP 2014 $billion
China	10,380.4	17,617.3
Brazil	2,353.0	3,263.8
India	2,049.5	7,375.9
Russia	1,857.5	3,564.5
South Africa	350.1	704.5
GCC	1,648.2	3,034.4
Other G20 Emerging Markets		
Mexico	1,282.7	2,140.6
Indonesia	888.6	2,676.1
Turkey	806.7	1,508.1
Argentina	540.2	947.6

Source: International Monetary Fund, *World Economic Output* (Washington: IMF, April 2015).

The rates of growth of the BRICS and GCC economies over a ten-year period have also been comparable. GCC GDP growth over the last ten years has been 5-6%, which is lower than those of China and India, comparable to Brazil and Russia, and above that of South Africa.

The composition of GCC GDPs, however, is substantially different from that of most of the BRICS countries. In the case of Russia, there is an element of similarity with GCC economies, as the Russian economy is also strongly dependent on hydrocarbons production and exporting. The degree of dependence in Russia's case, however, is substantially less than with the GCC countries. In 2012, before the imposition of sanctions had skewed the longer-term run of Russian statistics, the hydrocarbons sector accounted for 16% of Russian GDP, 52% of its federal budget, and 70% of total exports. The comparative figures for the GCC countries, taken together, have in recent years averaged around 30% of GDP, more than 85% of government revenues, and almost 90% of export revenues.[44] The Russian economy, therefore, is substantially more diverse and broadly-based than are the GCC economies. Another significant difference between the GCC and BRICS countries is in the make-up of the labour market. More than half of all labour employed in the GCC is expatriate, and this holds also for each GCC country taken individually.[45] Nothing comparable can be found in any of the BRICS countries.

While there are similarities between the size of the GCC and BRICS economies, it is also important to note that there are other G 20 "emerging market" countries which bear comparison to the BRICS countries, and for some of these the structural similarities bring them closer to the BRICS model. These countries are Argentina, Indonesia, Mexico and Turkey.[46] Their relevant GDP and PPP statistics for them can be found in the lower part of Table 1. All of them have, at various stages, shown an interest in BRICS membership, and some have attended BRICS meetings as observers.

7.2 *Assessment of Whether the Existing Economic Links Between the BRICS Countries and the GCC Countries are Indicative of a Strong Long-Term Economic Relationship*

The significance of the BRICS grouping's long-term economic relations with GCC countries will be assessed here through an analysis of the developing trading relations between them. While this constitutes only part of the economic relationship (the other key elements being investment and contracts), it does provide an accurate indication of how the overall relationship is developing. The main trends are documented statistically in Tables 1.2-1.55 below.

Tables 1.2-1.4 provide information on trade between all 8 Gulf countries and the Gulf's major trading partners, with the three BRICS countries which are not in the "major partners" grouping added on. This data, therefore, includes Iraq and Iran, as well as the GCC countries. It is important to take the pan-Gulf dimension into account, given that the BRICS countries are likely to assess their Gulf interests within the wider context.

Table 1.2: The Gulf's Trade with its Major Trading Partners, and BRICS Countries $ billion (2014)

	Bahrain	Saudi Arabia	UAE	Qatar	Oman	Kuwait	Iraq	Iran	TOTAL
China	1.53	66.90	57.10	13.31	23.92	12.86	27.32	51.74	254.74
India	0.92	43.70	61.23	17.91	4.28	15.01	15.49	15.08	173.64
Japan	1.45	51.56	48.40	35.24	7.46	13.34	2.80	5.90	166.15
South Korea	0.86	42.53	22.65	25.75	5.47	17.53	8.06	9.16	132.01
European Union	3.64	85.92	72.11	18.92	6.12	14.02	20.79	10.79	231.95
United States	2.05	63.21	26.86	4.03	3.11	15.41	14.78	0.20	128.65
Brazil	0.44	6.10	3.63	0.73	1.19	1.46	1.29	1.59	16.43
Russia	0.02	1.23	2.15	0.14	0.09	0.05	1.94	1.78	7.40
South Africa	0.11	7.68	3.08	1.66	0.57	0.31	0.40	0.14	12.95
WORLD	52.26	510.69	534.03	161.93	91.39	126.23	130.26	182.80	

Source: Calculations made by the writer, drawn from data found in International Monetary Fund, *Direction of Trade Statistics* (Washington: IMF, 2015), accessed June 2015. <http://elibrary-data.imf.org/finddatareports.aspx?d=33061&e=170921>.

From Table 1.2, it can be seen that the two largest BRICS economies now rank first and third among the Gulf's major trading partners. The European Union, which for most of the last two decades has been by far the largest trading partner of the Gulf, has fallen significantly behind China. India too now has a substantial share of Gulf trade, ahead of Japan which ranked second up to 2010. Given the rate at which trade has been increasing since 2008 (see Table 1.3), moreover, China and India are likely to increase their share further in the years ahead. This likelihood is, furthermore, strengthened by developments in global energy markets, where China and India are expected to have growing needs for imports of Gulf oil and gas, while US demand will decline and EU demand will remain fairly static.

The Gulf trade of the remaining three BRICS countries (Brazil, Russia and South Africa) is not sufficient for them to be classed as major trading partners. Nonetheless there are particular parts of their trade which have assumed some importance, specifically South Africa's oil imports from the Gulf, and Brazil's developing export trade with Saudi Arabia and the UAE. Overall, then, the economic relations between the BRICS grouping and Gulf countries are significant to the interests of both sides, although most of this significance lies in the trade with India and China.

Table 1.3: Percentage Increases/Decreases in Trade with the Gulf, 2008-2014, in ranked order: the Gulf's Major Trading Partners (2014 figure compared with 2008)

Trading Partner	Trade Increase/Decrease
China	+109.8%
India	+45.51%
South Korea	+16.9%
European Union	+8.6%
United States	+3.0%
Japan*	-5.6%

Source: Calculations made by the writer, drawn from data found in International Monetary Fund, *Direction of Trade Statistics* (Washington: IMF, 2015), accessed June 2015 at <http://elibrary-data.imf.org/finddatareports.aspx?d=33061&e=170921>.

The all-round strength of the Gulf's economic relations with China and India is reflected in the balance between imports and exports. Contrary to common belief, the trade does not consist only of Gulf exports of oil and gas. Most of the Gulf's trading partners maintain a negative trading balance with the Gulf, as do China and India, but they also enjoy substantial export markets in the region (see 1.4). 43.8% of China's trade with the Gulf consists of Chinese exports, and 35.7% of India's. Among the Gulf's major trading partners, only the European Union enjoys a positive balance of trade, with 66.2% of its trade consisting of exports. Brazil and Russia also enjoy positive trade balances with the Gulf. Given that they are themselves oil exporters, and therefore have no need for Gulf oil, this is not surprising.

+Figures for Brazil, Russia and South Africa are not given here. In view of the relatively low level of trade, annual figures are greatly affected by one-off contracts. Comparing any two years, therefore, would not be a good indication of long-term trends.

* The figure for Japan given here is affected by a freak condition related to 2008. For a variety of reasons, Japan needed to import more oil than usual in that year. This distorts the comparison with the 2014 figure. The overall trend indicates that Japan's trade has been growing, although slowly. It would be more realistic to place it above the US but below the European Union.

Table 1.4: Proportion of Trade with the Gulf of Trading Partners, Imports/Exports

	Percentage of Imports in Total Trade with the Gulf	Percentage of Exports in Total Trade with the Gulf
China	56.2	43.8
India	64.3	35.7
Japan	82.3	17.7
South Korea	78.5	21.5
EU	33.8	66.2
US	54.8	55.2
Brazil	40.6	59.4
Russia	11.4	88.6
South Africa	81.2	18.8

Source: Calculations made by the writer, drawn from data found in International Monetary Fund, *Direction of Trade Statistics* (Washington: IMF, 2015), accessed June 2015. <http://elibrary-data.imf.org/finddatareports.aspx?d=33061&e=170921>.

While the pan-Gulf dimension may be of particular relevance for the BRICS countries, the trading patterns particular to the GCC need also to be considered. The collective trade of Iran and Iraq with the outside world comes to less than two-thirds that of either the UAE or Saudi Arabia, but nonetheless the particular conditions affecting that trade (especially the US and UN sanctions on Iran) affect the overall pattern. In practice, China and to a lesser extent India have sought to maintain their economic links with Iran while Western countries, and more recently Japan and South Korea, have steadily reduced theirs. In 2014, China accounted for 28% of all Iran's external trade. Taking GCC trade by itself, the European Union emerges as the largest trading partner, with China and India holding the 2nd and 4th positions – and Japan in between at 3rd (see table 1.5). South Korea and the US retain the 5th and 6th positions which they hold in pan-Gulf trade. Given the rates of growth of trade since 2008, the gap between EU and Chinese trade is likely to narrow in the years ahead, with China reaching a position where it could overtake the EU. It is, also, significant, that the gap between Chinese and Indian trade with the GCC is not as great as is the case at the pan-Gulf level. In 2014, India's trade with the UAE, Qatar and Kuwait exceeded that of China.

Table 1.5: GCC Trade with its Major Trading Partners, and BRICS Countries, in ranked order

Trading Partner	Trade Total ($ billion)
European Union	200.37
China	165.68
Japan	157.45
India	143.07
South Korea	114.79
United States	113.67
Brazil	13.55
South Africa	12.41
Russia	3.68

Source: Calculations made by the writer, drawn from data found in International Monetary Fund, *Direction of Trade Statistics* (Washington: IMF, 2015), accessed June 2015. <http://elibrary-data.imf.org/finddatareports.aspx?d=33061&e=170921>.

7.3 Assessment of the Economic Benefits which the Two Sides Could Draw From GCC Membership of BRICS

Section 7.2 has established that a substantial economic relationship already exists between the BRICS grouping (or at least some members of that grouping) and the Gulf states. China and India, and to a lesser extent South Africa, will all be importing increasing quantities of Gulf oil and gas, increasing the level of mutual dependence between them and the GCC countries. Both sides will have an interest in tethering the hydrocarbons trade to a wider economic and perhaps political relationship, so as to ensure that the oil-importers can guarantee their supplies and the oil-exporters can be sure they can market their hydrocarbons. In China's case this has in fact been an established policy since the mid-1990s.[47] The oil-importers, moreover, will be seeking to ensure that they can boost their exports to the oil-importers so as to avoid excessive strain on their balances of trade. China and India also play a major role in contracting and investment in the GCC states, and this has potential to expand further. There is now, in addition, a significant flow of investment going in the opposite direction: from the GCC to China, India and most recently Russia. [48]

In the case of Russia and Brazil, the value of economic coordination arises from their role as oil producers – a major existing producer and exporter in the case of Russia, and a growing producer and potential major exporter in the case of Brazil. While there are other for a where Russia, Brazil and the GCC can meet to discuss oil-related issues, the BRICS context could have a dimension of particular value. Hydrocarbons issues can be discussed there within a wider context of economic exchange, coordination and development. Brazil, Russia and South Africa are also currently seeking means of increasing the flows of trade and investment between them and the Gulf states. While Russia's trade has been the lowest of all the BRICS countries, recent agreements with Saudi Arabia suggest that this is about to change.[49]

The ongoing expansion in economic relations has, of course, occurred without GCC membership of BRICS and it would no doubt continue without such membership. Nonetheless, the extensive nature of the existing economic relations, and the prospects for this expanding further in the future, suggest that both the GCC and the BRICS grouping would benefit from operating within a more coordinated economic framework – one where cooperation, exchange of ideas and perspectives, and a measure of policy coordination is actively promoted and encouraged. It would, for example, be advantageous to both sides for the GCC countries to be involved in the BRICS Contingent Reserve Arrangement, the BRICS Export Credit and Guarantee Agencies, and the new BRICS Development Bank. In all of the fields of practical BRICS cooperative activity mentioned earlier, moreover, GCC involvement would bring benefit to both sides. GCC representatives would bring distinctive perspectives, and learn from the perspectives of others, in the relevant BRICS committees covering cooperation in finance, trade, business, academic exchange, health, science and technology, security, agriculture and statistics. The BRICS connection would also help GCC countries engage with organisations and projects which, while not integral to BRICS, are critical to the interests and strategies of one or more BRICS countries, such as the Shanghai Cooperation Organisation, the India Brazil South Africa Dialogue Forum, the One Road One Belt Project,[50] and the Eurasian Economic Union.[51]

On the key BRICS issue of reform of the global institutions GCC engagement would also bring benefit to both sides. Given the huge external assets held by GCC states, the latter have both a strong interest in gaining a more substantial role in the running of these institutions, and a convincing basis on which to pursue the claim. GCC support for the ongoing changes in the institutional practice of the IMF will clearly be beneficial. To some extent, however, that support has already been provided within the context of G20 meetings.

Overall, then, there are substantial economic gains which the two sides could make by bringing the GCC into the BRICS grouping.

7.4 *Assessing whether the BRICS Global Political Orientation Is Shared by GCC Countries*

At surface level the politically-oriented issues which are raised in BRICS conferences, and which figure in the statements and declarations which follow them, are ones which GCC leaders could well support – although sometimes without the strength of conviction which existing BRICS members bring to them. They would be supportive of the strengthening of the United Nations, and would be unlikely to oppose the reform of UN institutions. They might well have concerns, however, over a more broadly-based Security Council, fearing that it would be less effective over issues which the GCC states see as key to their security (especially those concerning Iranian nuclear weapons). Most of the BRICS' positions on specific international issues which figure in the Fortaleza Declaration are at least compatible with the positions taken by GCC states, even though the GCC states tend to formulate their positions in different ways. On the Arab-Israeli conflict, despite the fact that some of the BRICS countries have strong relations with Israel, the Fortaleza Declaration takes a line which fully coheres with that of most Arab countries:

> We reaffirm our commitment to contribute to a comprehensive, just and lasting settlement of the Arab-Israeli conflict on the basis of the universally recognized international legal framework, including the relevant UN resolutions, the Madrid Principles and the Arab Peace Initiative.,. We

> call upon Israel and Palestine to resume negotiations leading to a two-State solution with a contiguous and economically viable Palestinian State existing side by side in peace with Israel, within mutually agreed and internationally recognized borders based on the 4 June 1967 lines, with East Jerusalem as its capital. We oppose the continuous construction and expansion of settlements in the Occupied Palestinian Territories by the Israeli Government, which violates international law, gravely undermines peace efforts and threatens the viability of the two-State solution... We recall with satisfaction the decision of the UN General Assembly to proclaim 2014 the International Year of Solidarity with the Palestinian People.[52]

The BRICS position on the need for a nuclear-free Middle East also coheres closely with the position of Arab countries:

> We express our support for the convening, at the earliest possible date, of the Conference on the establishment of a Middle East zone free of nuclear weapons and all other weapons of mass destruction. We call upon all states of the region to attend the Conference and to engage constructively and in a pragmatic manner with a view to advancing that goal.[53]

It is clear that the BRICS grouping would gain in global influence by the inclusion of the GCC. The GCC has economic attributes which render it important to the global economy generally: the largest accessible oil reserves in the world, financial assets which enable it to influence investment patterns in many parts of the world, and a growing share in the critically-important global market for petrochemicals. It would, moreover, fill a significant gap in the "representative" dimension of the BRICS network: adding an area of the developing/emerging markets spectrum (the Arab World/Middle East) which has so far been left out. This area moreover has the advantage, from the perspective of China, India and Russia, of being geographically well-situated for integration into their expanding commercial infrastructure (the Silk Road, the oil pipelines, etc).

Notwithstanding the apparent agreement on key issues in contemporary international relations, there is a major difference in how the GCC and the BRICS countries relate to the global system. The existing BRICS countries are all major regional powers. They are confident not only in their ability to maintain their own security, but also in their right and ability to defend their interests within their respective regions. While strongly advocating respect for state sovereignty in the global arena, they are nonetheless willing and able to use their weight and influence within their own regions.[54] They have the economic, military and diplomatic power to make such regional action effective. They do not seek support from global powers to defend themselves, and to varying extents seek to discourage global powers from excessive military engagement within their regions. The GCC states are not in this position. No doubt they seek regional leadership, but this is strongly challenged by other regional states (Iran in particular). To safeguard their own security, moreover, they are reliant on external powers for support (military, diplomatic and political). Regional threats to their security are at the top of their foreign policy agendas.

The different way in which the GCC states relates to their regional environment, and the manner in which that affects their position in the global order, is significant. While they may be able to agree with BRICS countries on individual global issues, they do not share the same global outlook.[55] This is likely to continue to be the case for as long as the GCC states are unable to reconcile their differences with Iran (and to some extent with Iraq, in whatever shape that emerges from the ongoing conflict there). For the GCC states to adopt a similar world outlook to the BRICS, they would need to achieve reconciliation on a basis where the collective security of the Gulf region is guaranteed regionally – probably through regional security structures comprising all states bordering the Gulf. There seems little likelihood of this happening in the short term, however inevitable it may be in the longer-term.

7.5 *Assessing the Institutional and Geopolitical Reasons which Could Facilitate/Complicate GCC Inclusion*

Whatever economic and political gains there may be for both sides, there are institutional and geopolitical reasons (in addition to that given at the end of the last section) which make GCC inclusion in the BRICS grouping both difficult and unlikely. The first is that any expansion of the BRICS grouping from its current basis would be problematic. It is currently a finely-balanced group, whose cohesion rests in part on the ascribed prominence given to each country in its own region. No member, moreover, has reason to oppose the membership of the other existing members. Each country can draw pride in the exclusivity of the grouping: it puts them (putatively) at higher level than other countries in its region. Diluting this exclusivity by admitting neighbouring regional countries would be against their interests. The GCC would pose no problems for this exclusivity as it is outside the regions of any of the existing members, but it would raise other issues: If the GCC were included, why should other countries (Argentina? Mexico? Nigeria? Indonesia? Vietnam? Pakistan?) whose economies and global orientation might fit in better with those of the BRICS not be admitted? If the GCC were accepted into membership, how would other regional states with which BRICS countries have close relations react? Most specifically, following the latter point, could the GCC be included without Iran[56] (and perhaps Egypt) also being brought in? What problems would arise from admitting a set of countries which are currently embroiled with ongoing conflicts within the Arab/Middle Eastern region? It is unlikely that these concerns could be resolved, at least for as long as current conflicts in the Gulf region are ongoing.

Second, the GCC is structurally unlike the existing BRICS states, being a loosely-connected collection of sovereign entities. Saudi Arabia is a member of the G20 grouping, but the others are not. While the GCC countries share some common attributes with each other, and have established significant fields of cooperation, their interests can differ critically and they do not operate as a single political actor in global politics. If they were represented in BRICS meetings, it would have to be either by the GCC Secretary-General – who would have limited scope to agree to anything without referring it back to the 6 governments, which would themselves not necessarily have a common position – or else by the leader of one of the component GCC states (presumably Saudi Arabia). The latter option might be workable for the BRICS, but would not necessarily be acceptable to all GCC countries – who might not feel bound by agreements reached in this manner. In short, the GCC does not have an institutional structure which would make its inclusion of value to the BRICS grouping. The only GCC country which could be considered for BRICS membership individually would be Saudi Arabia, but the extent to which there is any comparability between the Saudi and BRICS economies is much more limited than if the GCC is taken as a unit.

8. Conclusion

This paper has shown that the BRICS countries and the GCC have a strong interest in cooperating more closely together, and if possible seeking areas in which some of their economic activities can be coordinated. It would be in the interest of both the BRICS and the GCC if the latter could achieve an observer status at BRICS

Summits, and perhaps be brought into participation in some of the committees which bring the representatives of BRICS countries together.

While formal membership of the BRICS grouping would be good for the GCC, however, it would not serve the interests of the BRICS grouping, and is unlikely to be seriously envisaged. The institutional/geopolitical factors which complicate inclusion are too great.

Notes

1 The organisation adopted the name BRICS in December 2010, when South Africa joined the previously existing BRIC grouping. In this paper the term "BRICS" will be used throughout, except when the reference is specifically to the period before December 2010, when "BRIC" will be used.

2 Jim O'Neill, "Building Better Global Economic BRICs", Global Economics Paper No: 66 (New York: Goldman Sachs, November 2001).

3 While the paper should not be seen as a starting-point for the BRICS grouping, it is clear that the acronym BRIC came from that paper, and perhaps some of the analysis reinforced the belief among BRICS countries that they share common interests.

4 For texts of the Declarations following IBSA Summits, see IBSA, "Celebrating 10 Years of Partnership", accessed June 2015. <http://www.ibsa-trilateral.org/about-ibsa/ibsa-summits>. The IBSA declarations, however, put more emphasis than BRICS declarations on the member countries' shared commitment to democracy and human rights.

5 A useful summary of the motivations which BRICS countries have in maintaining the BRICS organisation can be found in the comments made by four experts from the BRICS countries, interviewed in the run-up to the Seventh Summit in Ufa, 2015. See "Why do Brazil, Russia, China and India Need BRICS?", accessed May 2015. <http://carnegie.ru/eurasiaoutlook/?fa=60636>.

6 BRICS, *The BRICS Report 2012* (New Delhi: OUP, 2012), 13-14.

7 International Monetary Fund, *World Economic Outlook, April 2015*, accessed 5 June 2015. <www.imf.org/ external /pubs/ft/weo/2015/01/>.

8 This target was set by the BRICS trade ministers, meeting shortly before the 4th BRICS Summit in 2012. See <http://indiatoday.intoday.in/story/brics-targets-$500-billion-intra-group-trade-by-2015/1/179822.html>.

9 International Monetary Fund, *World Economic Outlook, op.cit.*

10 *Ibid.*

11 The South African economy is not the largest in Africa. The Nigerian economy is significantly larger. The latter, however, reflects the large part which oil production plays in the Nigerian economy, while the South African economy is more balanced. The World Economic Outlook projections for 2015 showed that South Africa would be clearly positioned as being the second largest economy in Africa in 2015 – significantly ahead of Egypt and Algeria (in third and fourth positions), and twice as large as all of the economies of East Africa combined. See *Ibid.*

12 BRIC, "First Summit: Joint Statement of the BRIC Countries Leaders", accessed June 2015. <http://brics6.itamaraty.gov.br/category-english/21-documents/114-first-summit-2>.

13 BRICS, "Fifth Summit: eThekwini Declaration and Action Plan", accessed May 2015. <http://brics6.itamaraty.gov.br/category-english/21-documents/69-fifth-summit>.

14 The importance which BRICS countries attach to the fact that all of them being members of the G20 grouping, and their commitment to using this body as a means to protect and project their interests, is clear from the prominence given to this in all BRICS Summit joint statements and declaration. Indeed, it figures as the initial clause in the First Summit Joint Statement. The clause reads: "We stress the central role played by the G20 Summits in dealing with the financial crisis. They have fostered cooperation, policy coordination and political dialogue regarding international economic and financial matters". BRIC, "First Summit", *op.cit.*.

15 International Monetary Fund, ""Historic Quota and Governance Reforms Become Effective", accessed March 2016. http://www.imf.org/external/np/sec/pr/2016/pr1625a.htm.

16 International Monetary Fund, "Acceptances of the Proposed Amendment of the Articles of Agreement on Reform of the Executive Board and Consents to 2010 Quota Increase", accessed June 2015. <http://www.imf.org/external/np/sec/misc/consents.htm>.

17 Concern over how the IMF is seen by countries which are not "major advanced economies", however, is reflected in how the IMF responded to the issue of Greece's debts in the first half of 2015. It would have been difficult for the IMF to take a more lenient position towards Greece, for fear of being accused by the BRICS and others of showing discriminatory favour towards a European country while other countries in financial crisis were treated more harshly.

18 BRICS, "Sixth BRICS Summit – Fortaleza Declaration", clause 18, accessed May 2015. <http://brics6.itamaraty.gov.br/media2/press-releases/214-sixth-brics-summit-fortaleza-declaration>.

19 BRICS, "Sixth BRICS Summit", *op.cit.*, clauses 13-15.

20 *Ibid*, clause 20.

21 See, Carnegie Moscow Center, "*Another BRIC(S) in the Wall*", accessed 12 July 2015. <http://carnegie.ru/eurasiaoutlook/?fa=60628&mkt_tok=3RkMMJWWfF9wsRogu6%2FKZKXonjHpfsX56O8qX6eg38431UFwdcjKPmjr1YYHS8t0aPyQAgobGp5I5FEIQ7XYTLB2t60MWA%3D%3D>.

22 BRICS, "Sixth BRICS Summit", *op.cit.*, clauses 22.

23 BRIC, "First Summit", *op.cit.*, clause 6.

24 BRICS, "Fifth Summit", clause 3.

25 The main document from which the information presented here is drawn is Government of Brazil, "Main Areas and Topics of Dialogue Between the BRICS", produced at the time of the Sixth Summit Meeting in Fortaleza, accessed June 2015. <http://brics6.itamaraty.gov.br/about-brics/main-areas-and-topics-of-dialogue-between-the-brics>.

26 *Ibid.*

27 *Ibid.*

28 See "BRICS Ministers Discuss First-Ever Cooperation Strategy Ahead of Ufa Summit", 8 July 2015, accessed 10 July 2015. <http://sputniknews.com/politics/20150708/1024342560.html>.

29 *Ibid.*

30 *Ibid.*

31 *Ibid.*

32 *Ibid.*

33 There are some problems in this procedure, given that it is dependent on material produced by the central banks and that this may not be framed on the same basis for each country. In the *BRICS Joint Statistical Publication 2014* (Rio de Janeiro: Instituto Brazileiro de Geografia e Estatistica, p.39), for example, India is shown as having a rate of GDP growth which is approximately double that which is documented in IMF publications. A note on India's figures explains the different basis on which it was calculated, but it creates confusion when the other countries' figures follow the IMF pattern.

34 BRICS, "Sixth BRICS Summit", op.cit., clause 23.

35 The TPP which is currently under negotiation includes provisions for the break-up of State-Owned Enterprises in partner states, and for the introduction of inter-state dispute settlement (ISDS) which would enable global businesses to sue governments for "loss of expected profits" when the introduction of new laws would damage their economic interests. Such cases would not be held in local courts but in international tribunals. None of the BRICS countries currently allow ISDS clauses in international treaties to which they are party. SOEs, enjoying an element of protection from MNC competition, played a major part in the rapid development and development of East Asian economies.

36 BRIC, "First Summit", *op.cit.,* clause 12

37 BRIC, "First Summit", *op.cit.*, clause 14.

38 BRICS, "Seventh Summit: Ufa Declaration", accessed April 2016. <http://www.brics.utoronto.ca/docs/150709-ufa-declaration_en.html>, clauses 7-8.

39 BRICS, "Sixth Summit", *op.cit.*,, clause 25.

40 *Ibid*, clauses 29-44.

41 BRICS, "Seventh Summit), *op.cit*, clause 27.

42 A good account of the China-Pakistan relationship, and its critical importance to both sides, is to be found in Andrew Small, *The China-Pakistan Axis* (London: Hurst, 2015).

43 The Indian political scientist Girijesh Pant describes the Indo-Chinese relationship as having a "conflictual mode", while at the same time stressing India's desire to avoid confrontation in the Gulf. He states: "India

does see China in the Gulf region as a player with potential to undermine its strategic position. However, it would not like to endorse any competitive engagement with China in the region". Girijesh Pant, "Emerging Dynamics of US-Gulf Engagement: India's Policy Options", in Steve Hook and Tim Niblock, eds. *The United States and the Gulf: Shifting Pressures, Strategies and Alignments* (Berlin: Gerlach, 2015), 146.

44 Data from Tim Callen, Reda Cherif, Fuad Hasanov, Amgad Hejazi and Padamja Khandelwal, "Economic Diversification in the GCC: Past, Present, and Future" (Washington: IMF Staff Discussion Note, December 2014).

45 *Ibid*, Figure 1.

46 South Korea has sometimes been mentioned as a possible BRICS member, but the nature and structure of the South Korean economy makes it a better fit with the advanced industrial countries.

47 See Tim Niblock, "China's Growing Involvement in the Gulf: the Geopolitical Significance", in Simon Shen and Jean-Marc Blanchard, eds, *Multidimensional Diplomacy of Contemporary China* (Maryland: Lexington Books, 2010), 216.

48 In July 2015, an agreement was signed between the Public Investment Fund (PIF) of Saudi Arabia and the Russian Direct Investment Fund (RDIF) to create a partnership to invest $ 10 billion in projects in Russia. See "Saudi Arabia fund to invest SR37.5bn in Russia", *Arab News*, accessed 10 July 2015. <http://www.gulfinthemedia.com/index.php?id=757632&news_type=Economy&lang=en>.

49 The relatively low level, and low rate of growth, of GCC-Russian trade would, up to recently, have suggested that Russia's relations with the GCC are not in the same mould as the other BRICS countries. However, the visit of King Salman's son and Deputy Crown Prince, Prince Mohammad bin Salman Al Saud, to Russia, between 17 and 20 June 2015, and his talks with President Putin, have created speculation that economic relations between Saudi Arabia and Russia will be substantially boosted. On this occasion, agreements on oil, space and nuclear power were signed. President Putin has now been invited to visit Saudi Arabia, and has accepted the invitation. A significant increase in Saudi-Russian trade, especially one which involved defence sales (which have been the subject of speculation), would change the balance of GCC-Russian trade. See *Asia Times*, 1 July 2015, accessed 1 July 2015. <http://oilprice.com/Energy/Crude-Oil/Is-Saudi-Arabia-Leaving-The-US-Behind-For-Russia.html>.

50 The importance of the One Belt One Road (OBOR) project, and the manner in which this links in with the Central Asian focus of the Shanghai Cooperation Organisation, is worth considerable emphasis. The OBOR project is closely associated with President Xi Jinping, and has been pursued with determination ever since President Xi assumed the presidency in 2012. In effect China now has a strategic orientation towards Eurasia. The concerns of the Shanghai Cooperation Organisation are no longer limited to trade but now cover wider economic, security and political issues, and the geographical scope seems likely to expand to include India, Pakistan and Iran. For some analysis of this, as it relates to the Gulf region, see Jeffrey Payne, "China's Iran Belt" (Washington: Middle East Institute), 8 June 2015, accessed 9 June 2015.<http://www.mei.edu/content/map/china%E2%80%99s-iran-bet>. There would clearly be benefits for the GCC if its links with BRICS were of use in enhancing its engagement with the Eurasia project, and prospective losses if it is left out of the growing Eurasian infrastructural and commercial networks. The linkage which is developing between the OBOR and the Russian-led Eurasian Economic Union (EEU) is important to note here. During President Xi Jinping's visit to Moscow in May 2015, the two sides apparently agreed to formally link the EEU and the OBOR. President Putin stated: "The integration of the European Economic Union and Silk Road projects means reaching a new level of partnership and actually implies a common economic space on the continent". See, *The Diplomat*, "At Russia's Military Parade, Putin and Xi Cement Ties", accessed 14 May 2015. <http://thediplomat.com/2015/05/at-russias-military-parade-putin-and-xi-cement-ties/>.

51 It is worth noting that 5 of the 6 member-states of the GCC are founding members of the China-led Asian Infrastructure Investment Bank. The GCC states with the largest stakes are Saudi Arabia (2.59% of the total shareholding) and the UAE (1.21%). The shareholdings of China and India are, respectively, 30.34% and 8.53% of the $100 billion total capital stock. The concept of the Bank was first raised at the 2013 Asia-Pacific Economic Cooperation meeting held in Indonesia – which itself is an indication of how membership of one organisation can play a supportive role in developments in another. For a report on the UAE's inclusion as a founding member, see *Al-Khaleej*, 30 June 2015.

52 BRICS, "Sixth BRICS Summit", *op.cit.*, clause 38.

53 *Ibid*, clause 39.

54 This is most clear in the cases of China, India and Russia: China's assertion of its rights in the East and South China Seas, India's perception of its special position in the Indian Ocean, and Russia's special concerns with states which emerged from the Former Soviet Union.

55 As one (minor) element regarding differing global outlooks, it should be mentioned that the BRICS countries lack much of the cultural soft power enjoyed by Western countries in the Gulf. Of the five BRICS countries, India probably has most – due to historical factors and the presence of some 7 million Indians in the Gulf region – but even that has limited significance to the cultural life of GCC citizens. China's soft power is beginning to expand, with the presence of three Confucius Institutes in the GCC (the first opened in Dubai in 2011, and the two others subsequently opened in Abu Dhabi and Bahrain). They mainly engage in the teaching of Mandarin, but with some associated cultural events such as on Chinese medicine. There are currently 440 Confucius Institutes worldwide.

56 Iran in fact has something of an advantage over the GCC with regard to BRICS. Due to its central Asian dimension, there is more reason for it to be integrated into the networks of communications being developed by Russia, China and India in that region (in part through the Shanghai Cooperation Organisation). As Iran is an observer at SCO gatherings, President Rouhani was invited (with other Central Asian republic leaders) to attend the joint BRICS-SCO summit meeting in Ufa, July 2015. GCC heads of state/government were not invited.

References

Becker, Uwe, *The BRICS and Emerging Economies in Comparative Perspective: Political Economy, Liberalisation and Institutional Change* (London: Routledge, 2014), pp 223.

BRIC, "First Summit: Joint Statement of the BRIC Countries Leaders", <http://brics6.itamaraty.gov.br/category-english/21-documents/114-first-summit-2>. Accessed June 2015.

BRICS, "Fifth Summit: eThekwini Declaration and Action Plan", <http://brics6.itamaraty.gov.br/category-english/21-documents/69-fifth-summit>. Accessed June 2015.

Callen, Tim et al, "Economic Diversification in the GCC: Past, Present, and Future" (Washington: IMF Staff Discussion Note, December 2014).

Government of Brazil, "Main Areas and Topics of Dialogue Between the BRICS", produced at the time of the Sixth Summit Meeting in Fortaleza,<http://brics6.itamaraty.gov.br/about-brics/main-areas-and-topics-of-dialogue-between-the-brics>. Accessed June 2015.

BRICS, "Sixth BRICS Summit – Fortaleza Declaration",<http://brics6.itamaraty.gov.br/media2/press-releases/214-sixth-brics-summit-fortaleza-declaration>. Accessed June 2015.

BRICS, *The BRICS Report 2012* (New Delhi: OUP, 2012).

Government of Brazil, "Main Areas and Topics of Dialogue Between the BRICS", produced at the time of the Sixth Summit Meeting in Fortaleza. See <http://brics6.itamaraty.gov.br/about-brics/main-areas-and-topics-of-dialogue-between-the-brics>. Accessed June 2015.

IBSA, "Celebrating 10 Years of Partnership", <http://www.ibsa-trilateral.org/about-ibsa/ibsa-summits>.

Instituto Brazileiro de Geografia e Estatistica, *BRICS Joint Statistical Publication 2014* (Rio de Janeiro: Instituto Brazileiro de Geografia e Estatistica, 2014).

International Monetary Fund, "Acceptances of the Proposed Amendment of the Articles of Agreement on Reform of the Executive Board and Consents to 2010 Quota Increase", <http://www.imf.org/external/np/sec/misc/consents.htm>. Accessed June 2015.

International Monetary Fund, *World Economic Outlook, April 2015*, <www.imf.org/external /pubs/ft/weo/2015/01/>. Accessed 5 June 2015.

Niblock, Tim, "China's Growing Involvement in the Gulf: the Geopolitical Significance", in Simon Shen and Jean-Marc Blanchard, eds, *Multidimensional Diplomacy of Contemporary China* (Maryland: Lexington Books, 2010), 207-232.

Niblock, Tim, "Gulf-Asia Economic Relations: Pan-Gulf and Pan-Asia Perspectives", in Tim Niblock (ed) with Monica Malik, *Asia-Gulf Economic Relations in the 21st Century* (Berlin: Gerlach, 2013), 5-34.

O'Neill, Jim, "Building Better Global Economic BRICs", Global Economics Paper No: 66 (New York: Goldman Sachs, November 2001).

O'Neill, Jim, *The Growth Map: Economic Opportunity in the BRICS and Beyond* (London: Portfolio Penguin, 2011), pp. 254.

Pant, Girijesh, "Emerging Dynamics of US-Gulf Engagement: India's Policy Options", in Hook, S, and Tim Niblock (eds), *The United States and the Gulf: Shifting Pressures, Strategies and Alignments* (Berlin: Gerlach, 2015), 132-150.

Jeffrey Payne, "China's Iran Belt" (Washington: Middle East Institute), <http://www.mei.edu/content/map/china%E2%80%99s-iran-bet>, accessed 9 June 2015.

Small, Andrew, *The China-Pakistan Axis* (London: Hurst, 2015), pp. 319.

2

GCC-BRICS Strategic Cooperation in the New Era: The Dual Implications of Geoeconomics and Geopolitics[1]

Degang Sun

1. Introduction

Since the end of World War Two, the world economic and financial order has gone through fourmain historical stages: US predominance (1945-1971); US-Soviet rivalry (1971-1991); Western predominance (1991-2008); and co-governance by both established powers and the rising powers (2008-present). In the first stage, the US offered global public economic and financial goods through the founding of the IMF, the World Bank and GATT (later renamed WTO). In the second stage, due to the decline of the US, the G7 was founded following the collapse of the Breton Woods system in the early 1970s. The G7 then became the predominant player in the global economic and financial architecture, together with the Soviet Union, another economic powerhouse. In the following decade, after the collapse of the Soviet Union, the US, Western European countries, Japan, Canada and Australia were the predominant engines of world economic growth and the major suppliers of global public financial goods.

In the 21st century, however, the countries of the Global South have achieved an imbalanced development. The big developing countries, represented by China, Russia (now placed in this category), India, Brazil and South Africa (BRICS) have risen to become substantial economic powerhouses. However, BRICS does not represent all the developing countries. The 57 Islamic countries, which account for almost 50% of all developing countries, do not have a seat within the BRICS. While

Turkey, Egypt, Iran, Indonesia, Kazakhstan, Nigeria and Algeria might all be seen as candidates for the future Greater BRICS membership, the GCC as a bloc may have more potentiality to be a strategic partner for the BRICS and even to become a new member of the BRICS.

2. The Origins of the GCC-BRICS Cooperation

The GCC was founded in May 1981 following the outbreak of the Iran-Iraq war. In the following three decades, the six monarchies have become the most prosperous and stable area in the troubledMiddle Eastern/Islamic world. The six Arab monarchies, which comprise three constitutional monarchies (Qatar, Kuwait, and Bahrain), two absolute monarchies (Saudi Arabia and Oman), and one federal monarchy (the UAE), share very similar political cultures and historical narratives, and broadly similar political systems and values. They share the same general policy orientations, such as concern with creating a monetary union and the establishment of a security community to counter regional threats, including those coming from Iran, Yemeni Houthis, and "the Islamic State". Despite its internal and external hurdles, in the past decade the GCC has evolved from being a political organization into an emergent security community.

Since the commencement of the global financial crisis in 2008, with diminishing US and European energy imports from the Gulf, Saudi Arabia, Qatar, Kuwait, Oman, and the UAE have been seeking to increase their energy exports to the rising economies of China and India, as also to other developing economies. They are, moreover, inclined to "look East" for political reasonsto balance against western pressure for democratization, human rights and freedom. The BRICS states are their potential strategic partners in these regards.

Compared with other international institutions and economic blocs, the BRICS is relatively young, more or less an informal political forum instead of a fully-fledged organization, and its birth is the outcome of the post-2008 global financial crisis. The terminology "BRIC" was coined by economist Jim O'Neill from Goldman Sachs Asset Management in his article "The World Needs Better Economic BRICs" in 2001. With the relative decline of the US, Japan and the Western European countries, O'Neill highlighted the importance of Brazil, Russia, India and China, and designated them as "rising stars".

In 2003, Brazil, India and South Africa established the Forum of IBSA, whileChina and Russia (and more distantly India) were becoming increasingly congenial with each other within the context of the Shanghai Cooperation

Organization (SCO). The first BRIC summit was held in Yekaterinburg (Russia) in 2009. The economic term "BRIC" had become a real and new forum for international cooperation.

In April 2011, South Africa joined the bloc. The five heads of states had come together for the first time in Sanyain China's Hainan province, where they issued "the Sanya Declaration". Thereafter, the dialogue mechanism was renamed "BRICS".[2] The BRICS has since then attracted significant world-wide attention, mainly because the grouping boasted – at least over the years immediately following its creation –quite sound economic growth, alluring development opportunities, abundant human resources, and budding markets. The bloc has shown great potential in terms of developing as a "new power" vis-à-vis the G7 and the OECD. Perhaps more importantly, the 5 BRICS countries all pursue independent foreign policies, rejecting a role as "puppets" of the West, and they all call for the thorough reform of the IMF, the World Bank and the WTO to better serve their interests.

China is the largest economy in the BRICS representing about 50% of the total BRICS GDP. In March 2013, during his visit to South Africa, Chinese President Xi Jinping said that the BRICS and other developing countries should strengthen their cooperation and solidarity to make use of their respective advantages, to cope with various kinds of ventures and challenges, and to achieve inclusive economic development. Hepraised the remarkable role played by the rising developing economies and especially the BRICS grouping:

In recent years, the G20 summit has achieved great progress, and the IMF has undertaken the reform of its division of voting shares, which is a crucial step for the reform on the global economic governance system. It (the reform) conforms to the demand forraising world productivity, and is conducive to global common development. Particularly, BRICS cooperation helps to promote a more balanced world economic development, better global economic governance and more democratic international relations.[3]

The five members of BRICS are basically satisfied with the current framework and level of cooperation within their organisation, and they have declined the admission of otherpotential members such as Argentina, Indonesia and Egypt. Although new members' participationmight enhance therole of developing countries on the world arena, it could also complicate the internal structure of BRICS. That having been said, the GCC can be seen as a potential candidate for the BRICS to build a partnership with in the future. Given that it is the locomotive for economic development and social stability in West Asia and North Africa, the

GCC plays a crucial role not only in the Middle East but also in the Islamic world. It could perhaps serve as a representative of these regions in the future BRICS architecture.

Table 2.1: The Ranking of GCC and the BRICS Members' GDP (in PPP) in 2014

Rank in the World	Country	GDP in billion US Dollars
1	China	17,617.3
3	India	7,375.9
6	Russia	3,564.5
7	Brazil	3,263.8
14	Saudi Arabia	1,605.7
29	South Africa	704.5
32	United Arab Emirates	599.8
49	Qatar	320.5
52	Kuwait	284.0
67	Oman	162.4
96	Bahrain	61.9

Source: "Report for Selected Country Groups and Subjects (PPP valuation of country GDP)," IMF, Retrieved June 4, 2015.

The outbreak of the global financial crisis in 2008 constituted a watershed in the development of global economic relations. World economic and financial power is no longer as centralized as it was before. The international order has been reshuffled, with the established powers and the rising powers as two distinct pillars. In the post-crisis era, the established powers of the US, Canada, Australia, the EU and Japan have formed one power centre- the Global North - while China, Russia, India, Brazil, South Africa and the GCC countries, acting as pivots of the developing economies, have formed the new albeit fragilepower centreof the Global South. In the 2014 world GDP rankings (based onpurchasing power parity), China ranks number one, India number three, and Russia, Brazil and South Africa rank numbers 6, 7 and 29 respectively. As an outcome of this new reality, the G7 has given way to the coexistence of G7 and G20, indicating that the Western countries are no longer the sole players in global economic and financial affairs; the century-long western-dominated economic architecture is fading away.[4]

With the rise of the BRICS and the GCC, among other regional blocs, multi-polarization isjust over the horizon. Compared with the declining West, the rising developing economies seem to have brought more hopes for the future. China in East Asia, India in South Asia, Russia in Eurasia, Brazil in Latin America, South Africa in the African continent and the Saudi-led GCC in the Islamic world have become the new locomotives of world economic growth. They have set models for other developing countries in their respective regions, and they are marching from the "periphery" to the "core" on the world stage, unprecedented in the past two centuries.

The more diversified pattern of global political economy has led to China, India, Russia, Brazil, South Africa and the Saudi-led GCC countries becoming the new engines of regional development in East Asia, South Asia, Eurasia, Latin America, Africa and the Middle East respectively. The International Monetary Fund statistics shows that in 2014, China, India, Russia, Brazil, Saudi Arabia, South Africa and United Arab Emirates rank top among the 35 world economies (see table 1). The GCC-BRICS cooperation conforms to the trend of the times, which will have far-reaching geo-economic and geopolitical implications.

Geo-economically, the bilateral and multilateral cooperation between the GCC and BRICS will be increasingly close-knit. The GCC-BRICS cooperation can reshape the century-long global economic architecture of "core, semi-periphery and periphery", as put forward by Immanuel Wallenstein, contributing to a more balanced world economic and financial governance through reform in the structures of the IMF, the WTO, the UN Global Climate Change Conference, and the World Bank. With such a prospect in view, it is not surprising that since the outbreak of the global financial crisis in 2008, the rising economies of China, India, Russia, Brazil and South Africa have, to varying degrees, sought to build close ties with the GCC.

Geo-politically, the cooperation between the GCC and BRICS has the potential to foster a new balance of power between the Global North and Global South, accelerating political multi-polarization through the growing role of the G20 and other institutions. However, the GCC-BRICS does not have the capability or motivation to confront the West; it will not aim to seek geopolitical rivalry with the G7 either. Due to each member's divergent strategic priorities, and a variety of domestic problems, the GCC-BRICS cooperation may take the form of non-binding, issue-based and lightly-institutionalised links, consisting of complex and networked bilateral and multilateral ties, particularly in the domain of low politics.

3. The Dynamics of GCC-BRICS Cooperation

There are three main factors which provide the incentive for BRICS and the GCC to form some kindof "coalition" in the future. The first stems from their shared economic potential and strength. Since the outbreak of the global financial crisis, the GCC and the BRICS countries have had to cope with the economic challenges at home and abroad which have ensued. The sudden financial crisis has exposed the flaws inherent in a global economic order dominated by US, Japan and the EU countries, and have aroused the rising powers' aspirations to carry out an all-round financial reform ofworld economic governance. The GCC and BRICS members cover about 30% of world territory, constituting some 45% of the world population and 20% of global GDP. They have achieved remarkable results in spearheading world economic growth. From 2008 to 2013, the G7's proportion of global GDP has decreased from 52.8% to 46.4%, and the developing countries' GDP has risen steadily.[5] In 2012, based on purchasing power parity, the GDP of developing countries exceeded that of the developed countries for the first time.[6] According to one academic projection, by 2035 China's GDP will exceed that of the US, and by 2039 the total GDP of the BRICS will surpass that of the G7.[7]

Second, the GCC and the BRICS countries have complementary characteristics. China is famous as the "world factory" due to its abundant labor resources and manufacturing capability; India is regarded as the "world office" due to its advanced software technology; Russia is the "world natural gas station" because it boasts the largest natural gas reserve in the world; South Africa is "kingdom of diamonds";[8] and the GCC countries are regarded as the reservoir of world energy, with proven oil reserves representing about 29.4% of the global total.[9] Besides, almost all of the above countriespossess significant consumer markets, abundant foreign exchange reserves, and large middle classes. The complementary nature of their economies is also reflected —in Russia, GCC, Brazil and South Africa being natural resource powers, while China and India are human resource powers. There is a clear potential for effective financial cooperation. In the sixth summit of the BRICS in July 2014, the heads of government of the five states unanimously agreed to establish the BRICS Bank with an initial capital of $100 billion and with Shanghai as its headquarters. The GCC countries are well-positioned to participate in the BRICS Bank and expand their cooperation with BRICS financially. They can do this through using the resources of their sufficient sovereign wealth funds and petro-dollar reserves.[10]

There are in fact many opportunities for financial cooperation. Due to the relatively limited supply of capital made available by the World Bank, the Asia Development Bank and the IMF, the BRICS are seeking to develop their own financial institutions so as to meet the developing countries' demand for more capital for infrastructure. China for instance announced in 2015 that it would establish the Asia Infrastructure Investment Bank (AIIB) as a "world bank" for the Eurasian developing countries. So far, along with Russia, India, Brazil, and South Africa, five GCC countries (Saudi Arabia, UAE, Qatar, Kuwait and Oman) have joined the AIIB. Bahrain is the only GCC country which has not. Up to the present, about 50% of the GCC's funds held by sovereign wealth fund(about $2.5 trillion) has been invested in western countries. GCC-BRICS financial cooperation could change that balance in the future.

Table 2.2: The GDP Growth Rate of BRICS Members, 2000-2015

Year	China	India	Russia	Brazil	South Africa	The World
2015	6.9%	7.0%	-3.7%	-3.8%	1.3%	3.0%
2011	9.3%	6.9%	4.3%	2.7%	3.1%	2.7%
2010	10.4%	9.6%	4.3%	7.5%	2.9%	4.3%
2009	9.2%	8.2%	-7.8%	-0.3%	-1.5%	-2.2%
2008	9%	7.1%	7.3%	5.1%	3.1%	2%
2007	13%	9.1%	8.1%	5.7%	5.1%	3.8%
2006	11.6%	9.7%	7.4%	4%	5.3%	4%
2005	10.4%	9.4%	6.4%	3.2%	5%	3.5%
2004	10.1%	8.3%	7.1%	5.7%	4.9%	4.1%
2003	10%	8.4%	7.3%	1.1%	3.1%	2.7%
2002	9.1%	3.8%	4.7%	2.7%	3.7%	1.9%
2001	8.3%	5.2%	5.1%	1.3%	2.7%	1.5%
2000	8.4%	4%	10%	4.3%	4.2%	4.1%

Sources: <http://data.un.org/>; <http://www.brics.utoronto.ca/>; ShenXixi, "The Cooperation and Mechanism of BRICS," Thesis, Fudan University, October 2011, p. 14; Dong Wen, "The Cooperation among the BRICS States: Dynamics and Prospect,"Thesis, Foreign Affairs University of China, 2011, p. 12.

As individual states, the GCC and the BRICS countries have common interests in global financial reform. According to the 2010 IMF reform blueprint, the quota share and voting power of the BRICS' countries would increase from 11.499% and

11.03% to 14.807% and 14.139% respectively. The arrangement was delayed for a long time by opposition in the US Congress, but was finally accepted in January 2016.[11] Lobbied by the developing countries, the IMF has also agreed tonew regulations, such as the introduction of the flexible credit line (FCL) and precautionary and liquidity line (PLL).[12] During the G20 summit in Mexico in 2012, the BRICS countries announced that they would increase their capital in the IMF, China by $43 billion, Russia, Indian and Brazil by $10 billion each, and South Africa by $ 2 billion.[13] Within the G20 framework, the GCC and the BRICS should also have the opportunity to foster reform of the IMF and other international financial institutions and to facilitate a more balanced global economic governance.[14]

The third factor is their mutually compatible political attitudes and approaches. The member states of BRICS and the GCC have divergent national conditions and political values. Nevertheless, there is also a commonality in that the major members of the GCC and BRICS have ambitious international goals and are not willing to succumb to Western pressures. They are determined to pursue national rejuvenation rather than being simply lesser powers and "economic subjects". They are insistent that Western values and political systems should not be imposed on developing countries and thatthe rights of developing countries should be respected. The western predominance over the international economic order, they believe, is flawed, and Western interference in developing countries' internal affairs will bring more bloodshed instead of peace. Regional conflicts should be solved by peaceful means, while a "war to end all wars" is harmful and dangerous.

Unlike the G7 predilection for regime change, humanitarian intervention and democracy promotion, the GCC and the BRICS countries highlight the importance of equality, dignity, justice, the respect for national sovereignty, international law and multilateralism.[15] The GCC is strongly opposed to Iranian interference in the internal affairs of Iraq, Syria and Yemen (although they themselves, of course, are interfering in the internal affairs of these three countries), and this principle – perhaps interpreted in different ways – has been echoed by the BRICS countries. In March 2014, in face of the Ukraine crisis, the West proposed a UN resolution at the Security Council, criticizing Russian annexationof the Crimea. To the Western countries' surprise, the rising powers of China, India, Brazil and South Africa all abstained, and tacitly they maintained a positive attitude towards Moscow.[16] On March 24 2014, the G7 suspended Russian membership in what had been the G8, condemning Moscow for having strayed away from the beliefs and international responsibilities which Western powers shared. On the same day, the five Foreign Ministers of the BRICS issued a joint declaration, pointing out the BRICScountries shared common values found on "peace, security, development, cooperation and building a more equal and just world". The so-called "building a more equal and just world" was apparently a response to the G7 declaration against Russia.[17]

BRICS and GCC membersalso share common interests and similar attitudes towards some other critical issues in world affairs. Climate change has been one such "issue". In 2013, the world emission of carbon dioxide stood at about3,527 million tons, and the GCC and BRICS members accounted for about 45% of this (China: 1,033million tons; India: 207million tons; Russia: 180 million tons; Brazil: 48million tons; South Africa: 33 million tons; and Saudi Arabia: 49 million tons).[18] BRICS and GCC member states stood together on this issue. They effectively formed a policy coalition, pointing out that the developed countries had been giving out high emissions for several centuries, and that they should now take more responsibility in curbing global climate change. BRICS and GCC member states have also worked together in the G20 and WTO Doha round negotiations, compelling the developed countries to make a commitment to reduce subsidies on their agricultural products from a total value of $110 billion to $14.5 billion.[19]

The fourthfactor is their sense of shared identity. In themodern era, the US, Japan Australia, Canada, and the western European countries formed the core of the world system, while Asian, African and Latin American countries were perceived as the "semi-periphery" or "periphery" of the world, apparently marginalized. In the early 21st century, China, Russia, India, Brazil, South Africa and Saudi Arabia have all become members of the G20, representing the rising economies. They share a dissatisfaction with the old political and economic order, such as the monopoly position enjoyed byUS dollars and the current reality of Western-led agenda-setting, and they stress that the rising economies and other developing countries should be accordeddue position in the new global order. The GCC and the BRICS members all wish to have a larger voice and stronger presence in the international economic and financial architecture, and they call for the reform of the IMF, the World Bank, the world copyright regimes, the agendas of global climate change conferences, and some other global institutions and practices.

The cooperation between GCC and BRICS countries has the potential to create significant spill-over effects, strengthening their cooperation in a number of other multilateral fields. For instance, China hasplayed increasingly important roles in the Shanghai Cooperation Organization, the East Asia Forum, the ASEAN Regional Forum, the Conference on Interaction and Confidence-Building Measures in Asia, the AIIB, theIndian Ocean Association for Regional Development, the China-Africa States Cooperation Forum, the China-Latin American States Cooperation Forum, and the China-Arab States Cooperation Forum. Through China, the other

BRICS members are engaging with the above-mentioned multilateral mechanism. In the long run, GCC association with BRICS can enable GCC members to benefit in the same way, consolidating their shared identity as rising developing countries.

Table 2.3: Regional Organisations Related to the GCC and the BRICS Members

	SCO	East Asia Forum	ASEAN Regional Forum	CICA	ISBA	Indian Ocean Association for Regional Development	Asia Infrastructure Investment Bank	China-Latin American States Cooperation Forum	China-Arab States Cooperation Forum
China	√	√	√	√		*	√	√	√
Brazil					√		√	√	
Russia	√	√	√	√			√		
India	√	√	√	√	√	√	√		
South Africa					√	√	√		
Saudi Arabia							√		√
Kuwait				√			√		√
Qatar				√			√		√
Bahrain									√
UAE							√		√
Oman						√	√		√

"√": full member; " * ": observer. Source: Xing Kaixuan, "The Mechanism for Regional Financial Cooperation of BRICS," *Journal of Economic Survey*, No. 10, 2014, p. 104.

4. The Principles of GCC-BRICS Cooperation

As mentioned, since the outbreak of the global financial crisis Western countries have been in relative decline, failing to provide the public goods for the international community which would justify their global leadership. The rising economies, represented by the BRICS and the GCC, are now seeking to expand their international presence, actively seeking to institute reform. GCC-BRICS cooperation is conducive to creating a more balanced international economic and political order, where the developing countries will have more representation, and where international regimes and practices will be more responsive to developing countries' concerns and interests. It will be suggested here that 3 key principles should underlie this cooperation.

First, the GCC and BRICS should adhere to a low level of institutionalisation in their cooperation. BRICS has a global agenda while the GCC at present only has a regional agenda. For that reason each one should first develop its own institutionalization. Only later should they consider institutionalising the relationship between them.

The GCC is not monolithic. It has been confronted with internal crises in recent years, and territorial disputes exist between its members states, such asthose between Saudi Arabia and the UAE, and between Saudi Arabia and Kuwait. The recent disputes over the oil field which straddles the border of Saudi Arabia and Kuwait have sabotaged GCC solidarity. Oman, moreover, has shown some disinterest in the GCC as a regional bloc. Nonetheless, the GCC remainsone of the most critical regional organisations in the Middle East.

BRICS, for its part, is becoming increasingly institutionalised. It is evolving from a symbolic dialogue forum to a fully-fledged political and economic mechanism for world economic and financial governance.[20] Apart from the summit, the senior representatives for security affairs, the foreign ministers and ministers of finance have engaged ina variety of multilateral conferences covering their respective fields, and have issued joint declarations after each of the ministerial conferences. For instance, in March 2010, the first BRICS Ministers of Agriculture conference was held in Moscow.[21]

While BRICS and the GCC will gain from cooperation on the global level, their differences must be recognised. They incorporate divergent cultures, political systems, national conditions, economic development levels and policy orientations. Their cooperation should adhere to a kind of low level integration with limited sovereignty transference. These countries will not aim to build something akin to a G77 or non-alignment movement, nor will they seek confrontation with the Global North. Rather, they willseek balanced relations between the Global North and the Global South on an equal footing.

The GCC-BRICS cooperation, then, can best focus on the following fields: buildinga more balanced, just and multi-polar international order; carrying out international financial reformand building a more stable, predictable and multi-faceted international currency system; ensuring that the multilateral system will evolve towards a win-win cooperation between the developed and the developing countries; encouraging GCC and BRICS members to involve themselves in more transparent dialogue systems with other organizations, in an incremental manner; and jointly dealing with the problems of trade protectionism, climate change, environmental deterioration, and other global issues.[22]

Second, the GCC and the BRICS should seek common ground while putting aside differences, and should build *ad hoc* coalitions on a case-by-case basis. The commonalities of the eleven countries are that they are developing countries focused on steady economic development and social stability as their primary tasks. At the same time, they have multiple identities, and no country can afford to ignore their relations with the US, Japan and western European countries. They are mostly reliant on western markets, technological assistance and investment. To the GCC countries, military and security cooperation with the US and western European countries, and economic and energy cooperation with the BRICS are equally important, and sometimes the former is more crucial to their regime security and national solidarity. Since the Syrian crisis deteriorated, Russia and China have vetoed the UN Security Council resolutions three times, and their political positions in this regard are in conflict with those of the GCC members.

The eleven countries are so divergent in political systems and economic developments that it is out of the question to build a developing countries' version of "G7". The recent decline of oil and natural gas prices has had a great impact on the energy exporters of Russia, Saudi Arabia, UAE, Qatar, Oman and Kuwait. GCC-BRICS cooperation should stick to the principles of flexibility, inclusiveness, and openness. They should seek common goals in solving the domestic problems inherent in bettering economic development and social governance (with the improvement of their Human Development Index rating as the goal here). Their close ties will increase the bargaining power which each has with Western countries, but this does not necessarily imply forming an anti-western bloc or alliance.

The case of Brazil is instructive. Its ties with the BRICS and the GCC are only two components of its global strategy. In 2007, an EU-Brazil Strategic Partnership was established, and in 2014 an EU-Brazil summit was held successfully. The US and Brazil are also building a strategic partnership, where the two sides stress their obligation to promote human rights and democracy. Brazil, in this regard, is perceived as a Western-styled democracy. The Brazil-India-Japan-Germany alliance aimed at membership of the UNSC is also an important platform for Brazil in building a network of global diplomacy.

To Russia, the Eurasia alliance with Kazakhstan, Kirgizstan, Tajikistan, Belorussia, etc is more important than South Africa, Brazil and the GCC countries.

To China, the BRICS and its ties with the GCC are only a small proportion of its all-round diplomacy. To India and South Africa, their respective cooperation with the West isequally important too.

Therefore, there is no "zero-sum" game for GCC-BRICS cooperation. The eleven countries are geographically remote from each other, divergent in political systems, different in economic interdependence level, and there is also internal geo-economic rivalry (between Russia and the GCC) and geopolitical competition (between China and India; and between Russia and Saudi Arabia). Saudi Arabia and Russia are not only competitive in global energy supply, but also in a state of "cold peace" with each other due to their disagreements over the Syrian and Yemeni crises; China and India are cooperative in geo-economic profile, but are cautious towards each other due to their geopolitical rivalry and the enduringborder disputes. Within the GCC-BRICS framework, the countries are not equally important. While the value of Sino-Russian bilateral trade has exceeded $60 billion in recent years, the value of Russia-South Africa trade has stood at little more than$200 million.

Third, the GCC and the BRICS should build a network of multi-faceted bilateral and multilateral cooperation. In the past several years, some BRICS members have established quite close bilateral relations with the GCC, as seen in the China-GCC strategic dialogue and FTA negotiations (so far not successful), the India-GCC strategic negotiation, etc. These efforts should set the scene for a wider dialogue between the BRICS and GCC leaders. The GCCmight also be an observer in the BRICS meetings.

In the foreseeable future, both bilateral and multilateral cooperation are feasible. Four levels of cooperation can be envisaged. The top level of their cooperation could be constituted by a summit of the eleven countries' heads of states: presidents, prime ministers, kings or amirs. The second level would be ministerial conferences of senior representatives for security affairs, foreign ministers, presidents of central banks, and ministers of commerce, agriculture, public health, science and technology, education and customs. The third level is representatives from sister cities, enterprises, and working groups, and the fourth level would be forums of think tanks, economic exchanges, training, civilization and friendship.[23] Their cooperation should start with practical and feasible domains, such as energy, financial and tradecooperation. As to the trade facilitation among the GCC and the BRICS members, domestic trade facilitation committee and intergovernmental coordinating organization are needed, and priority needs to be given to areas such as customs and regulatory environment.[24]

5. Conclusion

As rising developing economies, China, India, Russia, Brazil, South Africa and the Saudi-led GCC are all pivotal and staunch forces in the Global South, representing Confucian, Hindu, Orthodox, Catholic, African and Arab-Islamic civilizations. Their rise is not only the token of their respective national rejuvenation, but also the symbol of the transformation of the world political and economic order. The age-old Western predominance over the political and economic order is giving way to a multi-polar world.

With the relative decline of the "West" and the rise of the "Rest", BRICS and the GCC are steadily prioritizing each other in their respective global strategies, and are playing increasingly important roles in the world economic, energy and financial architecture. The GCC and BRICS share complementary and crucial energy interests and similar political values. Different from the western-dominated regional organizations of G7, OECD, NATO, EU, etc., which highlight the western values of freedom, democracy, human rights, rule of law, alliance politics and Washington Consensus[25], the member states of GCC and BRICS place more emphasis on the values of economic development, political authority, incremental reform and non-interference in other's internal affairs.[26] The GCC-BRICS countries all stress justice and fairness globally, and regard development as their primary tasks in their respective strategies. Their mutual cooperation will accelerate world economic and political multi-polarisation.

That being said, GCC-BRICS cooperationwill inevitably encounter old and new hurdles. First, although GCC members regard economic collaboration with BRICS as their priority, their security and defence reliance on the West remains intact, somehow diluting their strategic cooperation with the BRICS. Second, BRICS has hitherto been a loose dialogue forum rather than a monolithic regional organization. Its members are geographically decentralized. They have in recent years, moreover, been suffering from steady economic slowdown, particularly Russia, South Africa and Brazil. This may reduce their motivation for prioritising cooperation with the GCC.[27] So far, the US, Japan and the EU are still the most important economic partners for both. Without cooperation and collaborationwith the West, the rising developing countries would find it difficult to build a new international economic system, let alone a global political system.

To sum up, as rising economic and political powerhouses, the GCC and the BRICS nevertheless face various "growing pains" and will no doubt encounter more unpredictable challenges both at home and abroad. The two institutionsmayserve as a bridge connecting the Global South and the Global North, embracing both the stagnant Western countries and small struggling and unstable developing countries. Hopefully, the GCC-BRICS cooperation will transform the century-long western governance into a more balanced and multi-faceted "East-West co-governance" of the globe.

Notes

1 The author is indebted to Professor Tim Niblock for his constructive suggestions and advice an the early version of the book chapter.

2 Wu Jingyun, "The Trade Complimentarity and Competitiveness of BRICS," *Journal of International Business*, No. 2, 2012, p. 21.

3 "President Xi Jinping Was Interviewed by the BRICS Media," <http://www.mfa.gov.cn/mfa_chn/zyxw_602251/t1022932.shtml>; Pang Zhongying and Wang Ruiping, "On the Relations between the BRICS Cooperation and the Improvement of Global Economic Governance: A Strategic Perspective," *Journal of Contemporary World*, No. 4, 2013, p. 6.

4 Huang Wei, "The BRICS Members' Cooperation: Bases, Dynamics and Progress," *International Economics and Trade Research*, Vol. 30, No. 12, 2014, p. 53.

5 Zhang Haibing, "BRICS' Cooperation under the World Economic Structure Adjustment," *International Survey*, No. 5, 2014, p. 22.

6 Zhang Haibing, "BRICS' Cooperation under the World Economic Structure Adjustment," *International Survey*, No. 5, 2014, p. 22.

7 Dominic Wilson and Roopa Purushothaman, *Dreaming with the BRICS: the Path to 2050*, Goldman Sachs, 2003, p. 99.

8 Ouyang Yao, Zhang Yabin and Yi Xianzhong, "On the 'Inclusive' Growth in Foreign Trade Between China and Other BRICS Countries," *Chinese Journal of Social Sciences*, No. 10, 2012, p. 70; Li Wei, "The BRICS Mechanism and the Reform on the International Financial Governance," *International Review*, No. 1, 2013, p. 36.

9 "The GCC Countries' Oil Reserves," BP, June 2014.

10 Huang Wei, "The BRICS Members' Cooperation: Bases, Dynamics and Progress," *International Economics and Trade Research*, Vol. 30, No. 12, 2014, p. 55.

11 You Hongbing, "On the Promotion and Consolidation of the BRICS Cooperation," *Journal of World Economic Cooperation*, No. 8, 2014, p. 35.

12 Zhu Jiejin, "On the Transformation of the Cooperative Mechanism of the BRICS," *International Survey*, No. 4, 2013, p. 71.

13 Zhu Jiejin, "On the Transformation of the Cooperative Mechanism of the BRICS," *International Survey*, No. 4, 2013, p. 68.

14 Wang Hao, "The Global Financial Governance and the BRICS Cooperation," *Financial Supervision*, Vol. 21, No.2, 214, p. 84.

15 XuGuoqing, "The BRICS Countries' Summit in Durban: The New Opportunities for Africa's Development," *West Asia and Africa*, No. 3, 2013, p. 18.

16 You Hongbing, "On the Promotion and Consolidation of the BRICS Cooperation," *The World Economic Cooperation*, No. 8, 2014, p. 36.

17 BRICS Information Centre, "BRICS Ministers Meet on the Sideline of the Nuclear Summit in The Hague", <http://www.g8.utoronto.ca/summit/2014brussels/hague_140324.html>;<http://www.brics.utoronto.ca/docs/140324-hague.html>, accessed April 2016.

18 Jos G. J. Olivier and Marilena Muntean, *Trends in Global CO2 Emissions: 2014 Report*, The Hague: PBL Netherlands Environmental Assessment Agency, pp. 42-43.

19 Zhao Kejin, "The BRICS' Cooperation in China's International Strategy," *International Review*, No. 3, 2014, p. 48.

20 Zhu Jiejin, "On the Transformation of the Cooperative Mechanism of the BRICS," *International Survey*, No. 4, 2013, p. 59.

21 European Commission and Netherlands Environmental Assessment Agency, "List of Countries by 2012 Emissions Estimates," EDGAR Database, 2012; Zhong Longbiao, "The BRICS States in the International System Transformation," *Journal of CPC Tianjin Party's School*, No. 5, 2011, p. 34.

22 Fan Yongming, "BRICS Cooperation and Diversified Development in Asia", *Fudan Journal (Social Sciences)*, No. 6, 2013, p. 153.

23 Zhu Jiejin, "On the Transformation of the Cooperative Mechanism of the BRICS," *International Survey*, No. 4, 2013, pp. 61-62.

24 Shen Minghui, "On the BRICS Cooperation Mechanism: In Prospective of Cooperation on Trade Facilitation", *The Pacific Journal*, Vol. 9, No. 10, 2011, p. 35.

25 In 2004, the "Greater Middle East Initiative" was officially launched at the G7 Summit, aiming to carry out democratic reform on the authoritarian Islamic countries.

26 On the non-interference principle, the GCC countries seem to have double standards. Such as on the Syrian crisis, the GCC countries band-wagoned the West in fighting against the Syrian regime and attempts to affect the Syrian peace process; on the Yemeni crisis, the GCC countries harshly condemn Iranian interference in Yemeni internal affairs.

27 Wang Yuhua and Zhao Ping, "The Cooperation Mechanism of BRICS: Mechanism, Problems, and Countermeasures," *Contemporary Economy Management*, Vo. 33, No. 11, 2011, pp. 26-27.

References

BP, "The GCC Countries' Oil Reserves," (London: BP, June 2014).

BRICS Information Centre, "BRICS Ministers Meet on the Sideline of the Nuclear Summit in The Hague", <http://www.brics.utoronto.ca/docs/140324-hague.html>. Accessed April 2016.

European Commission and Netherlands Environmental Assessment Agency, "List of Countries by 2012 Emissions Estimates," EDGAR Database, 2012.

Fan, Yongming, "BRICS Cooperation and Diversified Development in Asia", *Fudan Journal (Social Sciences)*, No. 6, 2013, p. 153.

Huang, Wei, "The BRICS Members' Cooperation: Bases, Dynamics and Progress," *International Economics and Trade Research*, Vol. 30, No. 12, 2014, p. 55.

Li, Wei, "The BRICS Mechanism and the Reform on the International Financial Governance," *International Review*, No. 1, 2013, p. 36.

Olivier, Jos G. J. and Marilena Muntean, *Trends in Global CO2 Emissions: 2014 Report*, The Hague: PBL Netherlands Environmental Assessment Agency, pp. 42-43.Pang, Zhongying and Wang Ruiping, "On the Relations between the BRICS Cooperation and the Improvement of Global Economic Governance: A Strategic Perspective," *Journal of Contemporary World*, No. 4, 2013, p. 6.

Shen, Minghui, "On the BRICS Cooperation Mechanism: In Prospective of Cooperation on Trade Facilitation", *The Pacific Journal*, Vol. 9, No. 10, 2011, p. 35.

Wang, Hao, "The Global Financial Governance and the BRICS Cooperation," *Financial Supervision*, Vol. 21, No.2, 214, p. 84.

Wang, Yuhua and Zhao Ping, "The Cooperation Mechanism of BRICS: Mechanism, Problems, and Countermeasures," *Contemporary Economy Management*, Vo. 33, No. 11, 2011, pp. 26-27.

Wilson, Dominic and Roopa Purushothaman, *Dreaming with the BRICS: the Path to 2050*, Goldman Sachs, 2003, p. 99.Wu, Jingyun, "The Trade Complimentarity and Competitiveness of BRICS," *Journal of International Business*, No. 2, 2012, p. 21.

Xu, Guoqing, "The BRICS Countries' Summit in Durban: The New Opportunities for Africa's Development," *West Asia and Africa*, No. 3, 2013, p. 18.

Yao, Ouyang, Zhang Yabin and Yi Xianzhong, "On the 'Inclusive' Growth in Foreign Trade Between China and Other BRICS Countries," *Chinese Journal of Social Sciences*, No. 10, 2012, p. 70.

You, Hongbing, "On the Promotion and Consolidation of the BRICS Cooperation," *The World Economic Cooperation*, No. 8, 2014, p. 36.

Zhang, Haiping, "BRICS' Cooperation under the World Economic Structure Adjustment," *International Survey*, No. 5, 2014, p. 22.

Zhao, Kejin, "The BRICS' Cooperation in China's International Strategy," *International Review*, No. 3, 2014, p. 48.

Zhong, Longbiao, "The BRICS States in the International System Transformation," *Journal of CPC Tianjin Party's School*, No. 5, 2011, p. 34.

Zhu, Jiejin, "On the Transformation of the Cooperative Mechanism of the BRICS," *International Survey*, No. 4, 2013, pp. 61-62.

3

Taking BRICS to the GCC: Shaping an Indian Initiative to Promote a BRICS Role in the Gulf Security Scenario

Talmiz Ahmad

1. Introduction

Over the last six years since the BRICS countries–Brazil, Russia, India, China and South Africa - have been meeting at summit level, the organisation has achieved an extraordinary cohesiveness and confidence, and has been able to articulate considered views on a variety of issues of global interest. This is besides expanding intra-BRICS cooperation in several areas, including trade, finance, and investment, among others. Its most significant achievements to date are the agreements to set up the New Development Bank and the Contingent Reserve Arrangement. Several more such concrete achievements can be expected as BRICS vigorously pursues new ideas in different economic and financial areas.

BRICS has been articulating considered positions on a number of serious political problem areas, particularly in West Asia and Africa, highlighting its central conviction that "development and security are closely interlinked, mutually reinforcing and key to attaining sustainable peace." It has emphasised the role of multilateral efforts to promote global peace and security, particularly through the United Nations (UN) system, and has decried unilateral military interventions and economic sanctions.

The situation in West Asia has been of particular concern to BRICS leaders, which is reflected in their remarks at BRICS and other fora, and in the Declarations of the BRICS summits. All BRICS members have an abiding stake in West Asian security: they all have very substantial energy and economic ties with the region, and in several instances their relations have also acquired a strategic value as they have shared concerns relating to terrorism, extremism, sectarianism, drugs and arms trafficking and piracy, all of which have bases in different parts of West Asia.

China and India have special reasons to be concerned about the deteriorating security scenario in West Asia since their long term energy security and economic interests are linked to the region. Again, India has an 8 million-strong community in the region, while China's Silk Road project ("One Belt, One Road", or OBOR) is connected to West Asia both on the land and sea routes. Given such high stakes in regional security, BRICS cannot be "mute spectators" in the region's security scenario.

This chapter proposes that India, with its 5000-years of unbroken ties with West Asia, its economic and political standing in the region, and the high level of cultural comfort it enjoys with the countries of the GCC, should shape and lead a BRICS diplomatic initiative to promote a structured BRICS-GCC dialogue, complemented by a dialogue with Iran, on the lines of similar discussions that have been held by BRICS with African and South American leaders. This should then be followed by a robust initiative to prepare a platform for the principal contending powers, Saudi Arabia and Iran, to interact with each other to build mutual confidence and address issues in a moderate and accommodative spirit.

The chapter examines the various challenges this initiative faces, such as the deep divide between the Kingdom of Saudi Arabia and Iran; significant differences between India and China that might come in the way of BRICS' efforts in the region; and, above all, the readiness of BRICS to play such a security role.

2. BRICS: Economic and Political Evolution

BRICS has rather modest roots[1]: the acronym was developed by the chief economist of Goldman Sachs, Jim O'Neill, who, in his paper, "Building Better Economic BRICs", published in November 2001, identified the "BRIC" countries—Brazil, Russia, India and China, as economic powerhouses; his intention was to question the standing of the G-7 and stimulate investment in these non-western countries.[2] Two years later, in his paper, "Dreaming with BRICS: The Path to 2050", O'Neill and his team of economists forecast that the joint output of the four BRIC countries would surpass that of the G-7 (minus Canada) by 2040.[3] However, putting the countries together as a structured grouping was the brainchild of President Putin, who proposed the creation of BRIC at the meeting of the foreign ministers of Russia, India and China (the RIC countries) in September 2006, on the margins of the G-8 Outreach summit in St Petersburg. The BRIC grouping was expanded to BRICS with the decision of the foreign ministers in September 2010 to invite South Africa as a member.[4]

The BRICS countries collectively constitute a substantial grouping: they account for one-fourth of the world's landmass, 43 percent of the world's population (over 3 billion), 20 percent of global trade and 53 percent of global financial capital. They have half of the world's gold and foreign exchange resources ($4 trillion). Since 2010, more than 40 percent of global growth has come from BRICS. They also account for 23 percent of global economic activity: BRICS produce a third of the world's industrial products and one half of agricultural goods. In 2014, the BRICS' economies attracted 20.5 percent of the world's total foreign direct investment, and 14 percent of capital investment.

In 2010, China surpassed Japan as the world's second largest economy. Brazil became the sixth largest in 2011, with India and Russia also in the top ten. Intra-BRICS trade is valued at only $240 billion, but it has been growing at 28 percent annually. The collective GDP of BRICS is $32 trillion, a 60 percent growth since BRICS was set up, and accounting for about 30 percent of global GDP; it is likely to have 40 percent of the global GDP by 2050.[5] China and India are two great success stories in BRICS: in 2000, China's GDP was $1.2 trillion; in 2014, it had become $10 trillion. India's GDP in 2000 was $463 billion; in 2013, it was more than $2 trillion.[6] In 2014, the combined output of BRICS almost matched that of the US; just eight years ago, the US economy had been twice the size of BRICS.[7]

BRICS meetings at leaders' level take place at annual summits and on the margins of the G-20 summits; meetings of foreign ministers are held on the margins of the United Nations General Assembly (UNGA), and regular ministerial meetings of different economic ministers (trade, health, agriculture, and science and technology) take place through the year, as also those of national security advisors. Senior officials meet regularly as well to discuss specific issues mandated by leaders and ministers. BRICS is also supported by three non-governmental dialogue platforms: the finance and business fora and the academic forum; the latter functions as the track-II "BRICS Think Tank Council" (BTTC).

BRICS' leaders first met at summit-level at Yekaterinburg in Russia in June 2009, after which regular summit meetings have been held annually. The first summit took place amidst the ongoing global financial crisis and called for a reform of global financial institutions. The second summit in Brasilia addressed global governance issues, including reform of existing institutions and increased global cooperation in the full range of economic concerns of developing countries.

At the third meeting in Sanya, China, BRICS exhibited considerable internal institutionalisation. It met under the theme, "Broad Vision, Shared Prosperity", and, while re-affirming earlier interest in global economic reform, also articulated firm positions on political matters such as the need for robust multilateral diplomacy with the UN at its centre, the UN Security Council role in the Libyan crisis, and international terrorism.[8]

The Delhi summit in March 2012 was marked by a new confidence and cohesiveness in this grouping as indicated by the content and tone of the Delhi Declaration.[9] This document encompasses all the principal economic and political issues which cause deep concern to the emerging economies, and, taken together, it constitutes a firm rejection of the West-dominated global scenario. The overarching theme of the summit, "BRICS Partnership for Global Stability, Security and Prosperity", clearly stated the core interests of the leaders as they set out to critique what they saw was wrong and provide corrective principles and approaches. Thus, they expressed concern about the current global situation and criticised the policies of some Western countries whose actions were having a negative effect in developing countries as well.

The Delhi summit was equally vocal in the political domain. It gave priority to "the stability, peace and security of the Middle East and North Africa", and urged that the longstanding Arab-Israeli conflict be addressed quickly, a criticism of American and Israeli attempts to ignore the peace process and focus on Iran and other aspects of the fallout of the Arab Spring. With regard to Syria, BRICS rejected outside interference and preferred "to facilitate a Syria-led inclusive political process." On Iran, the BRICS leaders insisted that the situation not be allowed to escalate into conflict, which would have "disastrous consequences".

The fifth summit in Durban, South Africa, agreed in principle to the setting up of the BRICS Development Bank and the Contingent Reserve Arrangement (CRA) as a financial safety net for member countries.[10] The Declaration criticised the economic policies of western countries that, propelled by domestic mandates, had an adverse impact on the economic well-being of developing countries. The summit also articulated firm positions on a wide variety of international political issues, such as: Syria, Palestine, Iran, Afghanistan, problems in Africa (Mali, Central African Republic, South Sudan and the Democratic Republic of Congo) and terrorism. The BRICS leaders also reiterated their commitment "to increasing our engagement and cooperation with non-BRICS countries" and announced that, after the summit, they would meet other African leaders under the theme

"Unlocking Africa's Potential", which would focus on infrastructure development in Africa.

The sixth BRICS summit at Fortaleza, Brazil, marked the commencement of the next full cycle of summit-level engagements. It was historic in that the agreement to set up the $100 billion New Development Bank and the treaty on the establishment of the $100 billion CRA were signed.[11] These were complemented with other path-breaking intra-BRICS economic cooperation agreements, such as the memorandum of understanding (MOU) on cooperation among BRICS Export Credit and Guarantees Agencies and on innovation as part of the BRICS Inter-bank Cooperation Mechanism. The summit also mandated experts to study cooperation in new areas such as insurance, re-insurance, taxation and tax evasion.

The setting up of the New Development Bank marks a significant milestone not only for BRICS but for attempts to pursue a reform of the world economic order. It has been seen as representing the eastward shift of economic and financial power and heralds an overdue corrective to present-day arrangements. This would include changes in the governance of existing global economic and financial institutions; a steady shift away from the dollar in favour of the Chinese renminbi, and the strengthening of local currency debt markets.[12] Following the precedent set in South Africa, after the Fortaleza summit the BRICS leaders had a joint session with leaders of South American nations.

The BRICS leaders met at their seventh summit at Ufa, Russia, and issued the Ufa Declaration and Action Plan on 9 July, 2015. The summit also adopted the Economic Partnership Strategy, which set out, in President Putin's words, "concrete agreements on the development of our [BRICS] association and the consolidation of its international status, and provided for comprehensive measures to deepen our coordination in foreign policy, and expand mutual trade, investment and technology exchange."[13] The leaders also agreed to set up a virtual secretariat through a special website. The action plan noted that 35 meetings had taken place under the Russian presidency and a further 25 events would take place till the end of its presidency in February 2016.

Taking into account the Declarations of the seven summits so far, the following are the main themes and approaches that have come to inform the BRICS agenda:

i. The need for a thorough reform of the existing global financial, economic and political institutions so that they more fairly reflect the changes that have taken place in the world order since these institution were set up several decades ago.

ii. BRICS leaders favour the multilateral approach, with global and regional issues being addressed through the UN and its agencies; hence, they call for the reform and strengthening of the UN system.

iii. BRICS is focused on enhancing intra-BRICS cooperation and interactions. In this regard, it is constantly looking for new ideas and opportunities, which are approved at summit level after they have been thoroughly examined at Track-II, official and ministerial levels. Every summit declaration is accompanied by an Action Plan for the next year which is then reviewed at summit level; thus, not only has the BRICS agenda constantly been expanded, new institutions for cooperation and new platforms for dialogue have been set up year after year.

iv. BRICS leaders are anxious to engage with other developing countries and groupings, having done so recently with African and South American nations.

v. Above all, BRICS leaders recognise that "development and security are closely interlinked, mutually reinforcing and key to attaining sustainable peace."[14]

BRICS has come a long way from its early years when it faced considerable derision in the West. Responding to the criticism in the *International Herald Tribune* that BRICS is "an artificial bloc built on a catchphrase", the veteran Indian journalist, Prem Shankar Jha, in 2012 placed the new grouping in historical perspective: he pointed out that BRICS was "a challenge to the two-century old hegemony of the West over the modern increasingly inter-dependent world."[15] The Delhi Declaration, according to him, was not just a comprehensive criticism of the failures of the West, it also offered an alternative blueprint for the better management of our inter-dependent world.

Not surprisingly, BRICS's robust intervention in world affairs and its criticism of several aspects of the contemporary order provoked severe criticisms from several Western commentators who saw the group's pronouncements as "anti-American hot air". Walter Ladwig of the Royal United Services Institute opined: "this focus on institution-building is misplaced. It is the fundamental incompatibility of the BRICS nations, not their lack of organisation, which prevents [them] acting as a meaningful force on the world stage."[16]

Commentators in the BRICS, nonetheless, have been deeply conscious of the significance of the grouping and the shift in global power structure it represents. For instance, according to *The Hindu*, the Delhi Declaration was "a clear signal that the [BRICS] states have global weight and mean eventually to use it"; this was a "new milestone", though the group would need to go much further before it could play an effective role in world affairs.[17] The Chinese scholar, Du Youkong, pointed out that "[f]rom being followers, BRICS countries are evolving into rule makers", and applauded the various dialogue and cooperation platforms that were being put in place.[18] The Indian economist, Rajiv Kumar, believed that "BRICS represents an alternative pole in global governance in an increasingly multipolar world", and emphasised the common interest of the countries concerned in promoting development, eliminating poverty, protecting the environment and maintaining a free and liberal trading order.[19]

3. The New World Order

Even as the BRICS countries have consolidated themselves institutionally and have taken firm positions on economic and political issues of global significance, the West-led world order, put in place after the Second World War and largely effective over the last 70 years or so, now gives every indication of fraying and of being much less resonant in world affairs.

Western writings over the last few years have been flush with references to the US in retreat. In a recent article, Ian Bremmer said, "Americans seem as uninterested as many Britons in a more ambitious foreign policy", and that, over the long term, they will not support commitments requiring more troops and dollars.[20] At the same time, he noted, "a growing number of governments have the self-confidence to resist Washington."[21] In this situation, Bremmer advocated that US allies "prepare for a world in which American power means less than it used to", and pursue other "constructive relations", including those with China and Germany.

The theme of US retreat from active international leadership has also been picked up by James Rubin, a senior official in the Clinton presidency, who noted the failure of its approach in West Asia, where, in his view, the US "has neither extinguished nor contained the wildfire of civil war and extremist terror."[22] In fact, Rubin even saw an all-round US failure in Europe where, he believed, Obama had failed to confront Putin, and in Asia where China has refused to back off on the Islands' issue.

Michael Klare believes that the US predicament is a result of "imperialist overstretch", described by Paul Kennedy as the situation in which "the sum total of the US's global interests and obligations is … far greater than the country's power to defend all of them simultaneously".[23] Klare concludes that this situation is not likely to be reversed and points out that

> China is far more powerful than it was 13 years ago, Russia has largely recovered from its post-Cold War slump, Iran has replaced the US as the dominant foreign actor in Iraq, and other powers have acquired significantly greater freedom of action in an unsettled world.[24]

While reducing its global responsibilities, Klare suggested that the US place greater reliance on allies. Here, he reflected Obama's own views: in a *New York Times* interview in April 2014, the US president had bluntly criticised China as a "free rider" in Iraq. According to Obama:

> They [the Chinese] are free riders. And they have been free riders for the last 30 years and it's worked really well for them.... Nobody ever seems to expect them to do anything when this stuff [the fighting in Iraq and Syria and the rise of extremist elements] comes up.[25]

The president's comment elicited a sharp rejoinder from the Chinese official media which described the comment as an instance of ingratitude and scapegoating. Referring to "the failure of the US Middle East policy", it described the US as an "invader and deserter", while China itself was a "partner and builder" in Iraq: after the US withdrawal from Iraq in 2011, it had contributed 60 percent of the reconstruction funds and 40 percent of the substantial facilities.[26]

While this exchange took place in the specific context of Iraq and Syria, which were then (as now) in the throes of large-scale civil conflict, the president's desire for increased responsibility-sharing by other countries is applicable to the region's other trouble spots as well. In the same interview that caused so much offence to the Chinese, the president, after reviewing the various problem areas in West Asia–North Africa, asked in frustration: "Do I have the partners—local and/or international—to make any improvements [that] we make self-sustaining?"[27]

This question needs to be answered not just by China but by every other BRICS member since each of them has a direct and abiding stake in Gulf security. However, with the US exercising a monopoly on the use of power and influence in the region for the last several decades, they have so far not been in a position to play an influential role in promoting the security of the region.[28] Now, with the US overwhelmed by the complexity of the competitions, conflicts and state-breakdown that its erstwhile policies have created in West Asia, and clearly unwilling to expend the human and financial resources required to address the region's confrontations, an opportunity may have opened for the BRICS members to play a role in stabilising the region.

4. The Gulf Security Scenario

Over the last 25 years, the Gulf has been in the throes of instability due to the following factors: (a) the US-led military intervention in Kuwait and Iraq in 1991; (b) its "dual containment" policies against Iraq and Iran in the 1990s; (c) its robust and ongoing military actions in the region after 9/11 as part of the global war on terror; (d) its assault upon Iraq in 2003; and, (e) till 2013, its confrontation with Iran and the frequent threats of military action. Further west, in the same period we have witnessed the failure of the Israeli-Palestinian peace process, the harsh Israeli response to the second Intifada in 2000, the assault upon Lebanon in 2006, and the attack upon Gaza in 2009. East of the Gulf, in South Asia, we see continued conflict in Afghanistan between the Taliban and a weak central authority, in tandem with Al Qaeda-fomented extremist violence which originates in Pakistan but whose destructive tentacles reach across South Asia, the Arabian Peninsula, large parts of West Asia, the Horn of Africa, and now much of north and central Africa as well.

The scenario has been further complicated by the emergence of the Islamic State of Iraq and Syria (ISIS) as a political and military power across large parts of Iraq and Syria, now proclaimed as the caliphate of the Islamic State (IS). Thus, high levels of turmoil, insecurity and uncertainty are apparent across the entire swathe of territory from the Western borders of India to Palestine on the Mediterranean, described by Gary Sick as a "perfect storm".[29]

In the wake of the Arab Spring, over the last five years West Asia has been experiencing what Philip Gordon has called "a period of tectonic and destructive change", with Syria, Libya and Yemen in the grip of widespread civil conflict, even as a military dictatorship has been restored in Egypt.[30] Gordon traces these developments to the interplay of major historic forces which have caused: (a) collapse of state authority and erosion of national borders; (b) a burgeoning sectarian divide emerging from Saudi-Iran rivalry for regional influence; (c) an intra-Sunni divide, primarily between those advocating the continuation of the authoritarian state order and those backing the reformist doctrines of political Islam, largely influenced by the Muslim Brotherhood and its affiliates; and, (d) absence of any progress in the Middle East Peace Process.

The most significant development in the Gulf, in the face of the challenge of domestic reform emerging from the Arab Spring, has been the decision of the GCC countries to abandon policies of moderation and dialogue and to actively oppose what they see as Iran's hegemonic intentions in the region. Thus, the GCC countries, which till recently had been bastions of low-key, accommodative politics, are today confronting Iran on sectarian and strategic bases, in Syria, Iraq and Yemen. The GCC role has included a direct military assault on Yemen, and provision of weaponry, training and logistical support to rebel forces in Syria, including to Salafi elements with ties to jihadi forces affiliated to Al Qaeda, some of whom are said to be cooperating operationally with the IS in Syria. In Iraq, the war against the IS has taken a sectarian colour, with the Shia militia, backed by Iranian forces, leading the fight against jihadis in that deeply fragmented country.

The silver lining in this grim scenario has been the dialogue between the P5+1 and Iran, culminating in the agreement on the nuclear issue in July 2015. However, both Israel and Saudi Arabia continue to see in a settlement with Iran a grave threat to their interests, and are mobilizing support in Washington to obstruct the full normalization of US-Iran ties. Thus, not only is the US paralysed in West Asia, its political order at home has also become increasingly divided and dysfunctional due to party political differences.[31]

5. Political Context of BRICS Outreach to the Gulf

The above discussion indicates that spaces and opportunities have been thrown up for BRICS to consider playing a role in the Gulf for the promotion of regional security and stability. Before defining such a role, it is important to review the BRICS-related political context at global and regional levels within which it would take shape. This is looked at in the following sections.

5.1 Sino-Russian Relations

The most significant development at the global level is the estrangement between Russia and the western countries, led by the US, in regard to Ukraine, commencing with the overthrow of President Viktor Yanukovych in February 2014. This issue has led to Putin abandoning his earlier "Greater Europe" project linking Lisbon with Vladivostok in favour of a "pivot" to Asia, particularly China.[32] Thus, over the last two years, Russia has robustly expanded its energy and economic links with China, not only providing China with much-needed energy resources but also strengthening financial, investment, technology, and even defence ties.[33] More importantly, Putin has also accepted an enhanced Chinese presence in Central Asia by linking China's Silk Road Economic Belt with his own Eurasian Economic Union (EEU) proposal.

In May 2015, Russia and China conducted joint naval exercises in the Mediterranean, signaling their tightening military and political ties. The Russian deputy defence minister, Anatoly Antonov, said these exercises conveyed a common understanding of "challenges and threats" and "the need to restructure the current world order".[34] By conducting these exercises in the eastern Mediterranean, the first time that the Chinese navy sailed in these distant waters, the two countries have taken their cooperation to the very edge of Eurasia.[35] These seas constitute the western end of China's New Silk Road, giving China the opportunity to upgrade Mediterranean ports such as those of Piraeus (Greece), Marseilles and Barcelona, besides building a railway line linking Haifa and Tel Aviv with Eilat on the Red Sea.

Gabuev points out that over time Sino-Russia ties will "become stronger and more comprehensive", though Russia could seek to balance these ties through increased cooperation with India and Vietnam, while China would retain a cooperative relationship with the US.[36]

5.2 China's Interests in West Asia

Besides the extension of Chinese presence into the waters of the Mediterranean, facilitated by its burgeoning economic, political and defence ties with Russia, China is also taking a fresh look at its interests in West Asia. China already has very substantial energy and economic ties with the region: West Asia provides 55 percent of its oil imports, with five of China's top suppliers coming from this region. West Asia will also be meeting China's increasing gas requirements in coming years, with Qatar having become its second largest supplier in 2013. China's two-way trade with West Asia is valued at $300 billion annually, while the total value of its contracts is $120 billion. Its FDI in the region is about $10 billion. With the setting up of the renminbi [RMB] clearing centre in Doha in April 2015, China has taken forward its plan to promote global trade in its currency instead of the dollar and thus realise its aspirations to become a global economic presence.[37] The Chinese currency has been further buttressed after the IMF has included it in its basket of benchmark currencies to calculate the exchange value of its Special Drawing Rights.[38]

Outside the BRICS framework, China has set up the Asian Infrastructure Investment Bank (AIIB): on 15 April 2015, China announced that 57 countries had joined as founding members. The bank is expected to provide funding for infrastructure projects that normally do not attract funding from the World Bank and the Asian Development Bank. Thus, it is expected to complement rather than challenge the existing institutions. Its funds will be mainly used to finance the ambitious road and rail projects that are part of the Silk Road initiative (i.e., One

Belt, One Road) across Eurasia. These investments will cover over 60 countries, with projects in Central Asia alone being valued at $50 billion.[39] All the BRICS and GCC countries (excluding Bahrain) have joined the bank, as have several EU countries, including Germany, UK, France, Italy and Switzerland. The only major exceptions are the US and Japan.[40] Jonathan Pollack describes the US and Japanese positions as "problematic at best and churlish at worst", emerging from US concerns that the initiative will promote Chinese interests and undermine existing institutions.[41]

One new factor has now become resonant in China's interests in West Asia: China's "Silk Road" proposals have a maritime dimension which links the Malacca Strait with India and Kenya, then north to the Horn of Africa and to the Mediterranean, before meeting the land route at Venice.[42] These plans place West Asia at the centre of the land and sea routes through Eurasia and the Indian Ocean. The Chinese special envoy for the Middle East, Gong Xiaosheng, has said that West Asia will be important to implement the project and may become "the earliest to see the results".[43]

China's traditional policy in West Asia has been one of non-intervention. But, recent developments have persuaded at least some Chinese policy makers that continued adherence to this approach could jeopardise China's interests.[44] They note in this regard that political turmoil in Syria, Libya and Iraq has directly affected China's energy and economic interests, since China had significant investments in all these countries. Again, in the case of Libya, China was required to evacuate 35,000 of its nationals to safety. The situation in Iraq is particularly difficult since China already imports 50 percent of Iraq's production and had planned to raise this to 70 percent [850,000 barrels per day] before the advent of the ISIS menace in mid-2014.[45] Besides the purchase of oil, Chinese companies have invested heavily in the exploration and development of major oil fields in Iraq. The threat to its interests in Iraq has compelled China to reach out to Iraqi Kurdistan.

The problem of Syria has forced China to take considered positions in alliance with Russia against western military intervention: in 2011, China opposed external interference in that country, saying that the conflict was an internal matter. Since then, China has exercised its veto four times to deter foreign involvement in the conflict, while participating with the UN-sponsored initiative to rid Syria of its chemical weapons.

While China has gone against the US and GCC positions in regard to Syria, it has been more accommodative of the US in respect of Iran by respecting American sanctions and drastically reducing its purchases of Iranian oil; however, China remains Iran's largest trade partner, with two-way trade amounting to $ 52 billion in 2014, a 31 percent increase over the previous year. Again, China has also maintained a steady rhythm of engagement with the GCC countries and the Arab world in general through well-established dialogue platforms. The most important of these is the "Strategic Dialogue" it has with the GCC countries, established in 2010. At the third dialogue meeting in 2014, the two sides agreed to work towards shaping a strategic partnership, the highest level of engagement from the Chinese perspective.[46]

The Chinese scholar Chaoling Feng has noted China's important stakes in West Asia, the possible harm to Chinese interests due to non-involvement, the US interest in a Chinese security role in the region, and, above all, the interest of the GCC countries themselves in a larger Chinese role in the region to balance the western presence.[47] He has explained China's reluctance to pursue a proactive policy (advocated by Feng himself) thus: (a) China is not as familiar with West Asian affairs as compared to the US or Europe; (b) given China's substantial ties with both Saudi Arabia and Iran, it is just not able to decide to pursue bilateral interactions or adopt a collective regional approach; it just does not have all the required information to take such a crucial decision; and hence, (c) it suits China not to challenge the incumbent powers in the region.[48]

5.3 India's Interests in West Asia

This lack of confidence on China's part to play a more proactive political role in West Asia, even when its interests demand that it do so, creates the space for India to initiate, craft and propel a BRICS engagement with the GCC and complement it with an interaction with Iran. The logic behind this initiative is compelling. Like China, India has an abiding interest in Gulf security: it obtains 80 percent of its oil from this region; this dependence will go up to over 90 percent by 2035. The GCC is also one of India's largest trade partners, with two-way trade being valued at $150 billion in 2013-14. India has already built very substantial investment and joint venture engagements with the GCC countries, with every indication that these will expand dramatically in coming years.[49]

But, in contrast to China, India has a unique asset and a responsibility in the region—the presence of its community. Indians now number about 8 million in the GCC, with about 3 million each in Saudi Arabia and the UAE, well over half a million in Oman, Qatar and Kuwait, and just below half a million in Bahrain.[50] In fact, Indians constitute the majority community in at least three GCC countries—the UAE, Qatar and Bahrain; they are also the largest expatriate community in every country of the GCC and are well ahead of the number two community.

The Indian work force in the GCC remits to India about $35 billion annually.[51] Assuming that one expatriate worker supports at least four others at home, it can be safely assumed that about 40 million Indians benefit directly from the Indian presence in the GCC. Again, Indians play a significant role in the economy of the GCC: besides the contribution of labour, technicians and professionals in developing the region's infrastructure, industry and the services sector, Indian business persons, tycoons and small and medium entrepreneurs are increasingly becoming an important force in the economies of the GCC countries in diverse sectors—infrastructure and real estate development, industry, retail and services (education, health, etc.).

This significant Indian presence in the GCC is no accident: for over 5,000 years there has been an unbroken connectivity between the cities of western India and the ports of the Gulf and the Arabian Peninsula. This engagement has been commercial, intellectual and spiritual, and has shaped the civilisational ethos of the Indians and the Gulf Arabs. For several centuries, there have been colonies of Indian merchants and their family members in Gulf towns, while Arabs have had a congenial home in the Malabar. These links were, in fact, strengthened during the period of British domination of India, the Gulf and the Indian Ocean, when Gulf affairs, political, military and commercial, were controlled and funded from India.

The welfare of the Indian community is of abiding interest to all governments in Delhi, and several state governments as well. On several occasions during periods of grave regional crises, the Indian government has mounted major rescue operations, mobilising substantial national resources for the purpose. The government also has an interest in ensuring that Indians continue to be recruited for employment in the Gulf; thus, the review of domestic procedures and engagement with GCC governments to address welfare measures is a constant effort of the government and its officials in the region. The one point on which there is full understanding in India is that no national effort would make it possible to bring millions of its citizens out of the region in the event of a conflagration directly involving the region's major powers. Hence, the primary responsibility of the Indian government is to ensure that such apocalyptic contingencies are *prevented* through diplomatic effort.

India thus enjoys an advantage in the Gulf that China does not have—deep familiarity with the region and its people, and a high level of cultural comfort that the two peoples have with each other. While India's political ties with the GCC states have had their fair share of ups and downs due to their different engagements during the Cold War—particularly the ties of GCC countries with Pakistan, their position against the Soviet Union in Afghanistan, and their participation in global jihad to combat the Soviet occupation in Afghanistan—since the early part of the last decade there has been a steady upswing in bilateral political ties.[52]

This is best exemplified by the visit to India of every GCC head of state or government in 2005–07, and reciprocal visits by Indian leaders, culminating in the visit of Prime Minister Manmohan Singh to Riyadh in February 2010. During this visit, the Indian prime minister and the Saudi monarch signed the Riyadh Declaration, which announced the commencement of a "new era of strategic partnership" on the basis of deeper political, economic, defence and security ties. This relationship emerged from the conviction of GCC leaders that they shared with India the threat from jihadi violence—dramatically illustrated by the Mumbai attacks of November 2008—and that this threat largely emanated from Pakistan.

From the GCC perspective, India represents a narrative of economic and technological achievement in a multicultural democratic order. India has the added advantage that, in its foreign policy posture, it adopts positions that are non-intrusive, non-prescriptive and non-hegemonic. India is thus well-placed to take the lead in setting up the proposed diplomatic engagement with West Asia. Given that BRICS is anxious to interact with other countries and groupings, and has already engaged with African and South American leaders, there should be no difficulty in setting up a dialogue between BRICS and the GCC, perhaps during India's presidency from February 2016.

5.4 BRICS-Gulf Dynamics

What attractions does engagement with BRICS hold for the GCC? First, with the GCC shrugging off the American embrace even as the US has signaled its desire to minimise its military commitments in the region, new opportunities to pursue other engagements have opened up for the GCC countries. In fact, their "Look East" policies announced over 10 years ago now have real opportunities to fructify, particularly when they already have deep and valuable ties with all the BRICS countries in the economic and energy areas.

Second, the BRICS' agenda is almost entirely in conformity with the GCC's own interests: they have been conscious of the inequities of the world economic order, which has failed to give them due recognition in its councils. More importantly, they know they will benefit from cooperation with the dynamic economies of the

BRICS countries, particularly with regard to financial flows, energy and food security, trade, transportation, industry, technical education, scientific research and development, and development of financial markets.[53]

Third, with respect to the BRICS' positions on international issues, there is much the GCC would be comfortable with, particularly its concerns relating to terrorism and extremism, piracy, narcotics, cyber security and climate change. The GCC may disagree with BRICS in regard to Iran and, linked with it, the overall situation in West Asia for which it holds Iran responsible. But, even here dialogue with the BRICS members would enable it to project its views and concerns.

Above all, engagement with BRICS would give the GCC the opportunity to become a role player in shaping the new world order that reflects changes in global economic and power equations over the last few decades; an era in which non-western countries are high growth entities and major consumers of global energy, have a major role in global trade, and are important repositories of global foreign reserves and sources of investments. UAE scholar, Dr Mohammed Al Asoomi, has stated the case for BRICS-GCC engagement thus:

> A GCC partnership with the BRICS would be an important move, for strategic, economic and political dimensions on the one hand and the reviewing of international relations on the other. This is important in light of the changing balance of power in the world; at a time when the West shies away from buying Gulf oil, the BRICS are drawing closer to the Arabian Gulf and its oil products and exports.[54]

BRICS would also benefit from this interaction. The GCC is at the heart of global energy scenario, has much synergy with energy producers Russia and Brazil, and is central to the energy security interests of both India and China. It is also a financial powerhouse, with substantial investible resources available to fund energy, industry and infrastructure projects in the BRICS countries, as also in areas of priority interest to BRICS, Africa and Latin America. Again, the support of the GCC would enhance BRICS's bargaining position in reforming global financial and economic institutions. Over the longer term, the region would be an integral part of the logistical land and sea connectivities being structured across Eurasia, thus reviving the age-old Silk Road and Spice Route ties that had seamlessly linked the Indian Ocean littoral and had placed the Gulf and the Arabian Peninsula as a central player in these trade and civilisational connections.

Besides engagement with the GCC, it would be desirable for BRICS to have a separate interaction with Iran as well. Notwithstanding its energy resources and economic potential, Iran enjoys considerable geopolitical significance, straddling as it does South and Central Asia and the waters of the Gulf. It has great influence in West Asia, and holds the key to stability in Iraq, Syria, Lebanon and Yemen. It also can be a major force against the twin regional threats—sectarianism and extremism. Iran is already an observer at the SCO and is expected to be a full member within a year or so.

While it clearly suits Iran to engage with BRICS, the latter would also benefit from formal interaction. First, since the world's major non-western powers would be Iran's interlocutors, they would carry considerable influence with Iran, ensuring that Iran fulfils all its commitments to the international community under the nuclear agreement, whenever it is finalised. It should be recalled here that, while BRICS has fully supported Iran's right to the peaceful development of nuclear power and has criticised the unilateral sanctions imposed by western countries, no BRICS member has countenanced the development of a nuclear weapons programme by Iran.

Again, Iran will be central to the success of the Eurasian logistical and economic initiatives sponsored by China and Russia, besides the specific advantage it would provide India in regard to its projects to reach Afghanistan, Central Asia and beyond. Finally, both China and India would welcome an Iranian role in stabilising Afghanistan and confronting extremist elements in the region.

6. Challenges before the BRICS-Gulf Engagement

While an interaction between BRICS and GCC on the one hand and Iran on the other, is quite feasible, this engagement would serve a much greater international purpose if it would lead to improving the security situation in the Gulf region by providing a platform for Iran-GCC dialogue and promoting mutual trust and confidence between them. Such an initiative would, however, have to address a number of important challenges:

(i) the first difficulty would be the deep divide between Saudi Arabia and Iran emerging from the Kingdom's sense of an existential threat from Iran, whose increasing influence across West Asia is viewed as a sectarian and strategic challenge;

(ii) within BRICS, the continuing differences between India and China and strengthening Sino-Pakistan relations; and,
(iii) the fact that BRICS has not played such a security-promotion role so far.

These issues are examined in the following sections.

6.1 Saudi-Iran Relations

Saudi Arabia's concerns pertaining to Iran have propelled it toward an active military role in West Asia to confront Iranian interests in different theatres: Syria, Iraq and Yemen. The present situation, thus, would appear to be rather unpropitious for a new, more accommodative diplomatic engagement between BRICS and the GCC. But, it seems unlikely that this battle between the Islamic giants can carry on much longer: while much destruction has been wreaked upon Syria, regime change, the Kingdom's cherished hope, does not seem near at hand. In Yemen, too, while several hundred people have been killed, it does not seem that the Houthis are anywhere near being defeated; a negotiated settlement seems to be the only way forward. In Iraq, while the Haidar Al Abadi regime is fragile, it is facing the daunting task of confronting the scourge of the "Islamic State" (IS). In fact, the IS is a common threat to all of West Asia and this fact alone should encourage Saudi-Iranian engagement, besides of course the long term threat posed by burgeoning sectarian discord.

While Saudi-Iran differences show no sign of abating, the recent attacks in Paris by ISIS, the proliferation of jihad across large parts of Asia and Africa, and the continued allure that jihad has for sections of Muslim youth even in western countries, all of these concerns should move Saudi-Iran ties in a positive direction in the coming months so that India during its presidency of BRICS could host a constructive dialogue with the GCC and Iran.

6.2 Sino-Indian Differences

While there is little doubt that Sino-Indian differences persist in spite of the recent exchanges of high-level visits, these have not so far had a negative effect on the BRICS agenda. The two countries have compromised on the BRICS's New Development Bank, agreeing that its headquarters will be in Shanghai, while India will provide the first president for a five-year term. Chinese has dropped its misgivings relating to India's membership of the SCO, so that India is poised to join this important regional security organisation in 2016, giving India a role in contributing to the security initiatives affecting Afghanistan and Central Asia, besides opening up opportunities to enhance energy links with the Central Asian nations. In February 2015, India joined Russia and China in announcing their joint commitment "to build a more just, fair and stable international political and economic order" and a "multi-polar" world. They also backed the Chinese call for "a modern security architecture" in the Asia-Pacific.[55]

India is certainly concerned about the recent upswing in China's ties with Pakistan, specifically the Chinese promise to invest $46 billion in the country to set up logistical connections as part of its OBOR project. With full Chinese control over Gwadar port at the mouth of the Gulf and the increasing presence of the Chinese navy in the Indian Ocean, India perceives a security threat.

However, these concerns need not be over-played: China's presence at Gwadar is readily matched by the substantial links that India has developed with Oman: India has regular biennial exercises involving all three wings of the country's armed forces. The Indian and Omani navies have been holding regular biennial maritime exercises since 1993; these now include complex seamanship drills, firing serials and tactical exercises. Over 150 Omani military personnel trained in India in 2014. Some Indian defence analysts have even pointed out that, given China's stakes in the Malacca Strait and the Gulf, its enhanced naval presence in the Indian Ocean is quite natural, and that it would be a good policy for India to engage with China on this subject. An excellent start in this regard has been the participation of the Chinese navy in the International Fleet Review hosted by India in Vishakhapatnam in February 2016.[56]

As far the Gulf is concerned, India should shed its timidity vis-à-vis China: the latter can just not match India's historic links, the high level of mutual comfort, and its assets in the shape of its community. While China has just experienced the challenge of evacuating 35,000 of its citizens from Libya, India has accomplished this feat several times, starting with the airlifting of over 150,000 of its nationals from Kuwait 25 years ago.

Again, the expansion of Sino-Pakistan ties and the integration of Pakistan into the OBOR should not alarm India. This should be seen as an attempt by China to contribute to Pakistan's stability. As former Indian diplomat MK Bhadrakumar points out:

> Pakistan's stability has come to be a matter of serious concern from the perspective of China's internal security, which is attributable not only to the spurt in terrorist activities in Xinjiang by groups that are to be traced

> to the Af-Pak region, but also out of China's emergent concerns as a stakeholder in regional stability that is an imperative need to advance its regional and global policies more optimally.[57]

Similarly, India should be more positive about the Chinese OBOR project. The project enjoys the support of all regional powers led by Russia, which has happily integrated it with its own regional cooperation proposals. With India expected to become a full member of the SCO in 2016, it makes little sense to remain outside the region's most important project. In this context, it is important to recall that for some years India has been pursuing its own dream project—the International North-South Transportation Corridor, a road and rail connection from Chahbahar port in Iran (outside the Gulf, just next to Gwadar in Pakistan) to Tukmenistan and Russia and then on to northern Europe, with links to the Iranian ports of Bandar Anzali and Bandar Amirabad on the Caspian Sea. A separate road from Chahbahar would link up with the existing Zaranj-Delaram highway in Afghanistan, which would then go on to Tajikistan and Uzbekistan.[58] The importance of these projects when realised would be significantly enhanced if they were to be part of the Chinese-sponsored OBOR project.

A historical perspective would helpful. The old Silk Road, which flourished from the 3rd century BC to the 18th century, was a network of hundreds of roads that linked the entire Asian continent, with numerous market towns emerging in China, Central Asia, India, Iran and West Asia to handle these extensive commercial engagements. As Subhakanta Behera has written, the Silk Road was

> a series of caravan routes, a network of trails, and trading posts, oases and emporia scattered all across the vast Eurasia ... All along this vast stretch, branch routes at different points led to destinations off to either side of the main road....[An] important branch left the southern route at Yarkand and travelled south and across the Karakoram passes to the towns of Leh and Srinagar, before finally reaching northwestern India and thus to other routes across India.[59]

Indian traders were in fact central to the Silk Road transactions, being middlemen for the China-Mediterranean trade as also between China and India: the Chinese traded silk goods with Indians for precious stones and metals, which the Indians then sold in western markets. The Silk Road was also the principal route for cultural and religious exchanges between India and other countries. This brief foray into early history should affirm the value of Indian participation in the modern-day incarnation of an ancient conduit that robustly enhanced India's own economic and cultural interests.

6.3 Can BRICS Promote Security in the Gulf?

Can BRICS now build on its strengths and achievements and cross the last frontier to pool its resources to bring security to the Gulf? The basis for this is already being prepared: on 22 May 2015, the BRICS deputy ministers of foreign affairs, meeting in Moscow, issued a joint communique on the situation in West Asia and North Africa. The communique called for international efforts to address the scourge of extremism and terrorism and criticised unilateral military interventions in the region. The document referred to all the major trouble spots in the region—Syria, Libya, Yemen, Palestine, the Iran dialogue—and agreed to hold regular consultations.

Given the deep divide in the Gulf, its comment on the region was most cautious: "They duly noted the importance of building a system of relations in the Gulf zone that would guarantee equal and reliable security to all States of the sub-region."[60] Briefing the media on this communique, the Russian deputy minister for foreign affairs, Sergey Ryabkov, said:

> I am sure that BRICS has a huge potential for work in all the regions that have problems.... The Middle East region is on fire. Of course, we cannot stay on the sidelines of this process as a cooperation format. ... The next step will be collective engagement of BRICS as a structure in the work on these directions.[61]

Within a few days of this unprecedented stand-alone comment on the West Asian situation, President Putin addressed the BRICS national security advisers. Besides referring to terrorism and financial crime, the only other problem area mentioned by him was West Asia and North Africa, specifically the IS. Recalling the US military attack on Iraq in 2003, he said: "The consequences are clearly grave and everything that happened in the past years on the international arena needs to be adjusted."[62] After the meeting of BRICS national security advisors, the secretary of the Russian Security Council called for increased military and technical cooperation among BRICS countries to combat terrorism, extremism, separatism and cross-border crime, as also what he referred to as "new challenges and threats".[63]

Perhaps, the strongest call for intervention has been recently made by the Indian Prime Minister, Narendra Modi, when he delivered his address at Tsinghua University during his visit to China in May 2015. Referring to the situation in India's neighbourhood, the prime minister said:

> We must also deal with the changing character of terrorism that has made it less predictable and more diffuse. We source a large part of our energy from the same region that faces instability and an uncertain future. India and China conduct their international commerce on the same sea lanes. The security of the sea lanes is vital for our two economies; and our cooperation is essential to achieve it.[64]

7. Shaping the BRICS' Diplomatic Initiative

While BRICS members, Russia, China and India, recognise that their own and larger regional and even global interests are in jeopardy due to the ongoing conflicts in West Asia, none of them has been able to flesh out the contours of a BRICS role in security-promotion and the next steps which need to be taken in this regard. India needs to take the lead to shape the BRICS' diplomatic effort.

Clearly, BRICS does not have the capacity to address all, or even most, of the issues that divide the Gulf countries at present. As noted above, these issues are a product of significant developments taking place in the region at the same time, resulting from serious debates (and differences) in most Arab countries about the national vision and the principles and institutions to support it. These discussions will consume national attention for several years to come. But, what BRICS cannot ignore is that this turmoil has also given rise to forces of extremism and sectarianism that threaten the region as a whole, and in turn adversely impact the interests of the wider international community. Hence, the BRICS diplomatic effort has to focus on providing a platform for interaction, principally for Iran and Saudi Arabia, so that they can build mutual confidence and trust.

The process of engagement will have three attributes:

i. it will be diplomatic: it is not envisaged that BRICS will deploy military might to promote security;

ii. it will be inclusive: to shape a truly cooperative security arrangement in the Gulf, BRICS would need to pursue an inclusive structure that would include the P5+1 countries; and
iii. it would be incremental: given the complexity of issues involved, the variety of interests and their advocates, and the sharp antagonisms dividing different groups at present, the Gulf interlocutors would retain their existing alliances and affiliations, which could be shed or diluted as confidence among the principal parties increases.

The next steps to implement this initiative would include: (a) internal meetings among BRICS officials and ministers to develop a consensual BRICS position on the content and approach to shaping the initiative; (b) use of special envoys or national security advisors to engage with counterparts and ministers of the countries concerned; (c) at the appropriate time, the convening by BRICS of a regional security conference, perhaps initially at officials' level; in doing so, working groups could be set up to address specific topics, with each of them being chaired by a BRICS member.

Given that BRICS already has an active Track-II forum, it would be useful for the first approach papers to be prepared by this forum. In order to identify the important issues that concern the regional powers, this forum could have regular close-door interactions with counterpart bodies. It is suggested that the Gulf governments concerned could be asked to nominate their institutions and scholars for this interaction so that the discussions are productive and broadly in line with government thinking, while giving the scholars the opportunity for independent thinking.

8. Conclusion

With its six years of engagement at summit level and nearly two dozen meetings that take place throughout the year at ministerial and senior officials' levels, BRICS has now acquired a clearly defined personality as a significant player in the global economic and political scenario. Its forays into institution-building in areas that, for nearly seven decades, have been the preserve of the West are already being seen as revolutionary. It has articulated views on a variety of global issues that have been principled and often at odds with western positions. Thus, it would be accurate to describe it as a fairly cohesive political entity.

Of course, BRICS member countries may have views on specific matters that are sharper or more strident than the consensual positions that emerge in the summit documents, even as members may have serious bilateral differences with other members. But, this is clearly seen as normal in a multilateral scenario, the important factor being the issues that unite all members for a shared purpose and interest. Here, BRICS, a conglomeration of very diverse entities, has shown far greater capacity for consensus than had been expected by its critics when it was taking shape in its early years. Of course, the discipline of multilateral engagement has inherent in it the ability to moderate both conduct and positions.[65] But, moderation and support for consensus also emerge from the confidence among the members who are convinced that greater success will come from working together rather than in ploughing a lonely furrow. This confidence among BRICS members is founded on real economic achievement, which has led to legitimate claims for a place on the high table of global institutions, both political and economic. The reluctance of the West to yield space has added to the sharpness of the debate and also encouraged efforts to develop institutions and positions outside the West-dominated framework.

This has also led to an explosion of creativity, so that every summit Declaration is replete with new ideas for intra-BRICS cooperation as also interactions with nations outside the conclave but still claiming its attention, as in the case of Africa, where the old order has left behind polities with inadequate capacities for governance, development and prosperity, or, as in Latin America, where the nations are anxious to be in the vanguard of economic and social development in a nascent democratic order. Thus, BRICS refuses to be a closed shop of newly rich and successful nations that were underdeveloped just a few years ago.

In coming years, BRICS will grapple with achieving a new global financial architecture, sustainable development, and peace and security. In fact, even as BRICS has built new institutions and developed consensus on a variety of global economic and political issues, it is acutely conscious of the need to be more active in the political arena. Thus, the Fortaleza Declaration stated:

> We recall that development and security are closely interlinked, mutually reinforcing and key to attaining sustainable peace. We reiterate our view that the establishment of sustainable peace requires a comprehensive, concerted and determined approach, based on mutual trust, mutual benefit, equity and cooperation, that addresses the root causes of conflicts. [Para 26]

In the very next paragraph, the BRICS leaders set out their political position more categorically:

> We will continue our joint efforts in coordinating positions and *acting* on shared interests on global peace and security issues for the common wellbeing of humanity. [Emphasis added]

No international issue has obtained as much attention from BRICS leaders as the situation in West Asia. The Fortaleza Declaration devoted considerable space to the issues relating to Syria (which had four substantial paragraphs), Iraq, the Palestine issue, Iran, Al Qaeda and extremism, the Middle East as nuclear weapon-free zone, and piracy. In his brief opening remarks at Fortaleza, Prime Minister Modi devoted at least half his speech to West Asia, saying:

> The region stretching from Afghanistan to Africa is experiencing turbulence and conflict. This is causing grave instability that is seeping across borders. This impacts us all. *Remainingmute spectators to countries being torn up in this manner can have grave consequences.* ... The situation in West Asia poses a grave threat to regional and global peace and security. India is particularly concerned because this affects the lives of seven million Indian citizens living in the Gulf region [Emphasis added].[66]

There can be little doubt that, as new political crises emerge or present problems get aggravated, BRICS will take cognizance of them, develop consensual positions and take action: there will be no room for 'mute spectators' as derided by Mr Modi in his remarks. However, it is not envisaged that BRICS will be a military alliance on the lines of NATO; it will be a force for peace and security on the basis of its recognised political and economic standing which will impart to its diplomatic effort the required muscle and influence.

In this background and taking into account the deep concerns that animate the BRICS' leaders and their understanding that urgent remedial action is required, the case has been made in this chapter for a BRICS diplomatic initiative, led by India (and perhaps organised during its presidency in 2016–17)to engage the GCC as a grouping and Iran bilaterally, on the lines of similar interactions held with African and South American leaders. This is to be followed by an active diplomatic effort to prepare platforms for dialogue between the contending parties to promote mutual trust and confidence. BRICS is both prepared and well-equipped for this initiative.

Notes

1 Some early sections of this paper are modified versions of material that was contained in this author's paper, "New Silk Roads of the 21st Century: GCC-Asia Economic Connectivities and their Political Implications", presented at GRM-2012, and published in Ranjit Gupta et al. (ed*), A New Gulf Security Architecture: Prospects and Challenges for an Asian Role,* (Berlin: Gerlach Press, 2014), 5-41.

2 Jim O'Neill, "Building Better Global Economic BRICs", Global Economics Paper No.66, Goldman Sachs, New York, November2001.

3 Mette Skak, "The BRIC Powers as Soft Balancers: Brazil, Russia, India and China", (paper presented at the 11th Annual Aleksanteri Conference, Helsinki, 9-11 November 2011).

4 For details relating to the ideational and organisational origins of BRICS, see Tim Niblock, "The Dynamics of the BRICS Grouping: Convergences and Disparities with the GCC's Global Posture and Stances", (paper presented at Workshop No. 3, Gulf Research Meeting [GRM] 2015, Cambridge, UK, 24-27 August 2015).

5 Jagannath P Panda, "BRICS and the China-India Construct: A New World Order in Making?", Institute of Defence Studies and Analyses, New Delhi, September 2013, p. 15; Du Youkong, "BRICS means cooperation", *China Daily/Asia Weekly*, 30 March–5 April 2012, p.15; Rajiv Kumar, "BRICS can provide a Fallback position", *China Daily/Asia Weekly*, 6-12 April 2012, p.15; remarks by President Vladimir Putin, Ufa, 9 July, 2015, at <www.brics.utoronto.ca/docs/150709-ufa-putin-transcript.html> (23 August 2015).

6 Evan Feigenbaum, "The New Asian Order", 2 February, 2015, at <carnegieendowment.org/2015/02/new-asian-order/i137> (19 February 2015).

7 Rakesh Krishnan Simha, "Five takeaways from the BRICS summit", *Russia & India Report*, 16 July, 2015, at <in.rbth.com/blogs/2015/07/16/five_takeaways_from_the_brics_summit> (24 September 2015)

8 Panda, n. 5, p. 19-22.

9 "Fourth BRICS Summit – Delhi Declaration", Ministry of External Affairs, New Delhi, 29 March, 2012, at <mea.gov.in/mystart.php?id=190019162> (21 May 2012).

10 "Fifth BRICS Summit Declaration and Action Plan", 27 March 2013, at <www.brics5.co.za/fifth-brics-summit-declaration-and-action-plan> (8 June 2015).

11 "Sixth BRICS Summit–Fortaleza Declaration", 15 July 2014, at <brics6.itamaraty.gov.br/media2/press-release/214=sixth-brics=summit> (8 June 2015).

12 Nasser Saidi, "The BRICS Bank Signals the end of the American Financial Empire and US Dollar Hegemony", 21 July 2014, at <www.huffingtonpost.com/dr-nasser-h-saidi/the-brics-bank> (28 May 2015)

13 Remarks of President Putin, n. 5.

14 Fortaleza Declaration, para 26, at <brics6.itamaraty.gov.br/media2/press-releases/214-sixth-brics>.

15 Prem Shankar Jha, "Delhi could be a turning point", *The Hindu*, 10 April 2012, p. 10.

16 Simon Tisdall, "Can BRICS Create a New World Order?", *The Guardian*, 29 March 2012, at <alexansary.wordpress.com/2012/04/14can-the-brics-create-a-new-world-order> (7 May 2012).

17 *The Hindu*, 31 March 2012.

18 Du Youkong, n. 5.

19 Rajiv Kumar, n. 5.

20 Ian Bremmer, "Britain should find some new friends; Uncle Sam is going home", *The Sunday Times*, 31 May 2015, p. 23.

21 Ibid.

22 James Rubin, "As America retreats from the world, Britain fumbles for a compass", *The Sunday Times,* 7 June 2015, p. 19.

23 Michael Klare, "The Desperate Plight of a Declining Superpower", 30 May 2015, at <www.truthdig.com/report/item/delusionary_thinking_in_washington_the _desperate_plight_of_a_decli_20150528> (10 June, 2015).

24 Ibid.

25 Bree Feng, "Obama's free rider Comment Draws Chinese Criticism", *New York Times,* 13 August 2014, at <sinosphere.blogs.nytimes.com/2014/08/13/obamas-free-rider> (11 June 2015).

26 "Obama labelling China as free rider in Iraq issue", *Xinhua*, 4 September 2014, at <www.chinadaily.com.cn/world/2014-09-04/content_18543889.htm> (11 July, 2015).

27 Thomas Friedman, "Obama on the World", *New York Times*, 8 August 2014, at <www.nytimes.com/opinion/president-obama> (11 June 2015).

28 The president's criticism of China as a "free rider" in the Gulf is unwarranted since the US itself adopted a unilateralist approach to the region's security issues: it mobilised an international coalition to undo the Iraqi occupation of Kuwait, but thereafter went its own way, outside the UN system, in regard to the sanctions-inspections regime and no-fly zones in Iraq, Kurdish autonomy, the dual containment of Iraq and Iran, the assault on Iraq in 2003 and its aftermath, and the stringent sanctions against Iran at the end of the last decade.

29 Gary Sick, "Saudi Arabia's Widening War", 4 June 2015, at <www.politico.com/magazine/story/2015/06/saudi-arabia> (14 June 2015).

30 Philip Gordon, "The Middle East is falling apart", 4 June, 2015, at <www.politico.com/magazine/story/2015/06/america-not-to-blame-for-middle-east-falling-apart-11861_full.html?VXIW_s9VhBc> (8 June 2015).

31 For details regarding the domestic political divide in the US, see Friedman [5 April, 2015]. In his earlier interview with Friedman [8 August, 2014], President Obama had been quoted as saying: "Our politics are dysfunctional.... [The terrible divisions of the Middle East are a] warning to us: societies don't work if political factions take maximalist positions. And the more diverse the country is, the less it can afford to take maximalist positions."

32 Alexander Gabuev, "A soft alliance? Russia-China Relations after the Ukraine Crisis", (London: The European Council on Foreign Relations, February 2015), p. 3; "Russia and China: An Uneasy friendship", *The Economist*, 9 May 2015, p. 2, at <www.economist.com/news/china/21650566-crisis-ukraine> (7 June 2015).

33 Gabuev, p.4-7; Elizabeth Wishnick, "Russia and China Go Sailing", 26 May 2015, at <www.foreignaffairs.com/china/2015-05-26/russia-and-china> (7June 2015).

34 *The Telegraph*, London, 11 May 2015, at <www.telegraph.co.uk/news/world news/europe/russia/1159685> (29 November, 2015).

35 Wishnick; Anita Inder Singh, "Unequal Partners: China and Russia in Eurasia", 3 June 2015, at <thediplomat.com/2015/06/unequal-partners-china-and-russia-in-eurasia> (7 June 2015).

36 Gabuev, p. 8; Dmitri Trenin, "Russia's Pivot to Asia–A Sino-Russian Entente?", 15 April 2015, at <Carnegie.ru/2015/04/15/Russia-s-pivot-to-asia-sino-russian-entente> (28 May 2015).

37 Mohammad Z Rakhmat, "China, Qatar, and RMB Internationalisation", 6 June 2015, at <thediplomat.com/2015/06/china-qatar-and-rmb-internationalization> (7 June 2015).

38 Veronica Smith, "IMF approves China's yuan as elite reserve currency", 30 November, 2015, at: <news.yahoo.com/imf-approves-chinas-yuan-elite-currency-171229> (17 December,2015).

39 F William Engdahl, "AIIB, BRICS Development Bank and an Emerging World", *New Eastern Outlook*, 10 April 2015; Javier Solana, "China and Global Governance", 30 March 2015, at <www.project-syndicate.org/print/china-multilateral-institutions-threaten-us-by-javier-solana-2015-03> (10 June 2015).

40 Atul Aneja, "Pressure mounts on Japan and US to join China-led bank", *The Hindu*, 22 March 2015, at <www.the hindu.com/news/international/pressure-mounts> (30 May 2015).

41 Jonathan D Pollack, "Joining the club", Brookings, 17 March 2015.

42 Lars Erslev Andersen and Yang Jiang, "China's Growing Economic Involvement in the Persian Gulf after 9/11", DIIS Report 2014: 29, (Copenhagen: Danish Institute for International Affairs, 2014, p. 27); Chaoling Feng, "Embracing Interdependence: The Dynamics of China in the Middle East", (Doha: Brookings Doha Center, April 2015, p. 2-3).

43 Tong Zhao, "China and the Iranian Nuclear Negotiations", 2 February 2015, at <carnegiesinghua.org/2015/01/29/china-and-iranian –nuclear-negotiations> (24 February 2015).

44 Chaoling Feng, p. 3

45 Andersen, p. 25.

46 Andersen, p. 35.

47 Chaoling Feng, p. 4.

48 Feng, p. 8-9.

49 For details see Talmiz Ahmad, n. 1.

50 In the GCC countries, China has 60,000 workers, including 35,000 in Saudi Arabia; it has another 10,000 in Iraq and 2000 in Iran. [See Andersen, p. 28.].

51 This is the full amount that goes to the Indian banking system as foreign exchange; contrast this with the fact that the cumulative value of China's projects in the Gulf is $120 billion, equal to Indian remittances of about

three or four years; again, the net gain to the Chinese exchequer from its project exports would be profit of 10–15 percent, if that.

52 For details see Talmiz Ahmad, "The Gulf Region", in David M Malone, C Raja Mohan and Srinath Raghavan (eds), *The Oxford Handbook of Indian Foreign Policy,* (Oxford: Oxford University Press, 2015), p. 437–451.

53 Ibn Khaldun, "BRICS and beyond", August 2014, at <www.gulfonline.com/Print.aspx?ArtID=6580> (28 May 2015).

54 Mohammad Al Asoomi, "In theory: GCC, BRICS, have a case for merger", *Gulf News*, 28 May 2015.

55 "India and Russia back China's call for 'new world order', 3 February 2015, at <www.scmp.com/print/news/china/article/1699900/india-russia> (8 June, 2015).

56 Abhijit Singh," Of white papers and dark intentions: Why China's new military strategy has India worried", 6 June 2015, at <atimes.com/>2015/06/06 (11 June 2015); Ruchi Bambha, "International Fleet Review 2016 curtain raiser", 15 October, The Economic Times, 15 October, 2015, at: <economictimes.indiatimes.com/news/defence/international-fleet-review -2016-curtain-raiser-6-things-to-know/articleshow/49375814.cms> (17 December,2015).

57 MK Bhadrakumar,"Pakistan, China, Iran and the remaking of regional security", 18 April 2015, at <atimes.com/2015/04/Pakistan-china-iran-and-the-remaking-of –regional-security> (11 June 2015).

58 Sujata Ashwarya Cheema, "India's Look West Policy and Iran: External and Domestic Imperatives", in Cheema, *Essays on Iran and Israel: An Indian Perspective*, (New Delhi: KW Publishers, 2014, p. 4–8).

59 Subhakanta Behera, "India's Encounter with the Silk Road", *Economic and Political Weekly*, 37:51 (21–27 December, 2002), p. 5077.

60 Press Release, Ministry of Foreign Affairs of the Russian Federation, 22 May, 2015, at <www.mid.ru/brp_4nsf/0/66F46F68D9A4F78E43257E400> (5 June 2015).

61 "BRICS coordinating Joint Stance on Middle East events: Russian diplomat", 23 May 2015, at <www.bernama.com/bernama/v8/wn/newsworld.php?id=1137269> (5 June 2015).

62 "Meeting of BRICS national security advisers", 27 May, 2015, at <foreignaffairs.co.nz/2015/05/27/meeting-with-brics-national-security-advisors> (28 May 2015).

63 "BRICS countries need to boost cooperation in military sphere—senior security official", *TASS*, 26 May, 2015.

64 Address by the Prime Minister at the Tsinghua University, Beijing (15 May 2015), at <www.mea.gov.in> (11 June 2015).

65 Georgy Toloraya's comment in this regard is instructive: "… politically, China does not seek (at least, for the time being) dominant positions in the group [BRICS], understanding that not only Western countries but also other BRICS members will disagree to accept a Chinese plan to reorganising the world, and this would ruin the association. On the contrary, let's be frank, without such a "controlling mechanism" as the BRICS, Beijing would be much freer in its actions and would need less to heed the interests of its partners." ("Why Does Russia Need BRICS?", 9 March, 2015, at: <eng.globalaffairs.ru/print/number/Why-Does-Russia-Need-BRICS-17373> [10 June, 2015]).

66 "PM Narendra Modi's Full Statement at BRICS Summit", 15 July 2014, at <www.ndtv.com/india-news/pm-narendra-modis-full-statement> (14 June 2015).

References

Andersen, Lars Erslev and Yang Jiang, "Is China Challenging the US in the Persian Gulf?", (Copenhagen: Danish Institute for International Studies, 2014).

Bhadrakumar, MK, "India tries to forge a new relationship with China", *Asia Times News and Features*, 18 May 2015

Bhadrakumar, MK, "Pakistan, China, Iran and the re-making of regional security", *Asia Times News and Features*, 18 April 2015

Engdahl, F William, "AIIB, BRICS Development Bank and an Emerging World", *New Eastern Outlook*, 10 April 2015.

Feigenbaum, Evan A, "The New Asian Order", (Carnegie Endowment for International Peace, 2015).

Feng, Chaoling, "Embracing Interdependence: The Dynamics of China and the Middle East", (Doha: Brookings Doha Center, 2015).

Friedman, Thomas, "Iran and the Obama Doctrine", *New York Times,* 5April 2015.

Friedman, Thomas, "Obama on the World", *New York Times*, 8 August 2014.

Gabuev, Alexander, "A 'Soft Alliance'? Russia-China Relations after the Ukraine Crisis", (London: European Council on Foreign Relations, 2015).

Gordon, Philip, "The Middle East is Falling Apart", *Politico*, 4 June 2015.

Gupta, Ranjit et al., *A New Gulf Security Architecture: Prospects and Challenges for an Asian Role*, (Berlin: Gerlach Press, 2014).

Klare, Michael, "The Desperate Plight of a Declining Superpower", <www.truthdig.com/report/item/deludionary_thinking_in_washington_the_desperate_plight_of_a_decli_20150528> (10 June, 2015).

McCoy, Alfred, "The Geopolitics of American Global Decline: Washington versus China in the 21st Century", *Tom Dispatch*, 7 June 2015.

Mirhosseini, Seyed Mohsen and Elham Rasoulisaniabadi, "The Milestones of the Persian Gulf Security Developments", *Sociology and Anthropology*, 3(2), March 2015, pp 116-121.

Niblock, Tim, ed., *Security Dynamics of East Asia in the Gulf Region*, (Berlin: Gerlach Press, 2015).

Saidi, Nasser H, "The Brics Bank Signals the End of the American Financial Empire and the US Dollar Hegemony", *Huffington Post*, 21 July 2014.

Shapiro, Jeremy, "The Chinese foray into global governance", Blog, Brookings, 1 April 2015, at <http://www.brookings.edu/blogs/order-from-chaos/posts/2015/04/01-china-global-governance-shapiro>.

Sick, Gary, "Saudi Arabia's Widening War", *Politico*, 4 June 2015

Singh, Anita Inder, "Unequal Partners: China and Russia in Eurasia", *The Diplomat*, 3 June 2015.

Skak, Mette, "The BRICS Powers as Soft Balancers", (paper presented at the 11th Aleksanteri Conference, Helsinki, 9-11 November 2011).

Tolaraya, Georgy, "Why Does Russia Need BRICS?", *Global Affairs*, 9 March 2015.

Trenin, Dmitri, "Russia's Pivot to Asia: A Sino- Russian Entente?", (Moscow: Carnegie Moscow Center, 15 April 2015)

Trenin, Dmitri, "From a Greater Europe to a Greater Asia?", (Moscow: Carnegie Moscow Center, 26 February 2015).

Wishnick, Elizabeth, "Russia and China Go Sailing", *Foreign Affairs*, 26 May 2015.

Zanitti, Francesco Brunello, "Russia, China and India building a new multipolar world", *Pravda*, 15 January 2015

Zhao, Tong, "China and the Iranian Nuclear Negotiations", (Beijing: Carnegie Tsinghua Center, 2 February 2015).

4

GCC and BRICS: Exploring the Nuclear Energy Cooperation Route

Stuti Banerjee

1. Introduction

The former Director-General of the International Atomic Energy Agency (IAEA), Mohammad ElBaradei, has rightly pointed out that, "The disparity in energy supply is directly related to the disparity in standards of living, which in turn creates disparities in opportunity and hope — and… leads to the sort of despair and insecurity that give rise to tensions in many regions…."[1] Energy is an important material base for the survival and development of human beings. With electricity instrumental to modern economies and post-modern lifestyles, energy security is becoming paramount to human security. The late economist E.F.Schumacher (1977) reflected that energy was "not just another commodity, but the precondition of all commodities; a basic factor equal with air, water, and earth." Thus, energy security is integral to modern society….[2]

National energy policies strongly impact most aspects of human life such as economic activity, employment, health and consumption. Policies that help secure a safe and secure environment for growth with competitive and assured supplies of electricity help attract investment and generate wealth. The increase in business profitability and consumer purchasing power that results from lower energy costs, further stimulate business investment, consumer spending, and employment growth. This in turn enhances economic prosperity. If it is accepted that electricity is closely linked to human development and economic growth, then the choice of which fuel sources will be most appropriate for generating electricity is clearly important. Nations will make individual choices in this regard.[3] Most countries use a mix of energy resources, both renewable and non-renewable. It is in this context that nuclear energy has gained prominence in recent years.

Nuclear energy offers countries access to a large-scale reliable base load source of power, with relatively low carbon emissions. With nuclear energy, however, it is critical that all measures be taken to mitigate any possible risks, given the unthinkable outcomes which might otherwise ensue.[4] Nuclear power has been used to produce electricity since the early 1950s. As of April 2015, 30 countries worldwide are operating a total of 443 nuclear reactors for electricity generation and 66 new nuclear plants are under construction in 15 countries. Globally, the nuclear energy industry now has about 15,000 reactor-years ofoperating experience.[5] With demand for electricity increasing, nuclear energy is fast becoming an essential part of the energy security policies of states.

In December 2006, the heads of the six Gulf Cooperation Council (GCC) states, Saudi Arabia, Oman, Kuwait, Qatar, Bahrain and the United Arab Emirates (UAE), declared that they wished to develop nuclear energy for peaceful purposes. Officials and foreign ministers of thesestates assured the international community that the development would not affect regional stability. The GCC states' interest in developing a civil nuclear programme stemmed from the need to diversify their energy resources. The eventual decline in fossil fuel resources, the growing awareness on climate change and the need to ensure that indigenous sources of energy can be preserved for the export market makes nuclear energy attractive. It can also be useful for building anuclear technology export base.

The GCC countries at present do not have either the human expertise or the technical knowledge to build the necessary infrastructures and/or to operate a nuclear power plant. To develop their nuclear programmes they need to turn to the international nuclear market. The BRICS (Brazil, Russia, India, China and South Africa) countries are among those which have suitable expertise. Russia is an established power in nuclear energy and China is developing nuclear reactors for export. India, has ambitions for becoming a nuclear technology exporter in the future, and is developing the technology needed for building thorium-based fast-breeder reactors. Currently it has excellent human resource training capability which it can share. Brazil and South Africa have developed their peaceful nuclear programmes and operate two plants each. The BRICS is a grouping in which all the member states, therefore, have a successful nuclear power programme.

Keeping in mind these underlying factors, this chapter will begin by highlighting the rationale behind the GCC states' decision to develop peaceful nuclear programmes, and describe their current status. It will then attempt to study the areas of convergences between the GCC and BRICS in the arena of civil nuclear cooperation and highlight the economic, political and strategic grounds for cooperation. The benefits and drawbacks, if any, of such cooperation will be assessed. It should be noted that at present the GCC and BRICS countries do not have any nuclear cooperation agreements as two distinct groups. The cooperation is between the individual member states. Of the GCC states, the UAE and Saudi Arabia have the financial capacity to invest in nuclear energy, and Russia and China have already established contacts with them in this field. Nonetheless, this does not forestall future developments from being multilateral in nature.

2. The GCC and the Nuclear Option

The Supreme Council of the GCC states in its closing statement at its meeting in Riyadh, Saudi Arabia(2006) announced its intention to initiate a joint programme in civil nuclear energy. The relevant part of the statement read:

> "The Supreme Council renewed its appeals to render the Middle East, including the Gulf region, free from the weapons of mass destruction, while at the same time, recognizing the right of countries of the region to own expertise in the field of nuclear energy for peaceful purposes, and that should be available to all within the framework of relevant international treaties. The Supreme Council ordered the undertaking of a joint GCC study to evolve a joint program in the field of nuclear technology for peaceful purposes in accordance with international standards and regulations."[6]

The need to develop peaceful nuclear energy was reiterated in 2009 in Kuwait and in 2010 in Abu Dhabi, where the summit statement stated, "... the right of countries to use nuclear energy for peaceful purposes under relevant international conventions and the standards and procedures set up by the International Atomic Energy Agency(IAEA)..."[7]

Questions have been raised about the rationale and the timing of the GCC states' declaration of interest in nuclear energy. Experts studying the region are of the opinion that the GCC states' interest is linked to Iran's nuclear power ambitions. To buttress their views they point to a proposal by Saudi Arabia in November

2007, which stated that the GCC should develop a regional capacity to enrich uranium which would be based outside of the MiddleEast, in a neutral, perhaps European country. States which participated in the programme would be able to rely on a guaranteed supply. Iran was invited to participate in the programme as an alternative to its own enrichment programme. It is significant that the GCC states were expressing their desire to develop civil nuclear energy at a time when Iran had been projecting its nuclear ambitions is important to note. The GCC states have been vocal supporters of a 'Middle East Zone that is free of Weapons of Mass Destruction' and have repeatedly expressed concern over Iran's desire to develop its capabilities in this field. The GGC states view the intention and the capability of the Iranian programme as a future threat. Given this disposition and the political environment of the region, there has been scepticism about the GCC states' motivations indeveloping civil nuclear energy. The ambition to explore nuclear technology has been viewed by many as an effort by thesestates to balance Iran's power.

Since the declaration, officials of the six GCC states have repeatedly tried to allay fears of a nuclear arms race in the Middle East or concerns that their plans for civil nuclear energy mightadversely affect regional stability. They have stated again and again that they do not wish to develop military nuclear capability. SaudiArabia'sForeign Minister Prince Saud Al-Faisal declared, "We will develop it openly, not in secret. We want no bombs; all we want is a whole Middle East that is free from weapons of mass destruction."[8]

Many have asked why these six states, which together have the largest proven crude oil reserves in the world (486.8 billion barrels) representing 35.7per cent of the world's total, and close to 24 per cent of its natural gas reserves, should feel the need to develop nuclear energy? Putting scepticism aside, their desire to develop nuclear energy stems from a wide variety of reasons. The most important of these is the need to diversify their energy sources.

The GCC economies are currently, of course, largely based on oil-exporting. The economic outlook of the GCC countries, including their ability to meet their major challenges, will be shaped most directly by factors influencing the demand for oil and oil products. In addition to the impact on government finances and the balance of payments, changes in oil earnings have broader implications for domestic economic activity in the GCC countries. Non-oil economic activity is heavily influenced by domestic government expenditure, which itself is dependent on oil revenue. Moreover, most large-scale economic activities in the public domain (petrochemicals and oil-based manufacturing) are closely linked to developments in the oil sector. A fall in energy prices over an unexpected long duration could have a detrimental effect on the spending by government on other non-energy related sectors.

The world today is seeking to develop technologies and find sources of energy beyond oil and coal. Renewable energy sources such as solar energy, hydro-electricity and wind power are being encouraged. This 'non-conventional energy' supply revolution may in the future reshape the more conventional energy markets and industry. The United States Energy Information Administration (EIA) estimates that in 2013 about 11 per cent of world marketed energy consumption was from renewable energy sources (bio-fuel, biomass, geothermal, hydropower, solar, and wind) with a projection for 15 per cent by 2040.[9] It cannot be denied that technology is being developed that would be more environmentally friendly and financially less of a burden on the exchequer than hydrocarbons are.

The other issue that the Middle East has to contend with is the rising competition from Latin America and the discovery of shale gas reserves in North America. The importance of Latin American countries in this field has grown over the past few years due to a steady increase in its declared reserves of hydrocarbon resources. According to the OPEC data on the share of crude oil reserves in 2013, Venezuela had 24.7 per cent of world crude oil reserves. Brazil is expected to be the world's sixth largest oil producer in the coming decade. Latin America is politically a more stable region and this is attracting Asia countries to invest in energy exploration there. The United States' determination to develop cost-effective and environmentally-safe technology to extract shale gas and oil poses a further competitive threat to the economies of the GCC States. The United States energy department has estimated that the United States has some 48 billion barrels worth of technically-recoverable shale oil, with Argentina having 27 billion barrels, and Venezuela and Mexico having an additional 13 billion barrels each. According to the BP Energy Outlook 2030 Report (2013), China is expected to have the largest reserves of recoverable shale gas outside of the United States. Global knowledge of shale gas reserves and the technology to extract them is still evolving but the sector is expected to see growth in the coming decades.

The GCC States also have to keep in mind the developments which have followed from the Iran-EU+3 nuclear talks. The 'Joint Comprehensive Plan of Action' (JCPOC) or Iran nuclear deal, signed by the EU+3 and Iran states that, "the United Nations Security Council resolution endorsing the JCPOC will terminate all provisions of previous UN Security Council resolutions on the Iranian nuclear issue...."[10] The EU will also terminate its nuclear related economic and financial sanctions. The same would be done by the United States, according to its laws. This is subject to Iran implementing its end of the deal. To quote the agreement:

> The removal of sanctions would remove efforts to reduce Iran's crude oil sales; allow investment, including participation in joint ventures, goods, services, information, technology and technical expertise and support for Iran's oil, gas and petrochemical sectors; purchase, acquisition, sale, transportation or marketing of petroleum, petrochemical products and natural gas from Iran; export, sale or provision of refined petroleum products and petrochemical products to Iran; transactions with Iran's energy sector; If the draft of the final agreement is acceptable to both governments of Iran and the United States, it would add Iranian oil and natural gas in the international market.[11]

It is possible that the GCC states are developing policies to overcome these changing international energy market scenarios; nonetheless, the major export industry of these States is energy exports. It is revenue generated from this industry that is fuelling their economies. While oil from the GCC states is likely to continue dominating the international energy markets, it is also true that many states are exploring means to reduce this dependence as much as possible and as quickly as possible.

The GCC states' interest in nuclear energy is also influenced by other domestic compulsions. They need to diversify their energy resources so as to meet the rising domestic demands for electricity and to keep the indigenous hydrocarbons resources largely for export income. In Saudi Arabia for example, electricity use is increasing at about 7.5 per cent annually, raising overall energy demand nationwide. By 2028 total energy demand could reach 8.3 million barrels of oil equivalent per day, potentially cutting export revenue significantly. The demand in the housing sector particularly remains strong, with the sector consuming 50 percent of the Kingdom's total electricity production.[12]

The reason for this high demand for energy is largely due to the climate, but it also stems from the low cost of electricity, which has unfortunately led to a culture of wastage and excess.[13] Energy efficiency has to be encouraged by the governments of these states, in the domestic, industrial and transportation sectors in order to secure long-term economic and environmental benefits.

The other sector which consumes excessive energy is the process of desalination. Devoid of natural water resources of much abundance, the desalination of sea water is necessary to meet the water needs of the citizens. With a growing population and a rise in the purchasing capacity of individuals, demand for water has also risen. The GCC economies account for 40 per cent of global desalinisation capacity. This process is energy intensive, and as demand rises it is expected that energy needed to provide this water will also grow exponentially. Given these needs and the necessity to build upon alternative sources of energy, the GCC states are increasingly getting attracted to nuclear energy.

Interest in nuclear energy also stems from the concern about greenhouse gas emissions combined with the talk of a '*nuclear renaissance*'[14] and its advertised advantages. Relative to fossil fuels, nuclear energy contributes little to greenhouse gas emission. The writer is notsuggesting that nuclear energy is a zero emission process, but nuclear power does emit a lesser amount of greenhouse gases than any source of power based on hydrocarbons. In fact, the complete nuclear power chain, from uranium mining to waste disposal, including reactor and facility construction, emits 02-06 grams of carbon per kilowatt-hour. Thermal power plant emissions cannot be wished away despite technological improvements and the implementation of stringent environmental measures.[15]

The eventual dwindling of fossil fuels and the threat to climate change together make civil nuclear energy a very viable option for the GCC states. An effort towards a common approach to developing nuclear energy in the GCC has been thwarted by disagreements over which country would host the reactors. It is relevant to point out here that the most optimistic statistics do not foresee nuclear energy contributing more than 15 per cent to world energy production by 2050. Despite this, nuclear energy is gaining acceptance as countries look towards diversifying their energy sources and moving away from dependency on fossil fuels alone. Proponents of nuclear energy worldwide, including the GCC states, see it as a reliable –and in the long run a cheap and clean - source of energy.

3. Current Status of Nuclear Programme of the GCC States

3.1 The United Arab Emirates (UAE)

The UAE is perhaps the only country among the GCC states that has made clear progress in its endeavour to establish a nuclear power programme. In April 2008, the UAE released its 'Policy on the Evaluation and Potential Development of Peaceful Nuclear Energy'.[16] The policy document states, "The UAE's interest in evaluating nuclear energy is motivated bythe need to develop additional sources of electricity to meet futuredemand projections and to ensure the continued rapid developmentof its economy. Recent analysis conducted by official UAE entities has concluded thatnational annual peak demand for electricity is likely to rise to morethan 40,000 MW's by 2020, reflecting a cumulative annual growthrate of roughly 09 per cent from 2007 onward."[17]

Allaying fears of the international community on possible proliferation concerns, the UAE has stated in its policy documents six principles that will guide its nuclear programme:

a) Complete operational transparency.
b) The highest standards of non-proliferation.
c) The highest standards of safety and security.
d) Working directly with the IAEA and conforming to its standards.
e) Partnerships with responsible nations and appropriate experts.
f) Long-term sustainability.[18]

In keeping with the above principles the UAE established the Emirates Nuclear Energy Corporation (ENEC) in 2009 to overlook the implementation of its nuclear programme. The ENECis developing the UAE nuclear power plants at Braka, the preferred site, in conjunction with its partners from the Korea Electric Power Corporation consortium. According to the ENEC, Unit 1 is expected to begin providing electricity to the grid in 2017. Plans are for the following three units to be completed in 2018, 2019 and 2020. These dates are not fixed and are subject to regulatory approval from the UAE Federal Authority for Nuclear Regulation. Among the nations that have signed nuclear cooperation agreements with the UAE is Russia, which signed an agreement in 2012.

The UAE is also a member of the Nuclear Non-Proliferation Treaty (NPT) and has ratified the safeguards agreements[19] with the IAEA. It has also signed the additional protocols[20] agreements with the IAEA.

3.2 Saudi Arabia

Saudi Arabia, along with the UAE, is the second statein the GCC with the capacity to carry forward a nuclear programme. In 2010, the government took the first steps towards defining its nuclear programme through a royal decree that stated: "The development of atomic energy is essential to meet the Kingdom'sgrowing requirements for energy to generate electricity, produce desalinated water and reduce reliance on depleting hydrocarbonresources".[21] Through royal order A/35 (April 2010), the government established the King Abdullah City for Atomic and Renewable Energy (K.A. CARE) with the aim to oversee safety, transparency, safeguarding of stakeholders and compliance with international standards and regulations. K.A.CARE is responsible for direct communication with the IAEA and with nuclear energy regulatory bodies in other countries. The government will establish an independent regulator, the Saudi Arabian Atomic Regulatory Authority, to oversee the Kingdom's civil atomic energy program and ensure all safeguards are in place for all stakeholders.[22]

SaudiArabia has signed bilateral cooperation agreements on nuclearpower with France, South Korea, Argentina and China; agreementswith other countries are reportedly under negotiation.

3.3 Bahrain

While the government of the Kingdom of Bahrain has stated that nuclear energy is a necessity for the country's future energy needs, it has not taken any concrete steps towards establishing a nuclear power capacity in the country.

After the announcement at the GCC Summit in 2006, the government signed an agreement with the United States to develop nuclear energy, but nothing has progressed beyond that. According to the government, the goal of incorporating nuclear energy into the energy mix of the country by 2017 has been postponed.

3.4 Kuwait

The State of Kuwait has twice attempted to develop and pursue a nuclear program for electric power generation. The first attempt was in the 1970's in coordination with and support from the IAEA and United Kingdom Atomic Energy Authority. The programme was cancelled after the Three Mile Island nuclear accident and due to the Iraq-Iran war.

The second attempt was as part of the declaration of the GCC in 2006. An Amiri decree was issued to form a committee, the Kuwait National Nuclear Energy Committee (KNNEC), to pave the way for the development of a nuclear programme. The progress in this second attempt achieved some results, in the form of economic feasibility and siting survey studies, the first draft of a nuclear law, international agreements (with France, Jordan, the United States of America and Japan), and sponsorship of about 30 students to pursue Bachelor and Master degrees in nuclear science and engineering. However, after the Fukushima Daiichi nuclear accident in Japan in March 2011, an Amiri decree was issued in July 2011, cancelling the Kuwait nuclear programme for electric power generation. The decree transfers KNNEC's programme to the Kuwait Institute for Scientific Research

(KISR). Thegoals of the programme were modified, such that they were now restricted to research and development.

3.5 Oman

Oman, like Kuwait, decided to halt its incipient nuclear power programmeas a result of the accident in Japan.

3.6 Qatar

The government of Qatar undertook a study into the viability of nuclear energy for the small nation. It subsequently announced that there was no strong case for the nation to pursue nuclear energy. This was mainly due to the non-availability of small reactors with varying capacity of 300-600 megawatt. The report indicated that Qatar had surplus energy, such that there was no immediate requirement to develop an alternative source of energy[23].Nonetheless, the government proposed a regional project for nuclear power generation that could benefit the smaller nations of the GCC.

Qatar has signed memorandums of understanding with Russia and South Korea in developing research on nuclear technology for peaceful use.

The major challenge facing Bahrain, Kuwait, Oman and Qatar is that they are geographically smaller in size than the UAE and Saudi Arabia, and have low populations and less demand for electricity. In such a scenario building large nuclear reactors could prove unviable economically. Some, moreover, do not have the financial resources necessary for nuclear energy programmes. The Fukishima accidents highlighted the issue of safety, and this too poses a particular problem for small countries. Nuclear reactors are typically built away from centres of population, thus sufficient space is needed. In case of an accident, moreover, the fall-out could prove to be disastrous for the populations of neighbouring states, as well as their own.

4. BRICS and Nuclear Energy

The world's energy consumption is set to grow an estimated 40 percent by 2040, and the BRICS economies will be responsible for most of that growth.[24]

The nuclear-related agenda of this influential group of countries is not limited to developing civil nuclear energy for their own consumption. They are also intent on strengthening the nuclear non-proliferation regime, in accordance with the goals of the Non-Proliferation Treaty (NPT) and other relevant agreements. They would like, in this context, to ensure that the civil use of nuclear energy is an option that can be exercised by any nation but without the growth of nuclear weapons development.

Over the past few years all these countries have decided to build their nuclear energy capacity. The BRICS grouping comprises states which have nuclear weapons and two which do not. Russia and China have signed the NPT as nuclear weapons states. Brazil and South Africa have signed the NPT as non-nuclear weaponsstates and along with Russia have ratified the Comprehensive Test Ban Treaty (CTBT), China has signed but not ratified the CTBT, whereas India while not having signed either of the treaties follows the principles of both in terms of nuclear non-proliferation and nuclear safety and security. Four BRICS countries (all except India) belong to the Nuclear Suppliers Group (NSG), set up to reinforce nuclear export controls. All five BRICS countries participate in the Geneva Conference on Disarmament and are engaged in developing, to varying extents, civilian nuclear power projects. Russia has 33 nuclear reactors, China has 14, India 20, and Brazil and South Africa have 2 nuclear reactors each. The Fukushima accident in Japan slowed the growth of nuclear energy but it did not halt its development, especially in India and China.

In China, the growth of nuclear energy is staggering. China currently has 14 reactors in operation. 28 more are under construction with firm plans for yet more. The state's 12th 'Five-Year Plan' foresees 70 gigawatts (GWs) of nuclear capacity by 2020, and the International Energy Agency (IEA) has increased its 2035 projection to a sizeable 110 GWs of Chinese nuclear capacity. China's own nuclear technology is as much a part of the domestic nuclear industry as areimported reactor models.

In India, installed nuclear generating capacity stands at 4.5 GWs, with a target of reaching 63 GWs by 2032. India is developing its own indigenous reactors to conserve fuel and reduce waste. It is also focussing on research on better technology for waste disposal, andcan claim to have experience in construction, operation and maintenance of a varied range of nuclear power plants-Light Water Reactors (LWR), Pressurised Heavy Water Reactors (PHWR), Fast Breeder Reactors (FBR) and Advance Heavy Water Reactors (AHWR). It has demonstrated the commercial capacity of its FBR at Kalpakkam and is an emerging leader in the development of reactors and associated fuel cycle technologies for thorium utilisation. A 30 KW research reactor, KAMINI, has been operating and is perhaps the only one of its kind that is operating on Uranium-233 based nuclear fuel.[25]

Domestic support for nuclear energy remains a prominent feature of Russia's nuclear industry. The Rosatom corporation is responsible for every aspect of nuclear technology research, development and deployment. Nuclear energy produces 17 percent of the country's electricity from the 33 units currently in operation.

Domestically, Russia can count another 10 units under construction while, according to Rosatom, Russia has contracts to build a further 21 abroad. This rapid expansion not only underlines Russia's firm commitment to nuclear energy within Russia, but the ambition to reach out as well.

Brazil signed a nuclear cooperation agreement with Argentina for the construction of one research reactor. This will be used to conduct tests on nuclear fuel and to produce radioisotopes – a crucial part of diagnostic medicine and now a product in demand with falling global supply. [26]

South Africa it is the only country in the world that has voluntarily given up its own accumulated nuclear arsenal. It has plans to develop nuclear energy to reduce South Africa's dependence on coal.

The economies of the BRICS nations need energy to fuel their development and growth plans. Nuclear energy is a viable option for them. The great advantage of nuclear power is its ability to wrest enormous energy from a small volume of fuel. More than 40 years of commercial nuclear power operations demonstrate that nuclear power is comparatively safer than fossil-fuel systems in terms of industrial accidents, environmental damage, health effects, and long-term risk. Within the grouping, there are countries that have a long history of civil nuclear energy development and thus the technology, knowledge and understanding needed to cooperate with the each other. Individually all these countries are contributing to the larger debates on nuclear non-proliferation and disarmament and the need to develop civil nuclear technology.

5. The GCC and BRICS Relationship

The energy relationship between the GCC States and the BRICS member States is undeniable. The GCC region is exceptionallywell-endowed with crude oil and natural gas reservesand, as such, it will continue to play a crucial role inglobal energy production in the coming decades. The rapid industrialisation of the BRICS economies is predicted to ensure that global demand for oil and natural gas does not dip. China and India have succeeded in displacing traditional economic powers such as Japan, the EU and the US from the list of the GCC's largest trading partners and it is likely that these relationships will continue to grow. Individually all the BRICS nations have economic ties with the GCC states. Further complementing India's ties with the GCC states, moreover, is the large number of migrant labourers from India working there.

A GCC partnership with the BRICS would have far-reaching strategic, economic, political and international significance. It would itself be an important reflection of the changing balance of power in the world. At a time when the West shies away from buying Gulf oil, the BRICSs are drawing closer to the Arab countries of the Gulf and increasing imports of their oil and other products.[27] The GCC States have, in return, the capacity to invest in substantial infrastructure development projects in the BRICS nations.

Nonetheless, the relationship cannot be confined just to energy resources. Over the past decade the Gulf region has witnessed much turmoil, with the US led war in Iraq, the civil war in Iraq and Syria, the rise of violent radical groups, etc. The countries of the region are now looking towards new opportunities and engagements rather than focusing narrowly on the distant United States. The BRICS countries have the opportunity, therefore, to deepen their existing relations. The two groupings share similar views on terrorism, piracy, cyber security and climate change. As high-income developing countries, the Gulf states have also been seeking a greater representation in global institutions such the IMF, an issue about which the BRICS has been proactive.

The BRICS nations have established the New Development Bank, and while the role of the bank is very similar to that of the IMF and World Bank, it is different in two respects. First, the bank has been established by developing economies; and second, it has laid much emphasis on sustainable development, especially development of renewable sources of energy. The joint statement released at the end of the Ufa Summit in Russia (2015) stresses on this:

> "... encouraging investment in priority areas such as... renewable sources of energy are a strategic goal for the sustainable growth of our economies..... the importance of transfer of technology and scientific knowledge to address climate change and its adverse effects and therefore agreed to conduct joint research on the priority issues of common interest."[28]

Diversification in its energy sources is a goal of the GCC States, with solar energy receiving prominence due to very obvious reasons. It is with this view that the GCC States are also exploring the possibility of nuclear energy in the region.

6. The GCC and BRICS: Nuclear Cooperation

As signatories of the NPT, the GCC states have the right to develop civil nuclear power. With the Iran nuclear negotiations culminating in a successful deal, the GCC States along with other Arab statesin the region are now giving renewed attention to their options. Suspicious about Iran's nuclear intent and its capacity, the GCC states are expressing their interest in being able to match the fuel enrichment capacity of Iran. They argue that, if the United States and the international community can agree to permit Iran to enrich uranium based on the knowledge that it would take Iran time to build a nuclear weapon, then they cannot credibly argue that the GCC states should not be permitted the same.

The question is, given their lack of expertise in nuclear technology how will the GCC States achieve this goal? The BRICS provides the GCC states with an alternative to the Westin developing their programmes.

Differences between the 'West' and the GCC have risen over the past year and a half. This provides the two groupings an ideal opportunity to develop Asia/BRICS-GCC cooperation. This may cause some discomfort, as the BRICS nations are challenging the status quo of the international order, an order created and dominated by allies of the GCC States. Nonetheless, BRICS-which is home to close to 43 per cent of the world's population and about 22 per cent share in global GDP, cannot be overlooked by the GCC States. Civil nuclear cooperation could prove to be a medium through which the two groupings may work together.

6.1 Challenges before the GCC in Developing Civil Nuclear Energy

Development of nuclear energy is not without its challenges, even for nations that have significant knowledge in nuclear technology. For the GCC States, it is a bigger challenge as they have neither the expertise required in the field nor a robust nuclear history.

One of the first challenges before the UAE and Saudi Arabia, the two nations of the six which have declared their intention to develop nuclear energy programmes, is the time factor. They have signed bi-lateral agreements for the development of nuclear energy, which is the first step in the direction of building a nuclear power plant. The next steps would cover such things as identifying the area where the plant would be constructed, a geological survey of the area concerned to ensure that it is not earthquake prone, environmental impact studies, and relocation of people, if need be. Plant construction itself is a time-consuming process and one which has to be monitored to ensure that all safety features are being incorporated.

The UAE's nuclear energy programme is the most advanced of the region and its success or failure will indicate the feasibility of nuclear power projects in the region. It is also being viewed as a successful example of a nuclear power ambition which does not encourage the spread of nuclear weapons. According to the UAE, its first nuclear power unit will be in operation by 2017. Saudi Arabia has made no such announcements.

Dual use technology poses a problem for the development of nuclear energy, in so far as it involves technology which can be used to develop nuclear weapons. States with nuclear know-how are extremely cautious in encouraging trade in this technology, especially to the Gulf states. The trade in nuclear technology and material is controlled by the export control regimes set up by the international community, in particular the following:

a) The Nuclear Suppliers Group (NSG), through its two sets of guidelines controls nuclear export and nuclear-related export. These guidelines are followed by 48 member states.
b) The Wassenaar Arrangement, which was established to promote transparency and greater responsibility in transfers of conventional arms and dual-use goods and technologies and has 41 member states.
c) The Fissile Material Cut-off Treaty (FMCT), which is a proposed international agreement that would prohibit the production of the two main components of nuclear weapons: highly-enriched uranium (HEU), and plutonium.

This is apart from the regulations established by the IAEA, in the form of safeguards and addition protocols, to'verify that a State is living up to its international commitments not to use nuclear programmes for nuclear-weapons purposes.' The global Nuclear Non-Proliferation Treaty and other treaties against the spread of nuclear weapons entrust monitoring of this to the IAEA as the nuclear inspectorate. The IAEA safeguards nuclear material and activities under agreements with more than 140 States.[29]

As there are few countries that are part of the global nuclear industry and have the capability, expertise and technology to build a nuclear power plant, delays are unavoidable. The United States, Russia, the United Kingdom, Canada, France and Japan are established powers in the global nuclear industry. China is a new entrant in the market and India wants to be a future exporter. Global capacity to produce vessels for nuclear reactors is currently limited to about six to eight a year. This creates a long lead time between when a vessel is ordered to when it would be produced. Thus, the vendors need time to meet the demand of new reactors.

Given this reality most vendors prefer nations which have a history of nuclear power, low political, economic or proliferation risk, and an established demand is for multiple reactors. The political instability of the Arab region has been one of the major issues that have been raised by countries that have entered into bilateral agreements with the GCC states. Internationally and regionally, the GCC states' nuclear power programmes have not been viewed optimistically. Two related reasons are typically cited: first, the risk of wider dissemination of nuclear technology proficiency and its subsequent proliferation to third party countries; and second, the risk of a nuclear arms race in the Middle East, given the threat that the Gulf states have expressed about Iran's nuclear programme[30] (although in the negotiations on the Iran nuclear deal Iran claimed that its nuclear programme was for peaceful use alone). Nuclear safety has also been raised as an area of concern, especially with regard to threats to the safety of nuclear power plants from terrorists and other non-state actors. This is a challenge that is not specific to the GCC states but is a common concern shared by all nuclear power states.

The second challenge is, very simply put, one of human resource. Nuclear power plants have to be operated by experts who have the knowledge to operate the power plant in normal times and the training to act during an emergency. As has been stated above, the GCC States have neither the human nor technical expertise to build oroperate a modern nuclear power plant. Embarking on a nuclear power programme requires theestablishment of a sustainable national infrastructure that provides governmental, legal, regulatory, industrial, technological, administrative and human support throughout the life cycle of aprogramme. A highly competent management is vital to the success at all stages of developing a safeand sustainable nuclear power programme. Building this highly reliable human resource is a time consuming process.

Nuclear power would provide the GCC states with large capacity from a very reliable base-load energy source. It is also a relatively clean and cheap source of energy. However, like all other sources of power it requires a capital-intensive programme, and while the GCC states would be in a position to finance the projects, it has to be kept in mind that cost over-runs and delays do happen, due to reasons beyond the control of the nuclear industry. For example, as a result of the Fukushima accident, all countries stopped construction of power plants, conducted intensive safety checks on existing operating power plants and ordered new safety features to be added to reactors ordered or in initial stages of construction. Increased safety and security requirements have considerably increased fixedoperating costs for existing nuclear power plants.

All these delays and changes add to the expenditure on power plants. The cost of the raw material or nuclear fuel is high as is the price of disposal of waste and decommissioning of nuclear power plants. As the nuclear power programme in the region would be a state-led and operated initiative, all of these costs would be borne by the national governments.

This combination of factors means that the economic viability of some smaller nuclear powerplants in a competitive electricity markets is in doubt. To achieve the best result, it has been recommended by experts that the GCC states revive electricity tariff plans and encourage energy saving. If electricity prices remain low andregulatory burdens continue to rise, it is quite possible that the operators of these reactors willdecide to shut them down early rather than invest in major equipment change-overs or in theother capital-intensive plant upgrades and maintenance that will be required to operate thereactors to the end of their licensed operating lives.[31]

For the GCC states, as they have neither the fuel nor the technology, nuclear power would also entail a number of non-commercial and invisible costs. On the diplomatic level, the acquisition of nuclear technology would need time, effort and the long term alignment of national interest with those of the countries and companies transferring technology. Indirect channels such as trade agreements, support at international forums etc are costs that cannot be quantified; nonetheless they are incurred by countries.[32]

6.2 Nuclear Diplomacy: The Need for Cooperation

As has been mentioned before, the GCC states, as yet, do not have the expertise in the field of nuclear technology and sciences to develop their nuclear programmes independent of support. In the BRICS grouping, Russia is the leading country in terms of nuclear capacity and technology. The Rosatom corporation is responsible for Russia's nuclear programme and would be a composite partner to any nuclear cooperation agreement. Russia has proven reserves of uranium, technology to produce enriched uranium needed as fuel in reactors, expertise to build reactors, the technology to dispose of the waste and assist in the decommissioning process. Among the BRICS nations, Russia can provide a 'cradle to the grave' service to its partners, from providing fuel to decommissioning solutions.

With experience of more than half a decade in the field of nuclear technology, "India is perhaps the only developing country that has demonstrated its capacity to design, build, operate and maintain nuclear power plants, manufacture all associated equipment and components, and produce the required nuclear fuel and special material."[33] India can claim to have experience in the construction, operation and maintenance of a wide range of nuclear power plants. This could prove to be advantageous for the GCC states as it would reduce the chances for proliferation as both enrichment of fuel and waste management would be the responsibility of supplier nation.

During the BRICS Summit in Brazil (2014), President Putin proposed the setting up of a BRICS/Russia fuel bank. This is not the first time Russia has proposed this concept. In 2006, Russia offered to set up an international uranium-enrichment and nuclear fuel centre in eastern Siberia, to break the deadlock in the Iranian nuclear dispute. The idea behind establishing a fuel bank is to limit the possibility of proliferation by encouraging new nuclear countries to forego uranium enrichment and reprocessing at the same time ensure control over enrichment and reprocessing technology, thus strengthening nuclear non-proliferation mechanisms.

Russia and Chinasigned a memorandum of understanding in 2014 on joint development of floating nuclear power plant technology. The power plants are to be marine nuclear reactors that would be placed on barges for civilian use. The advantage of these reactors would be that they would be small in size and could be used in remote and less densely populated areas. Russia is developing this technology to use it in the Arctic region to help in powering off-shore drilling and oil exploration grids. China has very similar interests. If successful, with this technology it would be possible to have small power reactors for less/low populated regions. The GCC states could collaborate in the development of this technology as it could be modified to address the question of economic viability of nuclear power for small nations. Given the interest in nuclear energy for peaceful purposes by the smaller countries of the GCC in the future, India has an opportunity to export its 220 megawattreactors. These would be ideally suited for the smaller electricity grids and low demand of these GCC states. The GCC countries can seek India's cooperation over these reactors, given that they have proved their competitiveness in capital and energy coast and have a demonstrated record of safe operation. [34]

Oman, Qatar, Bahrain and Kuwait have for the moment announced plans to halt their nuclear power programmes. Given their geographical size, grid network, power demand and economic strengthen, individual nuclear power programmes is not an ideal option. They have proposed the concept of a nuclear power programme for the GCC states, but not much progress has been made on this. However, these states can continue to develop as centres of learning and research in nuclear science. India, among the BRICS nations, could be a strong partner to collaborate on nuclear science and technology education. It is an indicationof India's nuclear expertise that it has been invited to participate in the multinational International Thermonuclear Experimental Reactor (ITER) being built in Cadarache, France to harness energy from nuclear fusion. While doing independent research on nuclear fusion, India is an emerging leader in the development of reactors and associated fuel technologies for thorium utilisation. It already has a small 30 KW (Th) reactor operational, the first of its kind in the world. India has also demonstrated its capabilities in enhancing the average capacity factor of its reactors.[35]

Collaboration between the BRICS and GCC countries, at bi-lateral or multi-lateral levels, would in the long run contribute to the growth of a highly skilled workforce for the GCC states. The GCC could become a centre for nuclear research and development centre globally. Such joint collaborations can lead to innovation in reactor designs; enhanced safety features in reactors, and the development of reactors that produce less waste. This would be an addition to the economic development of these nations. For example, India is building its capabilities to emerge as a low cost manufacturing destination for nuclear components. The development of a work force that is proficient and dedicated is an investment that can be used in future innovations in nuclear technology.

The BRICS and the GCC states can also collaborate on developing nuclear disaster management techniques and tools. The GCC states have entered into agreements with the IAEA to develop the national and regional programs in the areas of safety, security, research and development related to the uses of the nuclear energy in the Gulf states. The GCC states are developing a Regional Radiological and Nuclear Emergency Preparedness and Response (RRNEPR) Plan, which will be executed under the responsibility of the GCC Emergency Management Centre located in Kuwait, the organisation responsible for preparedness and response to radiological and nuclear events in the region. The IAEA has also conducted courses on nuclear energy management in the Gulf region. BRICS and the GCC could come together to establish more such regional centres of learning. The collaboration could extend to research and development in all aspects such as supply, storage, and consumption.

Agreements between the GCCstates and BRICS nations would also be important for the nuclear industry. Nuclear technology is a leading industry with applications in all spheres of the economy like power generation, agriculture, medical research and space explorations. A robust nuclear industry helps advance several importantdomestic priorities, such as reducing greenhouse gas emissions while supplyingaffordable, reliable energy and creating jobs. According to Rosatom, the Russian nuclear industry comprises over 400 companies with over 255,000 employees operating in the nuclear fuel cycle, power generation, and R&D sectors. The China National Nuclear Corporation (CNNC) website states that it has over 100 secondary member units across over 20 provinces, autonomous regions and municipalities with 100,000 employees. Fukushima continues to have a significant impact on nuclear developments, so maintaining nuclear energy infrastructure at home and a leadership role in the nuclear arena abroad is of interest for the BRICS governments. A strong domestic industry will deliver benefits for the people employed, directly and indirectly, by this industry.

Strategically, for the BRICS, nuclear cooperation agreements would have a bearing on its ability to advance anumber of crucial objectives, particularly with respect to non-proliferationandenergy security. Today, the largest numbers of nuclear power plants under construction worldwide are being built in the BRICS nations. Taking control of the commerce and availability of nuclear technology away from the trans-Atlantic system along with funding, would allow the BRICS nations to lead nuclear development. Collaboration with the GCC States would contribute to this goal. The BRICS nations have the ability to provide the fuel, technology and services on a reliable basis. In return they can impose strict conditionality to ensure that proliferation of material or technology is eliminated. The UAE and Saudi Arabia have signed agreements which include IAEA safeguards and additional protocols. To further dispel the fears of the international community they have agreed to transfer the spent fuel back to the suppliers. This can become a model for peaceful development of nuclear energy that can be followed in other regions as well. It would also reduce regional apprehensions and fears of future nuclear weapons development.

At the same time, the nuclear agreements could become the foundations of partnerships that could also focus on other 'sensitive' issues such as closer military and strategic ties, intelligence sharing, and cooperation on fighting terrorism. The nations of the two groups could come together to make strategic gains in addition to economic ones. It is possible that the BRICS nations could leverage their bi-lateral good relations and influence to help stabilise the region which is witnessing a rise in radical politics, growing influence of non-state actors and terrorist organisations. Saudi Arabia's agreement with China, reportedly for sixteen commercial nuclear power reactors, is being viewed largely as a strategic partnership rather than a purely transactional relationship, in an attempt to expand Chinese sphere of influence in a traditionally United States dominated region. It has also been viewed in the context of deepening Saudi Arabia-China military relations.

It has to be kept in mind that any nuclear agreement is not restricted to the countries buying or selling a few reactors. The agreements, if implemented, lead to assimilation into the international nuclear trade and technology regimes, constituting a step to leverage economic, strategic and political dividends for the country. Nuclear agreements can become an important pillar in consolidating and strengthening relations between nations.[36] Both the GCC and the BRICS countries have a common interest in weakening the nexus between economic growth, energy demand and environmental degradation.

Apart from the risk of proliferation, the BRICS countries would find very few drawbacks in exploring the route of nuclear energy cooperation to strengthen relations with the GCC States. The two notable issues that the author foresees are problems that may arise from competition within the BRICS nations to secure deals in the extremely competitive and small global nuclear industry. They also have to compete with the other nuclear trading nations such as South Korea, which already has agreements for developing nuclear projects in the GCC States. The other issue is the high expectations that the GCC states may have from nuclear energy. Nuclear collaboration has to be discussed keeping in mind realistic goals that can be achieved. Enhanced cooperation between the GCC and BRICS nations through various bi-lateral and multi-lateral forums would allow them to steer the global debates on international nuclear cooperation.

7. Conclusion

As countries move to explore 'non- traditional paths' to security, energy security has become an important component of the overall comprehensive security of nations. Ample energy is the prerequisite not just for economic growth but is a requirement for overall development of any country, needed for a stable political environment, social growth, economic development and strong defence. Thus, energy strategy is as important as economic strategy and military strategy.

Nuclear energy is rather unique as a source of energy. Unlike other sources of energy, an accident in a nuclear power plant anywhere in the world has a cascading impact on nuclear energy production worldwide. It could be said the nuclear energy is dependent on the safe working of plants all across the globe, because of the consequences that arise as a result of an accident anywhere in the world.

International terrorism, weapons of mass of destruction, collapsed states and organized crime are the most important elements in the new threat pictures along with the accumulation of significant amounts of nuclear waste, posing a potential security problem in addition to generating environmental concerns. Thus, cooperation among states is one of the most importantfeatures, both at the multilateral and bilateral levels. Cooperation between states includes early notification of nuclear accidents as well as preparedness to come together to contain the situation.

Nuclear power programmes are dependent on two factors. First, a clear formulation of the goals by the country concerned and a blueprint of the nuclear programme reflectingtime-bound phases of its implementation. Second, the ability to fulfil these goals through financial competitiveness, political will, resource building and ensuring the availability of all materials required for the realisation of the stated goals.

It has been established that the UAE and Saudi Arabia want nuclear energy for economic reasons. They need nuclear energy so that oil and natural gas use for domestic consumption can be minimised. Whether nuclear power is able to provide the GCC states an economic solution can only be assessed in a few years; nonetheless, it will be a reality in one GCC state (the UAE)in the near future.

Nuclear power for the GCC states is also about prestige and power. Iran's nuclear programme is as much a security concern as a political matter concerning the leadership position in the Middle East. However, the region itself has been volatile and has been subjected to repeated conflicts over the past few years. The fear of a nuclear arms race in the region is an ever-present risk. The agreements that have been signed by the UAE and Saudi Arabia have tried to address this concern, and are the best possible guarantee against proliferation.

Given this context, it would be prudent of the international community to address the security and safety questions that arise with regard to the GCC's nuclear ambition. After the Fukushima incident, national and regional security concerns have increased significantly. The densely-populated coastline of these nations and the close proximity of many of the nations of the region imply that an accident in any nuclear facility will have an impact on the neighbouring states as well. Thus, it is essential that the international community, including the BRICS nations, be involved in the development of nuclear programmes of the states of the region. Supplier nations have to be cautious in the transfer of technology and fuel.

The one possible assurance for non-proliferation is that the nuclear programme provides the GCC states with valuable political returns and they would not like to jeopardise the benefits or damage their reputations. The UAE has been described as a model for the region in how to develop nuclear power and a counter-example to the suspicions about Iran's nuclear programme. It seems unlikely that the UAE or Saudi Arabia would want to be compared to Iran. They can also learn lessons from India, which has an exemplary record of non-proliferation and safety, a prominent reason for the United States to agree to a nuclear deal with India and support its involvement in export control regimes.

To build civil nuclear cooperation between the BRICS and the GCC states, the best approach would be to establish bi-lateral cooperation agreements. Bi-lateral agreements are comparatively easier to negotiate on such contentious issues as nuclear energy. Russia hasalready signed agreements with Saudi Arabia and it can build on this foundation. China similarly can build upon its existing agreement to strengthen capacity-building in the GCC states. India can help address the issue of smaller nuclear reactors that are the requirements of the geographically smaller nations of the GCC. The BRICS nations have robust research and development institutions that can collaborate with the institutions in the GCC states. Collective effort can also be used to further boost the nuclear non-proliferation regime. The principle risk that is associated with nuclear energy is the possibility of an accident at the plant site or reactors. Natural calamities are taken into account during the survey and siting procedures. It is for this reason that reactors are built on sites that are far from population centres and in non-seismic active zones and incorporate new and advanced safety features within the reactor design. Precautions against man-made disasters are an ever-evolving process. It requires continuous training of security personals, security and background checks of the scientists and employees of the plant, conducting periodic drills to gauge the response time of the emergency systems etc. The need to secure these sites from attacks would also be of prime importance to the GCC states. Nuclear cooperation can extend to developing these skills. The BRICS nations can provide the GCC states with the expertise knowledge that they have acquired to ensure that nuclear installation sites are kept safe.

There is little doubt that nuclear energy is going to be an important element of the energy mix of the future. The GCC states want to look beyond oil to fuel their domestic economic needs; they have decided to explore nuclear energy. Thus, it is now the responsibility of the international community to encourage this development in an atmosphere of transparency and under the strict guidance of international regulations.

Notes

1 Dr. Mohamed ElBaradei, IAEA, "Nuclear Power: Preparing for the Future", Accessed on 29 May 2015, <https://www.iaea.org/newscenter/statements/nuclear-power-preparing-future>.

2 Benjamin K. Sovacool, "A Grounded Comparison of Energy Security in Denmark, Brazil, Bangladesh, and China", in *New Security Frontiers: Critical Energy and the Resource Challenges*, ed. Sai Felicia Krishna-Hensel, (Surrey, Ashgate Publishing Limited, 2012), 67.

3 Manpreet Sethi, "In the Wake of Fukushima: Implications and Lessons for India", in *Nuclear Power in the Wake of Fukushima*, ed. Manpreet Sethi, (New Delhi, Knowledge World Publication, 2012), 59.

4 Ibid, 59.

5 The Center for Strategic and International Studies, "Restoring U.S. Leadership in Nuclear Energy: A Security Imperative", (New York, Rowman & Littlefield, 2013), 01, Accessed 19 March 2015, <http://csis.org/files/publication/130614_RestoringUSLeadershipNuclearEnergy_WEB.pdf>.

6 Secretariat General, The Cooperation Council of the Arab States of the Gulf, "The Closing Statement of the Eighteenth Session of the Gulf Cooperation Council Supreme Council", 103, Accessed on 21 May 2015,<http://sites.gcc-sg.org/DLibrary/index-eng.php?action=ShowOne&F=Search&BID=179>.

7 Secretariat General, The Cooperation Council of the Arab States of the Gulf, "Closing Statement of the Supreme Council", Accessed on 21 May 2015, <http://www.gcc-sg.org/eng/indexcb9a.html?action=Sec-Show&ID=5>.

8 ArabianBusiness.com, March 27, 2007, <www.arabianbusiness.com/index.php?option=com_content&view=arile&id=9906> as cited by George Perkovichin *Nuclear Developments in the GCC: Risks and Trends, Accessed on 18 February 2015,* <http://carnegieendowment.org/files/perkovich_gcc.pdf>.

9 US Energy Information Administration, "How much of World Energy consumption and electricity generation is from Renewable Energy?, Accessed on 25 May 2015, <http://www.eia.gov/tools/faqs/faq.cfm?id=527&t=1>.

10 'Joint Comprehensive Plan of Action', Accessed on 16 July 2015, <http://www.theguardian.com/world/2015/jul/14/iran-nuclear-deal-full-text-of-joint-comprehensive-plan-of-action>, 11-12.

11 Ibid, 13.

12 International Energy Agency, "Summer Demand Taxes Saudi Power Sector, But Kingdom Is Working on Solutions", <http://www.iea.org/newsroomandevents/news/2014/august/summer-demand-taxes-saudi-power-sector-but-kingdom-is-working-on-solutions.html>, and Saudi Gazette, "Saudi electricity demand posts 8% annual growth", April 01, 2014, Accessed on 21 May 2015, <http://www.saudigazette.com.sa/index.cfm?method=home.regcon&contentid=20140401200466>.

13 Charles K. Ebinger and Sharon Squassoni, "Industry and Emerging Energy Markets" in *Business and Nonproliferation: Industries Role in Safeguarding Nuclear Renaissance*, ed. John P Banks and Charles K Ebinger, (Washington DC, Brookings Institute Press, 2011), 82.

14 Nuclear Renaissance is a term that is used to denote the revival or re-emergence of the nuclear industry that has been facing a slowdown in the last few decades.

15 ManpreetSethi, "N-Powering India: Opportunities and Challenges", in *Comprehensive Security for an Emerging India*, ed. KapilKak, (New Delhi, Knowledge World, 2010), 263- 264.

16 The Policy on the Evaluation and Potential Development of Peaceful Nuclear Energy document is available at <https://www.enec.gov.ae/uploads/media/uae-peaceful-nuclear-energy-policy.pdf>.

17 The Government of the United Arab Emirates (2008), "Policy on the Evaluation and Potential Development of Peaceful Nuclear Energy", (2008), i, Accessed on 21 May 2015, <https://www.enec.gov.ae/uploads/media/uae-peaceful-nuclear-energy-policy.pdf>.

18 Ibid, p. 1.

19 Safeguards are activities by which the IAEA can verify that a State is living up to its international commitments not to use nuclear programmes for nuclear-weapons purposes. Verification measures include on-site inspections, visits, and ongoing monitoring and evaluation.

20 The Additional Protocol is a legal document granting the IAEA complementary inspection authority to that provided in underlying safeguards agreements. A principal aim is to enable the IAEA inspectorate to provide assurance about both declared and possible undeclared activities. Under the Protocol, the IAEA is granted expanded rights of access to information and sites.

21 Ali Ahmad and M.V. Ramana (2014), "Too costly to matter: Economics of nuclear power for Saudi Arabia", Accessed on 27 May 2015, <http://www.princeton.edu/~ramana/Saudi-Nuclear-Economics-2014.pdf>.

22 King Abdullah City for Nuclear and Renewable Energy, "The Establishing Order", Accessed on 27 May 2015, <http://www.kacare.gov.sa/en/> and ----, "The Royal Decree Establishing King Abdullah City for Nuclear and Renewable Energy, Accessed on 27 May 2015, <http://kacare.gov.sa/en/wp-content/uploads/KACARE_Royal_Decree_english.pdf>.
23 Ashitosh Sharma, Nabil Sultan and David Weir, "Going Nuclear in the GCC Countries: Rational, Challenge and Politics", in *The GCC Economies: Stepping Up to the Challenge*, ed. Mohammad A Ramady, (New York, Springer, 2012), 61.
24 Moisès Naìm, "Will the BRICS change the global energy landscape?", *About Oil Magazine*, Accessed on 30 April 2015, <https://www.abo.net/oilportal/topic/view.do?contentId=2000196>.
25 Op. Cit XV MapreetSethi, 265.
26 Mark Ekstrom, "Nuclear Energy in the BRICS: An Overview", Accessed on 30 April 2015,<http://revolve.media/bric-nuclear-energy/>.
27 Mohammad Al Asoomi, "In theory: GCC, BRICS, have a case for merger", Gulf News, <http://gulfnews.com/business/analysis/in-theory-gcc-brics-have-a-case-for-merger-1.1004248>. Accessed on 04 July 2015.
28 Ministry of External Affairs, Government of India, "VII BRICS Summit: Ufa Declaration", Accessed on 16 July 2015, <http://mea.gov.in/Uploads/PublicationDocs/25448_Declaration_eng.pdf>, 29 and 40.
29 IAEA, "IAEA Safeguard Overview", Accessed on 25 May 2015<https://www.iaea.org/publications/factsheets/iaea-safeguards-overview.>
30 Laura El-Katiri, "The GCC and the Nuclear Question", *The Oxford Institute for Energy StudiesPapers*, (Oxford, University of Oxford, 2012), 05.
31 The Center for Strategic and International Studies, n.5, p. 4.
32 Laura El-Katiri, n. xxviii , p. 5.
33 Dr Chidambaram, Former Chairman, Atomic Energy Commission of India, as cited by Manpreet Sethi in N-Powering India: Challenges and Opportunities in *Comprehensive Security for an Emerging India*, ed. KapilKak, (New Delhi, Knowledge World, 2012), 265.
34 Ibid, 269.
35 Ibid, 265.
36 Vikram Singh Mehta, "Energy: A Solid Pillar upon which to build India-US Relations" in *The Modi-Obama Summit; A Leadership Moment for India and the United States*, (Brookings University Press, Brookings, 2014), 49.

References

Al Asoomi, Mohammad "In theory: GCC, BRICS, have a case for merger", Gulf News, <http://gulfnews.com/business/analysis/in-theory-gcc-brics-have-a-case-for-merger-1.1004248Accessed on 04 July 2015>.

Ahmad , Ali and M.V. Ramana (2014), "Too costly to matter: Economics of nuclear power for Saudi Arabia", Accessed on 27 May 2015, <http://www.princeton.edu/~ramana/Saudi-Nuclear-Economics-2014.pdf>.

Ebinger, Charles K. and Sharon Squassoni, "Industry and Emerging Energy Markets" in *Business and Nonproliferation: Industries Role in Safeguarding Nuclear Renaissance,* edited by John P Banks and Charles K Ebinger, 82, Washington DC, Brookings Institute Press, 2011.

ElBaradei, Dr. Mohamed. Nuclear Power: Preparing for the Future, Accessed on 29 May 2015, <https://www.iaea.org/newscenter/statements/nuclear-power-preparing-future>.

El-Katiri, Laura "The GCC and the Nuclear Question", *The Oxford Institute for Energy StudiesPapers*, 05, Oxford, University of Oxford, 2012.

Ekstrom, Mark "Nuclear Energy in the BRICS: An Overview", Accessed on 30 April 2015,<http://revolve.media/bric-nuclear-energy/>.

IAEA, "IAEA Safeguard Overview", Accessed on 25 May 2015, <https://www.iaea.org/publications/factsheets/iaea-safeguards-overview>.

International Energy Agency, "Summer Demand Taxes Saudi Power Sector, But Kingdom Is Working on Solutions", <http://www.iea.org/newsroomandevents/news/2014/august/summer-demand-taxes-saudi-power-sector-but-kingdom-is-working-on-solutions.html>, and Saudi Gazette, "Saudi electricity demand posts 8% annual growth", April 01, 2014, Accessed on 21 May 2015, <http://www.saudigazette.com.sa/index.cfm?method=home.regcon &contentid=20140401200466>.

King Abdullah City for Nuclear and Renewable Energy, "The Establishing Order", Accessed on 27 May 2015, <http://www.kacare.gov.sa/en/> and ----, "The Royal Decree Establishing King Abdullah City for Nuclear and Renewable Energy, Accessed on 27 May 2015, <http://kacare.gov.sa/en/wp-content/uploads/KACARE_Royal_Decree_english.pdf>.

Mehta, Vikram Singh "Energy: A Solid Pillar upon which to build India-US Relations" in *The Modi-Obama Summit; A Leadership Moment for India and the United States*, 49, Brookings University Press, Brookings, 2014.

Ministry of External Affairs, Government of India, "VII BRICS Summit: Ufa Declaration", Accessed on 16 July 2015, <http://mea.gov.in/Uploads/PublicationDocs/25448_Declaration_eng.pdf>, 29 and 40.

Naìm, Moisès "Will the BRICS change the global energy landscape?", *About Oil Magazine*, Accessed on 30 April 2015, <https://www.abo.net/oilportal/topic/view.do?contentId=2000196>.

Secretariat General, The Cooperation Council of the Arab States of the Gulf, "The Closing Statement of the Eighteenth Session of the Gulf Cooperation Council Supreme Council", 103, Accessed on 21 May 2015,<http://sites.gcc-sg.org/DLibrary/index-eng.php?action=ShowOne&F=Search&BID=179>.

Secretariat General, The Cooperation Council of the Arab States of the Gulf, "Closing Statement of the Supreme Council", Accessed on 21 May 2015, <http://www.gcc-sg.org/eng/indexcb9a.html?action=Sec-Show&ID=5>.

Sethi, Manpreet."In the Wake of Fukushima: Implications and Lessons for India", in *Nuclear Power in the Wake of Fukushima* edited by Manpreet Sethi, 59 New Delhi, Knowledge World Publication, 2012.

Sethi, Manpreet. "N-Powering India: Opportunities and Challenges", in *Comprehensive Security for an Emerging India*, edited by KapilKak, 263-265, New Delhi, Knowledge World, 2010.

Sharma, Ashitosh Nabil Sultan and David Weir, "Going Nuclear in the GCC Countries: Rational, Challenge and Politics", in *The GCC Economies: Stepping Up to the Challenge*, edited by Mohammad A Ramady, 61, New York, Springer, 2012.

Sovacool, Benjamin K. "A Grounded Comparison of Energy Security in Denmark, Brazil, Bangladesh, and China", in *New Security Frontiers: Critical Energy and the Resource Challenges* edited by Sai Felicia Krishna-Hensel, 67, Surrey, Ashgate Publishing Limited, 2012.

The Centre for Strategic and International Studies, "Restoring U.S. Leadership in Nuclear Energy: A Security Imperative", 01, New York, Rowman & Littlefield, 2013, Accessed 19 March 2015, <http://csis.org/files/publication/130614_RestoringUSLeadershipNuclearEnergy_WEB.pdf>.

The Government of the United Arab Emirates (2008), "Policy on the Evaluation and Potential Development of Peaceful Nuclear Energy", (2008), i, Accessed on 21 May 2015, <https://www.enec.gov.ae/uploads/media/uae-peaceful-nuclear-energy-policy.pdf>.

US Energy Information Administration, "How much of World Energy consumption and electricity generation is from Renewable Energy?, Accessed on 25 May 2015, <http://www.eia.gov/tools/faqs/faq.cfm?id=527&t=1>.

ArabianBusiness.com, March 27, 2007, www.arabianbusiness.com/index.php?option=com_content&view=arile&id=9906 as cited by George Perkovich in *Nuclear Developments in the*

GCC: Risks and Trends, Accessed on 18 February 2015,<http://carnegieendowment.org/files/perkovich_gcc.pdf>.

'Joint Comprehensive Plan of Action', Accessed on 16 July 2015, <http://www.theguardian.com/world/2015/jul/14/iran-nuclear-deal-full-text-of-joint-comprehensive-plan-of-action>, 11-12.

The Policy on the Evaluation and Potential Development of Peaceful Nuclear Energy document is available at <https://www.enec.gov.ae/uploads/media/uae-peaceful-nuclear-energy-policy.pdf>.

5

United Arab Emirates and Brazil: Ideas, Perceptions and Perspectives of Unlikely Allies[1]

Vânia Carvalho Pinto and Danielly Silva Ramos Becard

1. Introduction: Brief Introduction to the UAE and Brazil's (Lack of) Relations

Within the fields of Latin American and Gulf Studies, few studies have been conducted of bilateral relations between countries hailing from the two regions. This is mainly because dealings between them are comparatively few and tend to attract little media interest. There is little literature or information on which to base any analysis, and the few existing written works tend to focus on describing the evolution of trade links. In the cases of the UAE and Brazil, even though both countries have decades-long relations, the topic has so far not attracted much scholarly attention. Relations between Brazil and the UAE were formally established in 1974; Brazil's embassy in Abu Dhabi was opened in 1978; and the UAE' sembassy in Brasília only dates from 1991, its first embassy in Latin America.

The greatest increase in interactions between Brazil and the UAE (and the Arab world in general) in fact only came about in 2003 following former President Luiz Inácio Lula da Silva's visit to the country. By 2008, the UAE had become Brazil's second largest Middle Eastern commercial partner, just behind Saudi Arabia,[2] and in 2014 it surpassed Saudi Arabia.[3] Even though the Gulf was not prioritised in the same way as African or emerging countries were, the basic idea underlying this diplomatic push was that of reaffirming political-economic bonds with regions that were traditionally of little relevance to Brazilian foreign policy.[4] If economic motivations can explain some of the Brazil's diplomatic efforts towards the Gulf,[5] interactions between Brazil and the UAE can also be understood within the general context of diversification of partnerships so as to further their respective immersions into the international system. Indeed, both increasing the number of partners and expanding specific areas of engagement are traditionally important goals of Emirati as well as of Brazilian foreign policy. This has particularly been so during and since the presidency of Lula da Silva (2003-2010), although some changes have been made under Dilma Rousseff's tenure of the presidency (2010-2013; 2014-)[6] Despite a context of less presidential emphasis on expanding and deepening the country's foreign relations, economic cooperation between the UAE and Brazil has increased in the last few years. This is ascribed on the Brazilian side to an excellent bilateral relationship between the two countries and to a pronounced like-mindedness in a number of fields.[7] The writers of this chapter began their research convinced that their starting-point would be the very low level of interactions between both countries, but as research progressed, they realised that existing commonalities, at least on the issues taken for analysis here, justified a different perspective and research goal. From the initial goal of merely bringing together very different and, so we thought, almost unrelated countries, we switched to the challenge of exploring commonalities in a field of mutual interest: each country's general humanitarian discourses, with a particular focus on their flagship military engagements in Afghanistan (UAE) and Haiti (Brazil). What triggered our interest were the similarities in the ways both countries 'sold' their respective military operations. The overall aim of the chapter is thus to bring together the study of the UAE's and Brazil's foreign policies in this particular area. We hope that the approach can serve as a start-up for further academic enquiry. Our intention is to take the very first steps in overcoming the perception that because the UAE and Brazil are perceived as countries with little in common, examining their relationship would seldom be considered worthwhile.

2. In Search of a Theoretical Framework

Brazil and the UAE are radically different countries, in terms of their size, history, wealth, ethnic composition, political system and predominant religions. Brazil is a two hundred year-old republic based on a presidential system; whereas the UAE is a forty years old tribal monarchy. However, despite these differences, they both project themselves internationally as law abiding, trustworthy ethical countries. They have both striven to create the features of a role model in their respective regional diplomacies In the case of the UAE this has been particularly evident since the Arab Spring. In the case of Brazil, the projection was strongest during the Presidency of Lula da Silva, when the improvement of the economic situation combined with the enthusiastic personalities of the President and his Chancellor Celso Amorim, to drive Brazil's extensive 'charm' operation within the international system. Emboldened by what Sean Burges called 'rising self-esteem'[8], Brazil began projecting itself as a role model in a number of issue-areas such as regional integration, south-south cooperation, agribusiness, climate change and green energy. Underlying the UAE's and Brazil's self-proclaimed ethical stands in the international system is the very specific goal of building positive representations of themselves so as to foster international recognition of their capabilities.[9] This meant following a strategy of extensive participation in the institutions of the international system as well as adhering to the latters' practices and institutionalized rules as a means to acquire visibility and prestige.[10] Their actions and discourses in the humanitarian field are an ideal case study of these strategic efforts, as will be shown in the following sections.

3. Two Humanitarians in Comparative Perspective

A country's claim to the humanitarian mantle is usually predicated on the amount of humanitarian aid it bestows to other countries and organizations. Insufficient and/or unreliable data can hinder a country's ability to do this. The UAE government has since 2009, therefore, begun organising and duly publicising its humanitarian efforts. Brazil has only partially pursued this course. Interestingly, secondary literature on these countries' humanitarian policies displays a reverse tendency: whereas there are some works (not many) on Brazil's humanitarian policies, there is a dearth of analysis on the UAE's. The lack of academic interest in the Emirates' humanitarian activities can be ascribed to several factors. In addition to the already-mentioned factor of scarce data,[11] we should also take into account international policy-makers' and scholars' perceptions as regards the UAE's aid activities. Since Arab countries tend to be aid recipients rather than donors, less attention is paid to their humanitarian engagements, which results in little scholarly focus on their work.[12] The reasons for the absence of data on Brazil seems to be associated with the fragmentary nature of the Brazilian development cooperation structure, as well as to technical deficiencies associated to lack of monitoring and evaluation.[13] Corroborating the above assessment, made by the Overseas Development Institute, is the fact that there are in fact very few reports on these activities that are effectively compiled and issued. In 2013, the Brazilian government published a booklet entitled *Brazilian Cooperation for International Development: 2010* (Cooperação brasileira para o desenvolvimen to internacional: 2010). Focusing on the work done in that year (2010), the preamble reveals that the goal of the publication was to 'give greater disclosure and transparency to the Brazilian international cooperation,' since 'part of that effort (...) remains little known.'[14] Also from the preamble, we learn that this booklet was intended as an annual publication. However, further editions covering the past five years are still to be issued. Maybe the apparent lack of interest in further continuing the disclosure of Brazilian humanitarian activities can be traced to the decline in aid assistance that accompanied the worsening of the country's economic situation. Indeed, data from Global Humanitarian Assistance shows that Brazil's humanitarian aid decreased by 97 per cent in 2013.[15] Given that the initial aims underscoring the organisation and publication of these booklets were to garner prestige, it could be that having little to report may have dictated the end of the publications. But beyond this issue, several others should be mentioned, which should be seen in combination with the above mentioned scarce statistics and administrative difficulties. Of note is the fact that Brazil is not a member of OECD, does not follow Official Development Assistance (ODA) rules, and does not demand conditionality. Furthermore, humanitarian aid only became a clearly visible part of Brazil's foreign policy at the beginning of the twenty-first century.[16]

The peak in terms of international visibility of the UAE's and Brazil's humanitarian policies was reached in the mid- to late-2000s. This stemmed from leadership changes in both countries, and from the decision to make humanitarian poilices a discernible, strategic part of their international strategies. The political rationale underlying the decisions seems to have been, in both cases to build moral and diplomatic capital in the international arena, and to expand their networks of global relations.[17]Recognition of statehood and the strengthening of Arab solidarity were the main concerns guiding the UAE's early humanitarian policies within the first decade of the country's independence. In fact Khaled Almezaini claims that, without these resources, favourable international rapport would not have been possible for the UAE.[18] While the above factors continue to be key elements underscoring the Emirates' humanitarian policies, in later years the effort of organising the aid information has been primarily intended to 'help secure international recognition for the UAE's immense global humanitarian effort'.[19] The UAE has been among the largest Arab donors since the 1970s,[20] but more recently it has been establishing itself in international statistics as one of the top world donors.[21] The highpoint of the international recognition of this position was when the OECD declared the UAE to be the top aid donor (ODA/GNI) in the world for two consecutive years – 2013 and 2014, which clearly indicates a match between projection and performance.[22]

Similar strategic goals associated to international recognition also underscore Brazil's efforts in this area. Since 2003, the country has sought to build a regional platform for its leadership,[23] as a means eventually to secure a permanent seat at the UNSC. Humanism and solidarity were key themes in political and diplomatic speeches, and relations with the South – especially Latin America and the Caribbean – received particular mention.[24] Policies were justified in altruistic terms, with emphasis on sharing similar values with other southern countries as well as exercising a moral obligation to alleviate poverty.[25] The absence of expectations of reciprocity is something that is also highlighted by both governments. In the case of the UAE, Islam and Emirati national values are claimed to guide these altruistic policies; with Brazil it is the promotion of racial national reconciliation and southern solidarity.[26]

UAE aid to Afghanistan has been framed within the overall ethical and humanitarian context that underpins the UAE's foreign aid programme in general. Afghanistan has been among the top ten recipients of UAE aid at least since 2009 – which is when the UAE government began divulging this information.[27] Diplomatic discourse keenly emphasises the dimension of financial generosity as well as the lessening of suffering by improving the population's life conditions.[28] For many years, references to Afghanistan fell only within the purview of humanitarian assistance with no mention of military engagement. Since the UAE only acknowledged the military engagement publicly in 2012, this means that from an analytical point of view, it is possible to differentiate between the humanitarian and the military dimensions of Emirati engagement in Afghanistan. This is not the case of the Brazilian military intervention in Haiti, which received the humanitarian adjective from the very beginning. Consequently, the Brazilian engagement (both military and humanitarian) has been studied by reference to the concept of *Solidarity Diplomacy* ('Diplomacia Solidária'); whereas, to our knowledge, there is no similar conceptual tool to do the same exercise as regards the UAE in Afghanistan.

3.1 The Case Studies: ISAF and MINUSTAH

Coined by Ricardo Seitenfus, the concept of solidarity diplomacy is defined as the conception and application of an international collective action, under the auspices of the Security Council. It is performed by third states that intervene in internal or international conflicts, and their actions are moved solely by a duty of conscience. This means that these actions are devoid of material and strategic national interests. In order to make this absence of interests possible, it is necessary that the intervening state has had no special relations with the intervened country. This was precisely the case with Brazil and Haiti. The fact that the former was not directly involved with the latter's problems was conceptualized as awarding Brazil additional leverage vis-à-vis other actors; Brazil was thus posited as being *above* the conflict, unhampered by state interests and striving for a genuine solution.[29] Since, according to Seitenfus, there was no public pressure or material interests impelling Brazil to intervene in Haiti, the Brazilian policy brings about a 'valuable and original contribution' to the theory of solidarity diplomacy.[30] The government framed its intervention in terms of a contribution to the strengthening of Latin American and Caribbean identity as well as furthering the construction of a development agenda. In addition, Brazil's international responsibility towards less well-off countries was highlighted as a matter of 'non-indifference' (as opposed to interference).[31] Brazil's 'special attributes', which is a common theme in the diplomatic discourse, were once again highlighted as key in the promotion of more inclusive models of development as well as in the strengthening of cooperation among nations through more representative and legitimate governance mechanisms.[32] Diplomatic discourse emphasised that Brazil could create a new model of intervention, a new paradigm, out of the experience in Haiti. This was regarded as delivering obvious benefits for Brazil as the country would be able to participate in the big international discussions surrounding areas of development, peace and international security.[33] This, it was suggested, would lead to Brazil being finally recognized as a country capable of participating in regional and international decision-making processes. In the end, it was supposed to demonstrate both to the US and the international community that Brazil was able to provide the security goods expected of a potential permanent member of the UNSC.[34]

The UAE joined the International Security Afghanistan Force (ISAF)-NATO in 2003, the first Arab nation to do so and one of the few which contributed with troops to this contingent. The deployment involved more than 1,200 Emirati soldiers and they remained in Afghanistan until 2014.[35] Until recently, the UAE was reluctant to publicly acknowledge its participation due to political sensitivities.[36] Indeed, the UAE government's emphasis on the humanitarian dimension of this operation underscores a significant political effort aimed at downplaying the military aspect so as to make it more palatable to Arab and domestic audiences. This apprehension was warranted. Upon disclosure, perceptions in the UAE as regards this military engagement with NATO varied.

On the negative side, some in the UAE felt that the fact that UAE troops were engaged in combat operations was not acceptable because it was under NATO. In addition, there was also an erroneous perception that the UAE was the only Arab country involved, and that such engagement meant that the UAE wanted to be a NATO member (Personal interview, Dubai, 29.02.2012). Other evaluations included the idea that this was part of the UAE's global engagement strategy and that such participation was a way to do the big powers a favour and maybe obtain something in return at a later stage. All in all, one informant suggested, stabilizing Afghanistan was good anyway, since there were many Afghans in Dubai (Personal interview, Dubai, 28.02.2012). As regards Brazil and Haiti, as previously mentioned, there are no obvious economic, historical or political connections between those two countries. Even if this dearth of interactions is a key precondition for a relationship to be classified as solidarity diplomacy according to Seitenfus' criteria, it nonetheless generated extensive domestic criticism among some Brazilian commentators.[37]

Leading the military component of the United Nations Stabilization Mission in Haiti (Minustah) since 2004 with a mandate established by SC Resolution 1542, the Brazilian contingent has sought to go beyond the purely military aspects. This strategy included humanitarian assistance, election monitoring, promotion of development and the building of political and social institutions. As part of the overall diplomatic framing package, the soldiers were portrayed as impartial, moral individuals, reluctant to use violence, a perception replicated by and further divulged by some academic circles.[38] Videos of Brazilian soldiers playing soccer with Haitian children were frequently played on TV.[39] The Brazilian army also produced in 2011 a sixteen minutes short documentary about its mission in Haiti entitled *Haiti: The Brazilian experience in Minustah.*[40] The latter was narrated in creole by a Haitian girl, she briefly describes the historical struggles in her country as well as the positive role played by Brazilian soldiers in curbing violence. She describes the soldiers as curious, understanding and joyful. This portrayal of soldiers as fun, laid-back soccer-loving individuals sought to produce cultural resonance among the Brazilian public. It promoted the notion that the Brazilian soldier was 'different' from the others, and that from this singularity, a new 'Brazilian way of peacekeeping' had emerged, which was supposedly characterised by a high degree of impartiality and reluctance to use force.[41] The underlying notion within these ideational constructions was that Brazil's assumed innate pacifism[42] would make MINUSTAH a less imposing and more effective peace operation, in particular when measured against similar operations undertaken by the US.[43]

The UAE underwent similar efforts to portray its military contingent in a positive light. It produced a documentary aptly titled 'Winds of Goodness'[44] that followed the lives of Emirati soldiers, showcasing through interviews their heartfelt intentions and positive deeds while highlighting the risks associated with the mission. It also showed the interaction between the Afghans and the Emirati troops, emphasising the positive rapport that the common Muslim religion had produced among them. This was an aspect that was extensively highlighted in press articles about the Emirati contingent.[45] In both cases, Haiti and Afghanistan, there was an important underplayed dimension to the military engagements: that of guaranteeing soldiers from both countries real combat exposure. Whereas Brazilian diplomatic discourse accentuated the contribution the mission would bring to the improvement of Brazil's Peace Operations doctrine,[46] other critical voices emphasised less honourable goals. Specifically that the Haiti operation served as a training laboratory for Brazilian police forces. In Haiti, they could experiment with tactics and exercise a level of violence that they could latter replicate in Rio de Janeiro's shantytowns (favelas). It was argued that they could do things in Haiti they could not try in Brazil due to media interest and public opinion.[47] In the Emirati case, domestic as well as regional security concerns were at play. Whereas internally, this experience would aid soldiers fight domestic terrorism,[48] abroad it would prepare them to face Iran, if necessary.[49]

4. Conclusion

This chapter has sought to bring together the analysis of the foreign policies of the two countries that are seldom (if ever) brought together for comparative analysis. Our focus was on Brazil's and the UAE's humanitarian policies, with a particular focus on their flagship military initiatives: MINUSTAH in Haiti, and ISAF in Afghanistan, respectively. It was shown that their humanitarian policies are an important part of both countries' strategies for international recognition in the international arena. Consequently, both seek to portray themselves as ethical countries, an intention which is reflected in their self-proclaimed principled polices. Their participation in these military engagements was important for them both; it was the first time that Brazil led a UN Operation and this was perceived as an opportunity to showcase its credentials as an important international actor. For the UAE, to be recognised as a valuable country was also an important goal, which in this case was complemented by the objective of fighting terrorism, a key concern of the Emirati government.

The UAE and Brazil faced a similar challenge as regards the perceptions of their domestic audiences. For the UAE, it was problematic that this intervention occurred within the territory of a fellow Muslim country but under the banner of a 'western' operation, which Arab audiences perceive as occupation. As regards Brazil, not only had the country always cultivated an image of a peace-loving nation, but leading the mission in Haiti ran counter to traditional diplomatic politics of non-interference. Maybe because of that, the ways both countries justified their engagements were remarkable similar, even though the elements they utilized derived from their respective cultural worldviews, a strategy that sought to maximise resonance among their respective audiences. They both deployed the ideas of helping fellow countries in need (Muslim in the case of the UAE; southern in the case of Brazil); and stressed that ethical individuals were involved in these interventions: good Muslims (UAE); and laid-back cheerful soldiers (Brazil).

If both countries' foreign policy goals were to portray themselves as effective and valuable international actors (a good ally in the case of the UAE; a regional power in the case of Brazil), the former seems to have been more successful than the latter. As regards Brazil, even though domestic discourse (mostly diplomatic and some academic) constantly emphasises the successes of the mission, the extent to which this will actually translate into greater international prestige and effective diplomatic gains remains to be seen.

Notes

1 Acknowledgements: With thanks to FINATEC (Grant: 98/2015) that partially funded Vânia Carvalho Pinto's travel to the 2015 GRM meeting where this chapter was first presented. We are very indebted to Raíssa Vitório Pereira for her invaluable research assistance. Our thanks also go to Mirella Vaz Castro that assisted with the final editing of this work.

2 Brasil, Ministério das Relações Exteriores (MRE), "Emirados Árabes Unidos: Comércio Exterior" (Brasilia: MRE, 2015b), accessed 20 May 2015, <http://www.brasilexport.gov.br/sites/default/files/publicacoes/indicadoresEconomicos/INDEmiradosArabesUnidos.pdf>.

3 Interview with Diplomat Carlos Leopoldo (Chief of the Gulf Affairs Subsection at MFA), Brasília, 10 June 2015.

4 Sean W. Burges, *Brazilian Foreign Policy after the Cold War* (Gainesville et al: University Press of Florida, 2009), 161-184; Brasil, Ministério das Relações Exteriores (MRE), "Emirados Árabes Unidos" (Brasília: MRE, 2015a), accessed 20 May 2015, <http://www.itamaraty.gov.br/index.php?option=com_content&view=article&id=5103: emirados-arabes-unidos&catid=155&lang=pt-BR&Itemid=478>.

5 Elodie Brun, "Relations between Brazil and the Arab Countries of the Gulf: Renewed Context, Persistent Objectives," in: *The Gulf and Latin America: An Assessment of Expectations and Challenges,* ed.Alejandra Galindo (Cambridge: Gulf Research Centre, 2013), 158-160.

6 Amado Cervo and Antônio Carlos Lessa, "The fall: the international insertion of Brazil (2011–2014)," *Rev. Bras. Polít. Int. RBPI,* 57, no. 2 (2014): 133; Carlos Frederico Pereira da Silva Gama, "Conquistas e desafios da política externa de Dilma Rousseff," *Carta Maior,* 16 November 2014, accessed 24 May 2015 <http://www.

cartamaior.com.br>; Maria Regina Soares de Lima, "Entrevista. Maria Regina Soares de Lima," Interview by Wilson Tosta, *Jornal Estadão*, 10 November 2014, accessed 24 May 2015,<http://politica.estadao.com.br/noticias/geral, dilma-precisa-adotar-proatividade-de-lula-afirma-pesquisadora-imp-,1590522>.

7 Interview with Carlos Leopoldo.

8 Burges, *Brazilian Foreign Policy after the Cold War*, 169-171.

9 See Vânia Carvalho Pinto, "From 'follower' to 'role model': studying the transformation to the UAE's international self-image," *Journal of Arabian Studies*, 4, no. 2 (2014): 231-142, as regards the case of the UAE; and Luis L. Schenoni, "Ascenso y hegemonía: pensando a las potencias emergentes desde América del Sur," *Rev. Bras. Polít. Int. RBPI*, 55, no. 1 (2012): 31-48, for the case of Brazil.

10 This argument derives from Mervyn Frost's claim that states are enmeshed in a network of inter-subjective interactions, and that their international standing derives from the degree of recognition they receive from other states. This recognition arises from each state's degree of compliance with the rules that govern international politics. See Mervyn Frost, *Anarchy, Freedom and International Relations* (London and New York: Routledge, 2009), 1-53. For specifics of these positive representations in foreign policy see, on the UAE Abdulla Al-Suwaidi, "The United Arab Emirates at 40: A Balance Sheet," *Middle East Policy* 18, no. 4 (2011): 41; on Brazil see Amado Cervo, *Inserção Internacional: formação dos conceitos brasileiros* (São Paulo: Editora Saraiva, 2008).

11 Debra Shushan and Chris Marcoux offer a set of justifications to account for this underreporting: the first is associated to the domestic system; there are difficulties in distinguishing between public and royal funds so accounting is not transparent. Secondly, they claim that Arab countries have not been socialized to follow certain norms of international transparency; and finally, giving is an important cultural norm, members of the royal families may feel that announcing it would be inappropriate. In: Debra Shushan and Christopher Marcoux, "The rise (and decline?) of Arab aid: generosity and allocation in the oil era," *World Development, 39,* no. 11 (2011): 3. Incidentally, some of the reasons mentioned above – such as lack of publicity and the weight of cultural norms – were mentioned by Saudi Arabia in the wake of recent accusations conveyed in the media that the Gulf countries were not doing their share in helping Syrian refugees. According to an official from the Saudi Government, "The Kingdom of Saudi Arabia does not intend to speak about its efforts to support Syrian brothers and sisters during their distress." See Barın Kayaoğlu, "Why the Gulf isn't to blame for Syrian refugee crisis," *Al-Monitor*, 15 September 2015, accessed 25 September 2015, <http://www.al-monitor.com/pulse/originals/2015/09/syria-gulf-countries-respond-criticism-over-refugees.html#ixzz3mkHDtXPG>.

12 Momani and Crystal, "Between caution and controversy", 605; Patrícia Vilarinho Tambourgi, "O Brasil e a assistência humanitária internacional: prática, discurso e tendências." (Master's Diss., Pontifical Catholic University of São Paulo, 2012), 40-45.

13 The Briefing Paper further adds that since projects are analysed from an administrative point of view rather than against internationally recognised performance criteria that has compromised Brazil's ability to review experiences and generate good practices. See Overseas Development Institute, *Brazil: an emerging Aid Donor. Lessons on emerging donors and south-south and triangular cooperation*, Briefing Paper 64 (October 2010): 2-3, <www.odi.org/resources/docs/6295.pdf>.

14 Instituto de Pesquisa Econômica Aplicada-Agência Brasileira de Cooperação, *Cooperação Brasileira para o Desenvolvimento Internacional: 2010* (Brasília: IPEA: ABC, 2013), <www.abc.gov.br/api/publicacaoarquivo/561>.

15 Global Humanitarian Assistance, "Brazil: Key Figures 2013," accessed 22 August 2015, <http://www.globalhumanitarianassistance.org/countryprofile/brazil>.

16 Tambourgi, "O Brasil e a assistência humanitária," 40.

17 On the UAE see: Frauke Heard-Bey, *From Trucial States to United Arab Emirates: A Society in Transition* (London: Longman, 1996), 381; Faria and Paradis, "Humanism,",8-9.

18 Almezaini "The UAE and Foreign Policy", 49, 101-115.

19 WAM, "UAE praised for issuing foreign aid annual report. Local and foreign officials laud commitment of country's leadership to global humanitarian and development issues," 3 August 2010, accessed 29 May 2015, <http://www.emirates247.com/news/emirates/uae-praised-for-issuing-foreign-aid-annual-report-2010-08-03-1.274492>. This article in particular also offers multiple positive receptions of the UAE international aid that show a match between projection and reception.

20 Almezaini "The UAE and Foreign Policy," 1, 17, 113, 115.

21 WAM, "UAE world's 20th most generous donor," 12 February 2013, accessed 29 May 2015, <http://www.emirates247.com/news/uae-world-s-20th-most-generous-donor-2013-02-12-1.494730>.

22 OECD, "Development aid stable in 2014 but flows to poorest countries still falling," 8 April 2015, accessed 25 May 2015, <http://www.oecd.org/dac/stats/development-aid-stable-in-2014-but-flows-to-poorest-countries-still-falling.htm>.

23 Carlos Aurélio Faria and Clarisse Paradis, "Humanism and Solidarity in Brazilian Foreign Policy Under Lula (2003-2010): Theory and Practice", *BPSR*, 7, no. 2 (2013): 15.

24 Faria and Paradis, "Humanism," 21; Tambourgi, "O Brasil e a assistência humanitária", 7. The cancelling of debts was highly controversial in Brazil. One of the countries concerned was Mozambique. Even though the Brazilian government framed this pardon as a gesture of altruism, other financial considerations were said to be at stake. Namely, Brazilian companies who depended on loans from the National Bank of Economic and Social Development (BNDES) could not continue to do business with countries in arrears with Brazil. This was thus a way to lend a helping hand to these companies so that they could continue pursuing their business interests (Interview with Prof. Pio Penna, University of Brasília, 28 April 2015).

25 Faria and Paradis, "Humanism," 16-17.

26 Patriota, "Um país sul-americano convicto,"4-5.

27 See the relevant information on the following reports: *UAE Foreign Aid Report 2009*, n.d., accessed 27 May 2015, <https://www.google.com/maps/d/viewer?oe=UTF8&gl=uk&ie=UTF8&msa=0&mid=zxMGP2gtkTt0.k5ADLEHlnh44>; UAE OCFA, "United Arab Emirates Foreign Aid 2010" (Abu Dhabi: UAE OCFA): 47, accessed 5 December 2012, <http://www.ocfa.gov.ae/ResourcesGuidelines/UAE%20Foreign%20Aid%20 2010%20-%20EN.pdf; UAE OCFA>, "United Arab Emirates Foreign Aid Report 2011" (Abu Dhabi: UAE OCFA): 31, accessed 5 December 2012, <http://www.ocfa.gov.ae/ResourcesGuidelines/UAE_Foreign_Aid_2011_EN.pdf>; UAE Ministry of International Development and Cooperation, "UAE Foreign Aid 2013", *Mini Report, October 2014* (Abu Dhabi: Micad): 13, accessed 5 July 2015<https://micad.gov.ae/resources/pdfs/UAE_Foreign_Aid_Report_2013.pdf>; UAE Ministry of International Development and Cooperation, "UAE Foreign Aid 2012," *Mini Report, September 2013* (Abu Dhabi: Micad): 31, accessed 30 July 2015, <https://micad.gov.ae/resources/pdfs/UAE_Foreign_Aid_Mini_Report_2012.pdf>.

28 UAEinteract, "UAE confirms its support to afghan efforts for achieving national unity and stability," 29 November 2012, accessed 15 December 2012, <http://www.uaeinteract.com/docs/UAE_confirms_its_support_to_Afghan_efforts_for_achieving_national_unity_and_stability/52183.htm>.

29 Ricardo, Seitenfus, "Elementos para uma diplomacia solidária: a crise haitiana e os desafios da ordem internacional contemporânea", n.d., accessed 10 August 2015, <http://www.seitenfus.com.br/arquivos/elementos-diplomacia(1).pdf>.

30 Valler Fillho, "O Brasil e a crise haitiana", 224.

31 Ibid, 176-177.

32 Antônio de Aguiar Patriota, "Um país sul-americano convicto, um ator global,"Discurso proferido por ocasião da cerimônia de transmissão do cargo de Ministro de Estado das Relações Exteriores. Brasília, 2 de janeiro de 2011", *Política externa brasileira. Discursos, artigos e entrevistas (2011-2012)* (Brasília: Funag, 2013), 37.

33 Valler Filho, "O Brasil e a crise haitiana," 171, 175; Robert Muggah, "Reflexões sobre a contribuição da Minustah à segurança e estabilidade (2004-2014)," in: *Brasil e Haiti: Reflexões sobre os 10 anos da missão de paz e o futuro da cooperação após 2016,* ed. Eduarda Passarelli Hamann(RJ: Instituto Iguarapé, 2015), 14.

34 Correa, "Minustah e diplomacia solidária," 151; Filipe Nasser, "Paz Brasiliensis: Projeção de Poder e solidariedade na estratégia diplomática de participação brasileira em operações de paz da Organização das Nações Unidas," in: *O Brasil e as Operações de Paz em um Mundo Globalizado: entre a tradição e a inovação,* ed. Kai Michael Kenkel and Rodrigo Fracalossi de Moraes (Brasília: IPEA, 2014), 217; Burges, "Brazilian Foreign Policy", 179.

35 Rajiv Chandrasekaran, "In the UAE, the United States has a quiet, potent ally nicknamed 'Little Sparta'," *Washington Post*, 9 November 2014, accessed 7 December 2012, <http://www.washingtonpost.com/world/national-security/in-the-uae-the-united-states-has-a-quiet-potent-ally-nicknamed-little-sparta/2014/11/08/3fc6a50c-643a-11e4-836c-83bc4f26eb67_story.html>.

36 Bruce Campion-Smith, "Canada's spat with U.A.E. risks key alliance: Wikileaks cables," *The Star,* 24 January 2011, accessed 7 December 2012, <http://www.thestar.com/news/canada/article/927443--canada-s-spat-with-u-a-e-risks-key-alliance-wikileaks-cables>.

37 See, for example, Azevedo, Reinaldo, "Brasil no Haiti," 22 May 2015, accessed 22 September 2015, <http://veja.abril.com.br/blog/reinaldo/geral/brasil-no-haiti-mais-uma-obra-genial-de-lula-gasto-de-r-13-bilhao-ganho-militar-e-politico-zero-soldados-doentes-e-130-mil-imigrantes-miseraveis/>.

38 See Robert Muggah, "Reflexões sobre a contribuição da Minustah", 14.

39 TV Morena, *Bombagay – gente boa no Haiti*, accessed 8 May 2015, <https://www.youtube.com/watch?v=Lrrb7aMK9LU>.

40 Accessed 24 September 2015, <https://www.youtube.com/watch?v=vG3KxIaMRnw>.

41 Muggah, "Reflexões," 14. The myth of the 'good soldier' propagated both by soldiers themselves as well as by their respective political leaders is common in several cases of military intervention around the world. See, for example, Helena Carreir as' work on the self-perception of Portuguese soldiers that were stationed from 1997 to 1998 in Bosnia-Herzegovina. In the same chapter, she also presents excerpts of Portuguese diplomatic discourse where the humane characteristics of Portuguese soldiers are portrayed as bestowing them a comparative advantage vis-à-vis soldiers from other parts of the world. Of note is the utilization of the expression 'the strategy of smile', meaning that Portuguese soldiers are capable of easily connecting with other cultures and peoples, they are humane and solidary. See Helena Carreir as, "A dimensão sociológica das intervenções militares externas: As forças armadas portuguesas em missões internacionais," in: *Consolidação da paz e a sua sustentabilidade. As missões da ONU em Timor Leste a contribuição de Portugal*, coord. Maria Raquel Freire (Coimbra: Imprensa da Universidade de Coimbra), 144-145.

42 The idea that Brazil is a peaceful country is quite common in Brazilian literature on Brazilian foreign policy.

43 Correa, "Minustah e diplomacia solidária," 130.

44 Mission: Winds of Goodness, Documentary. David Eberts and Khaled bin Lahej Al Falasi (Directors). (Abu Dhabi: Presidential Guard, 2011).

45 See, for e.g., Ola Salem, "UAE aid to Afghanistan is a trusted help," *The National*, 23 July 2012, accessed 7 December 2012, <http://www.thenational.ae/news/uae-news/uae-aid-to-afghanistan-is-a-trusted-help>.

46 Patriota, "Um país sul-americano convicto," 4.

47 Interview with Prof. Pio Penna. The Brazilian soldiers' excessive use of force in Haiti is well documented. For a synthesis see Correa, "Minustah e diplomacia solidária," 151- 158.

48 Campion-Smith, "Canada's spat with U.A.E.".

49 Chandrasekaran, "In the UAE, the United States has a quiet, potent ally".

References

Almezaini, Khalid S, *The UAE and Foreign Policy: Foreign Aid, Identities* (Abingdon: Routledge, 2011).

Al-Suwaidi, Abdulla, "The United Arab Emirates at 40: A Balance Sheet," *Middle East Policy* 18, no. 4 (2011): 44-58.

Azevedo, Reinaldo, "Brasil no Haiti", 22 May 2015, <http://veja.abril.com.br/blog/reinaldo/geral/brasil-no-haiti-mais-uma-obra-genial-de-lula-gasto-de-r-13-bilhao-ganho-militar-e-politico-zero-soldados-doentes-e-130-mil-imigrantes-miseraveis/>. Accessed September 2015.

Brasil, Ministério das Relações Exteriores (MRE), "Emirados Árabes Unidos" (Brasília: MRE, 2015a), <http://www.itamaraty.gov.br/index.php?option=com_content&view=article&id=5103:emirados-arabes-unidos&catid=155&lang=pt-BR&Itemid=478>. Accessed May 2015.

Brasil, Ministério das Relações Exteriores (MRE), "Emirados Árabes Unidos: Comércio Exterior" (Brasília: MRE, 2015b), <http://www.brasilexport.gov.br/sites/default/files/publicacoes/indicadoresEconomicos/INDEmiradosArabesUnidos.pdf>. Accessed May 2015.

Brun, Elodie, "Relations between Brazil and the Arab Countries of the Gulf: Renewed Context, Persistent Objectives." In: *The Gulf and Latin America: An Assessment of Expectations and Challenges,* edited by Alejandra Galindo, 143-172(Cambridge: Gulf Research Centre, 2013).

Burges, Sean, *Brazilian Foreign Policy after the Cold War* (Florida: University of Florida Press, 2009).

Campion-Smith, Bruce "Canada's spat with U.A.E. risks key alliance: Wikileaks cables," *The Star*, 24 January 2011, <http://www.thestar.com/news/canada/article/927443--canada-s-spat-with-u-a-e-risks-key-alliance-wikileaks-cables>. Accessed December 2012.

Carreiras Helena, "A dimensão sociológica das intervenções militares externas: As forças armadas portuguesas em missões internacionais." In: *Consolidação da paz e a sua sustentabilidade. As missões da ONU em Timor Leste a contribuição de Portugal,* coordinated by Maria Raquel Freire, 121-153 (Coimbra: Imprensa da Universidade de Coimbra).

Carvalho Pinto, Vânia, "From 'follower' to 'role model': studying the transformation to the UAE's international self-image," *Journal of Arabian Studies*, 4, no. 2 (2014): 231-142.

Cervo, Amado, *Inserção Internacional: formação dos conceitos brasileiros* (São Paulo: Editora Saraiva, 2008).

Cervo, Amado and Antônio Carlos Lessa."The fall: the international insertion of Brazil (2011–2014)." *Rev. Bras. Polít. Int. RBPI,* 57, no. 2 (2014): 133-151.

Chandrasekaran, Rajiv, "In the UAE, the United States has a quiet, potent ally nicknamed 'Little Sparta'," *Washington Post*, 9 November 2014, <http://www.washingtonpost.com/world/national-security/in-the-uae-the-united-states-has-a-quiet-potent-ally-nicknamed-little-sparta/2014/11/08/3fc6a50c-643a-11e4-836c-83bc4f26eb67_story.html>. Accessed December 2012.

Correa, Paulo Gustavo Pellegrino, "Minustah e diplomacia solidária: criação de um novo paradigma nas operações de paz." In: *Operações de Manutenção de Paz das Nações Unidas*, edited by Vanessa Braga Matijascic, 129-158 (São Paulo: Editora Unesp, 2014).

Faria, Carlos Aurélio, and Paradis, Clarisse, "Humanism and Solidarity in Brazilian Foreign Policy Under Lula (2003-2010): Theory and Practice." *BPSR*, 7, no. 2 (2013): 8-36.

Mervyn Frost, *Anarchy, Freedom and International Relations* (London and New York: Routledge, 2009).

Gama, Carlos Frederico Pereira da Silva, "Conquistas e desafios da política externa de Dilma Rousseff," *Carta Maior*, 16 November 2014, <http://www.cartamaior.com.br>. Accessed May 2015.

Global Humanitarian Assistance, "Brazil: Key Figures 2013", <http://www.globalhumanitarianassistance.org/countryprofile/brazil>. Accessed August 2015.

Heard-Bey, Frauke, *From Trucial States to United Arab Emirates* (Abu Dhabi: Motivate Publishing, 2005).

Instituto de Pesquisa Econômica Aplicada-Agência Brasileira de Cooperação, *Cooperação Brasileira para o Desenvolvimento Internacional: 2010* (Brasília: IPEA: ABC, 2013), <www.abc.gov.br/api/publicacaoarquivo/561>. Accessed August 2015.

Kayaoğlu, Barın, "Why the Gulf isn't to blame for Syrian refugee crisis", *Al-Monitor*, 15 September 2015, <http://www.al-monitor.com/pulse/originals/2015/09/syria-gulf-countries-respond-criticism-over-refugees.html#ixzz3mkHDtXPG>. Accessed 25 September 2015.

Lima, Maria Regina Soares de, "Entrevista. Maria Regina Soares de Lima", Interview by Wilson Tosta, *Jornal Estadão*, 10 November 2014,<http://politica.estadao.com.br/noticias/geral,dilma-precisa-adotar-proatividade-de-lula-afirma-pesquisadora-imp-,1590522>. Accessed May 2015.

Mission: Winds of Goodness, Documentary. Directed by David Eberts e Khaled bin Lahej Al Falasi. (Abu Dhabi: Presidential Guard, 2011).

Momani, Bessma, and Crystal, A. Ennis, "Between caution and controversy: lessons from the Gulf Arab States as (re-) emerging donors." *Cambridge Review of International Affairs*, 25, no. 4 (2012): 605-627.

Muggah, Robert, "Reflexões sobre a contribuição da Minustah à segurança e estabilidade (2004-2014)." In: *Brasil e Haiti: Reflexões sobre os 10 anos da missão de paz e o futuro da cooperação após 2016*, edited byEduarda Passarelli Hamann, 9-14 (RJ: Instituto Iguarapé, 2015).

Nasser, Filipe, "Paz Brasiliensis: Projeção de Poder e solidariedade na estratégia diplomática de participação brasileira em operações de paz da Organização das Nações Unidas." In: *O Brasil e as Operações de Paz em um Mundo Globalizado: entre a tradição e a inovação*, edited by Kenkel, Kai Michael, and Rodrigo Fracalossi de Moraes, 213-243 (Brasília: IPEA, 2014).

OECD, "Development aid stable in 2014 but flows to poorest countries still falling," 8 April 2015, <http://www.oecd.org/dac/stats/development-aid-stable-in-2014-but-flows-to-poorest-countries-still-falling.htm>. Accessed 25 May 2015.

Overseas Development Institute (ODI), *Brazil: an emerging Aid Donor. Lessons on emerging donors and south-south and triangular cooperation*, Briefing Paper 64 (October 2010): 2-3, <www.odi.org/resources/docs/6295.pdf>. Accessed September 2015.

Patriota, Antônio de Aguiar, "Um país sul-americano convicto, um ator global", Discurso proferido por ocasião da cerimônia de transmissão do cargo de Ministro de Estado das Relações Exteriore, on 2 January 2011, Brasilia. In: *Política externa brasileira, Discursos, artigos e entrevistas (2011-2012)* (Brasília: Funag, 2013). Salem, Ola, "UAE aid to Afghanistan is a trusted help," *The National*, 23 July 2012, <http://www.thenational.ae/news/uae-news/uae-aid-to-afghanistan-is-a-trusted-help>. Accessed December 2012.

Sean W. Burges, *Brazilian Foreign Policy after the Cold War* (Gainesville et al: University Press of Florida, 2009), 161-184.

Seitenfus, Ricardo, "Elementos para uma diplomacia solidária: a crise haitiana e os desafios da ordem internacional contemporânea", n.d., <http://www.seitenfus.com.br/arquivos/elementos-diplomacia(1).pdf>. Accessed August 2015.

Schenoni, Luis L., "Ascenso y hegemonía: pensando a las potencias emergentes desde América del Sur." *Rev. Bras. Polít. Int. RBPI*, 55, no. 1 (2012): 31-48.

Shushan, Debra and Christopher Marcoux. "The rise (and decline?) of Arab aid: generosity and allocation in the oil era." *World Development*, 39, no. 11 (2011): 1969-1980.

Tambourgi, Patrícia Vilarinho, "O Brasil e a assistência humanitária internacional: prática, discurso e tendências.", Master's Diss., Pontifical Catholic University of São Paulo,2012.

TV Morena, *Bombagay – gente boa no Haiti*, <https://www.youtube.com/watch?v=Lrrb7aMK9LU>. Accessed May 2015.

UAE Foreign Aid Report 2009, n.d., <https://www.google.com/maps/d/viewer?oe=UTF8&gl=uk&ie=UTF8&msa=0&mid=zxMGP2gtkTt0.k5ADLEHlnh44>. Accessed May 2015.

UAE Ministry of International Development and Cooperation, "UAE Foreign Aid 2012," *Mini Report, September 2013* (Abu Dhabi: Micad), <https://micad.gov.ae/resources/pdfs/UAE_Foreign_Aid_Mini_Report_2012.pdf>. Accessed July 2015.

UAE Ministry of International Development and Cooperation, "UAE Foreign Aid 2013," *Mini Report, October 2014* (Abu Dhabi: Micad), <https://micad.gov.ae/resources/pdfs/UAE_Foreign_Aid_Report_2013.pdf>. Accessed July 2015.

UAE OCFA, "United Arab Emirates Foreign Aid 2010" (Abu Dhabi: UAE OCFA): 47, <http://www.ocfa.gov.ae/ResourcesGuidelines/UAE%20Foreign%20Aid%202010%20-%20EN.pdf>. Accessed 5 December 2012.

UAE OCFA, "United Arab Emirates Foreign Aid Report 2011" (Abu Dhabi: UAE OCFA): 31, <http://www.ocfa.gov.ae/ResourcesGuidelines/UAE_Foreign_Aid_2011_EN.pdf>. Accessed 5 December 2012.

UAEinteract, "UAE confirms its support to afghan efforts for achieving national unity and stability," 29 November 2012, <http://www.uaeinteract.com/docs/UAE_confirms_its_support_to_Afghan_efforts_for_achieving_national_unity_and_stability/52183.htm>. Accessed December 2012.

Valler Fillho, Wladimir, *O Brasil e a crise haitiana. A cooperação técnica como instrumento de solidariedade e de ação diplomática* (Brasília: Funag, 2007).

WAM, "UAE praised for issuing foreign aid annual report. Local and foreign officials laud commitment of country's leadership to global humanitarian and development issues," 03 August 2010, <http://www.emirates247.com/news/emirates/uae-praised-for-issuing-foreign-aid-annual-report-2010-08-03-1.274492>. Accessed May 2015.

WAM, "UAE world's 20th most generous donor," 12 February 2013, <http://www.emirates247.com/news/uae-world-s-20th-most-generous-donor-2013-02-12-1.494730>. Accessed May 2015.

Cited Interviews:

Pio Penna Filho, University of Brasília, 28.04.2015.

Carlos Leopoldo, Itamaraty Palace, Brasília, 10.06.2015.

6

Russia and the GCC Countries: Hard to be Friends but Impossible to Remain Foes

Nikolay Kozhanov

1. Introduction

During the last decade, Russian relations with the Gulf Cooperation Council (GCC) countries have experienced several stress-tests. Periods when the Gulf monarchies declared their readiness to improve their dialogue with Moscow swiftly changed into periods when relations seriously cooled between them and Russia. The events of the Arab spring and the active support provided by Moscow to the regime of Bashar Assad were expected to turn Russia into one of the main geostrategic opponents of Riyadh, Doha and Abu Dhabi. Unexpectedly, in 2013, the dialogue between the countries resumed and demonstrated a tendency for normalisation.

Traditionally, the idea of reaching the warm waters of the Gulf and Indian Ocean was a part of the Russian geostrategic agenda. However, until the 2000s, any attempts to establish a solid Russian presence in the region resulted in clear failure. At different times, the Russian Empire and the USSR managed to spread their influence to Iran and Iraq, but any significant contact with the lands of the Arabian Peninsula was unachievable. Direct diplomatic relations with the countries of the GCC have been established relatively recently. In most countries, Russian (or Soviet) embassies were opened during the last decade of the Soviet era or immediately after the fall of the USSR. Thus, the Russian diplomatic mission in Saudi Arabia was opened in 1991, in Oman in 1987, in the UAE in 1986, in Bahrain in 1993, and in Qatar in 1989. The only exception was Kuwait, with which diplomatic relations were established in 1963. Moreover, until the 2000s, the level of cooperation between Moscow and the GCC remained extremely low.

For the 1990s, this could be explained by the domestic political and economic turmoil in the Russian Federation and by the Western orientation of Russian diplomacy under President Boris Yeltsin (1991–1999). However, some developments did occur. During these years, the Russian government and its Gulf partners signed a number of official agreements and memorandums of understanding which formed the judicial base for economic cooperation and political dialogue between them. The latter helped to boost bilateral relations after the election of Vladimir Putin as Russian president in 2000.

2. Russian Relations with Saudi Arabia, Qatar and the Other GCC Members before the Arab Spring

Qatar and Saudi Arabia were opened up for Russia by the successor of Yeltsin, Putin, who tried to implement the Russian doctrine of a multipolar world by establishing close and friendly ties with non-European and non-Western countries. Thus, in 2003, during his visit to Malaysia, Putin stated that Russia would cooperate closely with the Islamic world. Later, he declared the Arab countries to be one of the main vectors of Russian diplomacy. In 2007, Putin backed this statement up with official visits to Saudi Arabia and Qatar. The choice of countries was not accidental: Doha and Riyadh were seen by Moscow as the main regional leaders. Nonetheless, the dialogue with them was built within the broader framework of the broader Moscow's intention to intensify Russian contacts with the GCC countries.

The above-mentioned trips of Putin were not merely a demonstration of Russian interest in dialogue with the countries of the Gulf. On the contrary, Moscow sought to become deeply involved in developments in the region. Thus, in 2007, the Russian government increased its focus on the region with a document entitled *The Concept for Ensuring Security in the Region of the Persian Gulf*. The main principles proposed in the document implied the settlement of conflict situations by solely diplomatic means, the conduct of peacekeeping military operations only in accordance with UN resolutions, the participation of all sides involved in emerging issues in a decision-making process, and the implementation of agreements achieved by the regional countries in strict compliance with international documents regulating relations in the region of the Gulf.[1]

The settlement of the issue of the Iranian nuclear programme and the stabilisation of the situation in Iraq were named in the document as the first stage in the practical implementation of the Russian initiative. These steps were aimed at the creation of mutual trust between the countries of the region. It was also supposed that the Gulf states would confirm their loyalty to their international legal obligations by being transparent in the development of their military capacities, banning the use of force for the settlement of conflicts, adopting multilateral treaties on arms control, paying attention to the observation of the non-proliferation regime, creating a WMD-free zone in the Middle East, and signing agreements on counteractingterrorism, criminal activities, drug, human and arms trafficking. According to the *Concept*document, the second stage of the implementation of the Russian initiative would involve the creation of an organisation for security and cooperation in the Gulf which would become an element in a new multilateral security system in the Middle East.[2]

This idealistic and probably naïve initiative aroused some interest among the smaller GCC members, but mostly as an eloquent theoretical speculation. Its practical implementation was obviously hampered by mounting Arab concerns over the Iranian nuclear programme, the continuing instability in Iraq, and the US hegemony over the Gulf. However, the initiative achieved one of its main goals: it demonstrated the Russian intention to have a presence in the region and to try to stay there for the long-term.[3] The trips of Putin to the Gulf also served as a signal for Russian officials and the private sector that the members of the GCC were worth dealing with. Since 2007, both the economic and the political relations of Russia with the members of the GCC have been substantially intensified.

However, Moscow failed to keep up with the initial high tempo. The factor of the personal influence of Russian leaders on the foreign policy of the country accounted for this. Putin's influence was crucial in establishing the dialogue between the RF and the Gulf countries. His decision to establish close relations with Arab countries and to declare this vector of Russian diplomacy as important, however, remained only a spoken commitment. It was not added as an amendment to any of the official concepts used by the RF to determine the general long-term strategy of foreign policy. Subsequently, whenDmitry Medvedev, who is known for his pro-Western orientation, took the presidential office (2008), Medvedev seems to have considered the development of a dialogue with Arab countries as the personal idea of Putin. He never supported it. As a result, under Medvedev Russian activities in the region became less intense.

In addition to that, Russian relations with the Arab monarchies of the Gulf during the period 2009 – 2011were challenged by a number of confusing political incidents. For example, in 2009, the ex-commander of the Russian Military Special Battalion "Vostok", Sulim Yamadayev, was killed in Dubai. Although, this murder was probably a result of a personal blood feud between Yamadayev and the clan of the current president of the Chechen Republic, Ramzan Kadyrov, it reminded the UAE authorities of the assassination of Chechen terrorist Zelimkhan Yandarbiyev which had taken place in Doha in 2004. He was allegedly killed by one of the Russian secret services. Under these circumstances, the probable political background of Yamadayev's killing caused serious concerns in the government of Dubai and the federal government of the UAE. Another unfortunate incident took place in 2011 when the security forces atDoha airport attacked and seriously injured the Russian ambassador to Doha, Vladimir Titorenko, while he was accompanying diplomatic mail bags. This incident seriously aggravated Russian relations with Qatar. Moscow temporarily downgraded its relations.

Nevertheless, the push given by Putin to the Russian dialogue with the GCC in 2007 prevented Russian-Arab contacts returning to the low level of the 1990s. The development of relations continued. On 1 November 2011, the Russian minister of foreign affairs met for the first time with his counterparts from the Gulf Cooperative Council in a summit meeting. Since then, Moscow has managed to hold three meetings of this kind (the last one was held on 19 February 2014 in Kuwait). These so-called GCC-Russia strategic dialogue meetings allowed Moscow to state clearly and to discuss its strategic interests in the Gulf with the Arab monarchies of the region, outlining the direction of future partnership. During the first meeting, Moscow demonstrated that Russian positions on the majority of regional and international issues were relatively close to those of the GCC member states. Russia had consistently supported the creation of an independent Palestinian state, and had striven to support the peace and stability of the region. The Russian authorities also emphasised that they maintained an "open doors" policy: the RF was ready to conduct a dialogue with any country of the region as long as this dialogue corresponded to Russian national interests.[4]

However, in 2011–2012, differences in Russian and GCC views on political developments in the Middle East caused certain tensions between Moscow and the Gulf Arabs (at first, between Russia and Qatar). This, in turn, put the continuation of the Russia-GCC dialogue under question. Being seriously disappointed the unwillingness of the GCC states to continue dialogue with the Assad regime in order to find a peaceful solution, their unofficial support for foreign military intervention in Syria, and their evasion of a dialogue with Moscow on the issue, the Russian authorities had difficulty in finding a common language with the Gulf Cooperation Council members and in preserving the existinglevel of cooperation with them.

3. The Arab Spring and Russian relations with Saudi Arabia and Qatar

In 2011–2012, the growing confrontation between Moscow and the Gulf monarchies caused by the Russian position on Syria tangibly limited Russian options for strengthening cooperation with the GCC. For instance, during 2010–2011, Russia offered to involve Qatar in a number of investment projects worth$10–12 billion in different fields of the Russian economy (especially in the oil and gas, construction and gold mining sectors). However, all these proposals were ignored by Doha. Political factors (such as Russian-Qatari differences over approaches to the Arab Spring and the Syrian conflict) were, according to some analysts, critical in determining the lack of a response.[5] Moscow's contacts with the other GCC countries also became problematic. Even the UAE, where the Russian presence was probably the strongest in the GCC, was considered as an unreliable partner from the beginning of the Arab Spring. As stated by one of the leading Russian experts on the economy of the Middle East, Eldar Kasaev:

> the UAE is a member of the GCC whose main ideologists, Saudi Arabia and Qatar, are famous for their anti-Russian feelings. ... [As a result,] it should not be assumed that the Emirates will continue to develop relations with Moscow if the Qataris and Saudis start waging an [undeclared] war against Russia.[6]

Moscow also realized that Qatar and Saudi Arabia could create troubles for Russian interests outside of the Middle Eastern region. Thus, Qatar was seen as one of the main Russian rivals in the gas market. After the beginning of the Arab spring, this unofficial confrontation received an ideological base. Additional troubles were created by the fact that both the RF and Qatar are members of the Gas Exporting Countries Forum (GECF). The political confrontation often influenced the behaviour of these players within the framework of that structure. Thus, in 2011, Russia deliberately sent to the summit of the leaders of the GECF countries in Qatar a delegation whose level was far below thatrequired by protocol. In 2013, the Qataris responded in the same way when the meeting was held in Moscow.[7] Taking into account that the two other members of the Forum, Libya and Egypt, were busy with their domestic situations, the behaviour of Moscow and Doha made the GECF a less effective organisation. This, in turn, harmed the interests of all participants.

By 2013, Riyadh and Saudi Arabia managed to defeat Moscow onthe Middle Eastern front of the information war. The crucial role in this process was played by the newspapers and TV channels supported by Qatar and Saudi Arabia. Taking into account the influence which *Asharq Al-Awsat, Al-Hayat* and *Al-Jazeera* have on public opinion in the region and outside, Moscow was inevitably doomed to lose the information war for the Middle East. Due to the efforts of these media channels, by the end of 2012, Russia had become closely associated with all things the Arab Spring was supposedly confronting: violence, dictatorship and bloodshed.

The mediasources backed by Saudi Arabia and Qatar also effectively used the Russian position on Libya to present Moscow in a negative light. On 17 March 2011, the Russian government withheld vetoing UNSC resolution 1973, and this paved the way for the US and EU intervention in the Libyan conflict. Subsequently, the RF imposed sanctions on Libya and was the first of Libya's armssuppliers to stop exporting weapons to the regime of Qaddafi. In the eyes of the pro-Western grouping in the Russian ruling elite, these steps were worth making: Moscow still hoped to reset relations with Washington, and Russia's military contracts with France also played a role. Nevertheless, this time the losses did not justify any gains. Medvedev's decisions on Libya probably determined the destiny of Qaddafi. In other words, in 2011 Russia betrayed the regime of Qaddafi which was supposedly one of the last allies of the Kremlin in the region. Under these conditions, the image of the RF in the Middle East suffered heavy losses. According to the traditions of the region, a treachery (no matter who is the betrayed person) is never forgotten.[8] This perception was immediately propagated by pro-Qatari and pro-Saudi media channels. The treachery was portrayed as a sign of weakness.

The strategy of balancing between different forces was also seen as a sign of weakness: a strong player can afford to demonstrate clearly his preferences. This, in turn, gave the opponents of Russia in the region confidence that in other cases the opinion of Moscow could generally be ignored. Since the very beginning of the Arab Spring, the Qataris have in fact been periodically repeating the idea that the RF has long lost its status as a centre of power in international politics, but it still tries to return to it by playing the role of a minor troublemaker and supporting the dictatorial regimes.[9]

Apart from that, the stance of Moscow on the Arab Spring provided an opportunity for the Saudi and Qatari media to discuss other topics which were sensitive to Russia, such as the state of democracy and Muslim minorities in Russia. In July 2012, *Al-Jazeera* voiced concerns about the domestic policy of Putin and called him 'the dictator of the 21stcentury'. The active polemics on these issues in the Arab press led to the further demonising of the image of Russia. Subsequently, on 12 October 2012, in an interview onQatar's state TV channelone of the leading religious figures of the Middle East, Yusuf al-Qaradawi, called Russia "enemy number one" of Islam and Muslims.[10]

The statement by al-Qaradawi constituted a very bad signal for the Kremlin, indicating that Riyadh and Doha could use their influence to undermine Moscow's dialogue with the religious leaders of the Middle East. The positive development of these relations was traditionally seen by Moscow as one of the factors directly influencing the political stability of the country. The Russian authorities believe that for as long as the majority of Muslim religious leaders considered the situation of the Russian Muslim community as normal, moral and financial assistance to radical Islamists acting in the South of Russia from abroad would be limited. Thus, in May 2012, the Russian authorities supported the convening in Moscow of an international meeting of Islamic theologians from 23 countries. The event was held under slogan 'Islamic doctrine against radicalism'. The list of invited participants included such prominent figures as the secretary general of the World Council of Muslim Scholars, Ali al-Qaradagi, and the vice-president of this organization Abdallah Bin Bayyah. The meeting ended with the adoption of adeclaration condemning religious radicalism and a call forMuslim theologians to be very careful when using such terms as caliphate (khilafa), jihad and takfeer since these could justify the activities of religious extremists. The issuing of this declaration was considered to be aserious diplomatic success byMoscow. The impact of this achievement was undermined when, in 2013, a similar meeting was held in Cairo. This time, the gathering blessed the activities of the Syrian opposition and called the civil war in this country 'a jihad'. The statement indirectly affected Russia by logically placing it as a country supporting the side against which holy war was being waged. It could hardly have been a coincidence that the organizing committee of the Cairo meeting had sought to include as many of the participants of the Moscow meeting as possible in the list of invited people.[11]

Under these circumstances, it was not surprising that in 2011–2012 Moscow became deeply concerned about the apparent efforts by Qatar and Saudi Arabia to support the most radical factions in Syria. Russian officials believed that the situation in the region was directly influencing domestic stability in Russia by provoking Russian religious extremists to undertake more aggressive anti-government actions. In 2011–2012, Moscow's security services reported on the increased financial help from Qatar and Saudi Arabia going to Russian Islamists. Moscow wasparticularly concerned with the participation of Chechens in the conflict on the side of the Syrian rebels who the Russians believed were sponsored by Saudi and Qatari citizens. Prominent Russian expert on Syria, Yuri Shcheglov in, stated that Chechens formed the second largest grouping of foreign nationals after Libyans fighting against the Damascus regime.[12] These Chechens were mostly associated with separatist movements in the Northern Caucasus. Thus, in the early 2013, Russian media reported the death of Rustam Gelayev, who was the son of one of the most high-profile Chechen terrorists killed in Russia in 2004. Gelayev was allegedly killed in Syria when fighting against government troops as a member of a Chechen military grouping headed by Abu Omar Shishani[13] (although Gelaev's relatives state that his death was a result of a tragic accident).[14] Shcheglov in pointed out that the active participation of the Chechens in the conflict made the Turkish, Qatari and Saudi sponsors of Chechen fighters increase funding of these radical groupings, despite this having been substantially limited after the Second Chechen war.[15] Under these conditions, the main question for the Russians was whether the above-mentioned sponsors would stop their financial support after the fall of Assad or continue it in order to enable the jihadists to come to Russian soil.

These concerns were not baseless. By September 2013, Russian analysts observed several negative trends related to the participation of Russian Muslims in the Arab uprisings.[16] They were concerned at the widening range of nationalities from the RF taking part in the Syrian jihad. Thus, apart from Chechen radicals, the so-called Russian grouping of jihadists (its size was estimated asat least 250 people) includes representatives of different minorities of the Northern Caucasus and the Volga region. There was some evidence of participation by Tatars from the extremist organization Jamaat Bulgar in the Syrian conflict. The latter development would mean the activisation of Islamic radicals in regions which were much closer to Moscow than the Caucasus. Syria was becoming the ground for networking between the different extremist groupings. Previously separated and scattered, the various groupings were forming a united front, establishing ties with international terrorist organizations and, thus, becoming part of the global extremist network. Russian experts and officials did not doubt that upon the return of these radicals to the RF, their connections, together with their battle experience, would be used against the central authorities.[17]

4. Russian Relations with Saudi Arabia and Qatar after the Arab Spring

However, the Arab Spring did not lead to the end of Russian dialogue with Saudi Arabia and Qatar. On the contrary, if the period 2011–2012 was the time of a serious stress-test for Moscow, the events of 2013–2014 demonstrated that Russia still had every chance to preserve its presence in the Gulf region.

First and foremost, by 2013 Moscow had reconsidered its approaches towards the Middle East. This was probably partly related to the return of Putin to the presidential seat in 2012. As opposed to his predecessor, Putin appeared to be less pro-Western and more pragmatic. He was seriously disappointed by the failure of the attempted reset in relations between Moscow and Washington under Medvedev and, consequently, more determined to develop relations with non-Western countries. As a result, Moscow became more deeply involved in the protection of its interests in the Middle East.[18] The Russian foreign policy on the region became tougher in defending its red lines and, at the same time, more astute.

Thus, Moscow started to look at the domestic situation in the region more carefully. Currently, Russia does not conceal its interest in a dialogue with almost all forces in the Middle Eastern arena. For instance, over the past two years, Russia has established contacts with the different groups of the Syrian opposition.[19] Thus, if until the summer of 2012 the Russian authorities were dealing mostly with semi-legal and moderate opposition forces, such as members of the National Coordination Council, by autumn 2012 the Russians were looking for contacts with members of the Syrian National Council (SNC). And in 2013contacts with the SNC were established at different levels.[20] On the other hand, Moscow made several steps to re-establish its contacts with the Saudis and Qataris whom the Kremlin saw as the main supporters of the Syrian opposition. Thus, on 22 November 2013, Moscow appointed an ambassador to Doha without receiving official excuses for the incident with Titorenko, despite the fact that the Russians had initially insisted on this as a precondition for the arrival of a new ambassador. On 10 February 2014, a high ranking delegation of Russian parliamentarians headed by Mikhail Margelov visited Doha. In February 2014, Sheikh Tamim Bin Hamad Al Thani, Emir of Qatar, visited the Olympic Games in Sochi. At the same time, Russia became involved in a dialogue with Saudi Arabia on the situation in Egypt.[21]

Meanwhile, the tactics are not the same as the open doors policy which Russia had used before the Arab Spring. Russia is ready for dialogue with many regional groupings, but not with all of them. Connections with the radical Islamic groupings were not an option for the Russian authorities. This principled position regarding the unacceptability of any dialogue with the extremists contrasted sharply with the behaviour of some Western countries which could apply radically different labels to the Islamists fighting in Afghanistan, Iraq, Mali, Libya or Syria. With the return of Putin, the role of the Middle East as a bargaining counter in Russo-American and Russo-European relations became less obvious. On the contrary, Moscow set certain red lines (such as the unacceptability of foreign military intervention in Syria) whose crossing by the West could bring retaliatory measures from the Russian government. This Russian stubbornness brought some success for the Kremlin's diplomacy in 2013.

Thus, Moscow received support for its stance on Syria from China, India and a number of other countries. In September 2013, Russia undermined US attempts to form a coalition for military intervention in Syria and stepped in with an initiative for the termination of the Syrian chemical arsenal. The latter proposal allowed Moscow (at least, temporarily) to neutralise American efforts to use the WMD of Assad's regime as a pretext for the military operation against Damascus. Finally, whenever Putin raised the Syrian issue on the sidelines of the meetings of the leading world powers such as the G8 Summit at Lough Erne (17-18 June 2013) and G-20 Summit atSt.-Petersburg (5-6 September 2013) he was always more persuasive and eloquent than his opponents. This was recognised by public opinion in the Middle East. Qatar and Saudi Arabia were compelled to recognise the Kremlin as an important player whose opinions should be taken into account. Thus, such influential newspapers as *Asharq Al-Awsat* and *al-Hayat* considered the failure of Obama to persuade Putin to change the Russian stance on Syria during the G-8 summit at Lough Erne as a pure victory for Russia whereas the U.S. administration was accused of 'opportunism and weakness'.[22]

In 2013–2014, the growing energy independence of the United States, Washington's intention to bridge relations with Tehran, and the US failure to use force against Bashar al-Assad created grounds for Washington split with its traditional allies – the Arab monarchies of the Gulf. The potential division between the US and GCC created new opportunities for Russia, which had been trying unsuccessfully to increase its presence in the Arab part of the Gulf since 2003. The rumours about US withdrawal from the region compelled Saudi Arabia and its Gulf partners to look for other non-regional countries capable of compensating for a future decrease in the US presence. As a result, some attention was nowpaid to Moscow, and, in spite of all existing contradictions, the members of the GCC were compelled to continue the dialogue with Russia. The visits of Saudi prince Bandar Bin Sultan to Moscow on 31 July and 3 December 2013 were, probably, the most noted examples of this. As mentioned by analysts, Moscow and the GCC shared issues which could benefit from constructive dialogue. These included regional political stability as well as bilateral cooperation in the fields of energy and space. In November 2013, the Saudis expressed their willingness to help the Egyptian authorities buy Russian weapons in order to compensate for the decrease in the supply of US munitions. For both the Russians and the Saudis this deal was intended to improve the positions of the Egyptian secular authorities and, thus, lead to the stabilisation of the situation in the Egyptian republic.

The intention to re-establish relations was mutual. Not only was Russia making steps towards Saudi Arabia and Qatar, but Doha and Riyadh had decided not to close the doors before the Kremlin. The details of the talks between Putin and Prince Bandar during the latter's last two visits were kept secret. Nonetheless, analysts argue that the talks constituted an unofficial attempt to bridge relations between Russia and the Kingdom, creating a constructive dialogue in areas of common interest to both. In the energy field, Lukoil Overseas had in 2004 signed a contract with Saudi Arabia, whereby the Saudi government had granted the company a 40-year concession forthe exploration and development of the gas field in the Rub-al-Khali desert.[23] For the implementation of this project, Lukoil Overseas and Saudi Aramco had established a joint company, Lukoil Saudi Arabia Energy Ltd. (LUKSAR). The share of the Russian company was80%. In 2006, the exploration works of LUKSAR resulted in the discovery of a new hydrocarbons field whose estimated resources reached 85 million tons in fuel-equivalent. LUKSAR continued work to assess the scale of the reserves discovered in order to begin the development of the field. By August 2011 the accumulated investments of the Russian company had reached$300 million.[24] The Russian and Saudi governments, therefore, had strong reason to seek to maintain a workable relationship.

Some analysts believe that, during the visit of Prince Bandar, the Saudi side sought to use their energy leverage to influence the behaviour of Moscow. The Saudis allegedly guaranteed that the GCC countries would not raise obstructions forRussian gas exports to the EU, in exchange for the Kremlin refusing to support the Assad regime. Riyadh was reported as promising to start full-scale imports of Russian arms. This information, however, has never been officially confirmed.[25] After the visits of Prince Bandar to Moscow, however, Russian relations with the Gulf monarchies did noticeably improve. A further factor in the improvement was the Saudi government's condemnation of radical movements in the Middle East, articulated in February–March 2014. The statements by the Saudi officials clearly demonstrated to Moscow that the Kingdom would not contemplate funding separatists operating in the South of Russia.[26]

5. Prospects for Economic Cooperation

In 2016, Russian economic ties with the GCC countries remain underdeveloped. Yet, in 2015, both Moscow and the Gulf monarchies clearly demonstrated their interest in boosting bilateral trade and investments. For instance, during the period 25 – 30 May 2015, the Russian Chamber of Commerce organized an investment exhibition "Russian Road Show" in Jeddah. In June 2015, a high-level Saudi delegation, led by the son of King Salman, the deputy crown prince and defence minister Mohammed bin Salman, was received by Russian President Vladimir Putin in St.Petersburg and signed a series of agreements and memorandums, including ones on peaceful nuclear cooperation, infrastructural development and investment. On 11 August 2015, these agreements were reconfirmed during the visit of the Saudi minister of foreign affairs, Adel Al-Jubeir, to Russia. Apart from Saudi Arabia, Moscow also continued to develop a political and economic dialogue with the UAE. On 25 August 2015, the Crown Prince of Abu Dhabi, Sheikh Mohammed bin Zayed, visited the Russian air and space show MAKS-2015 and held an official meeting with Putin to discuss the prospective for Russian-Emirates economic cooperation. Moreover, in August 2015, Moscow prepared all necessary documents to open a trade mission in the UAE in order to facilitate the development of bilateral trade and investments.

5.1. Russian Trade Relations with the GCC

Since 2000, the volume of trade between Russia and the GCC countries has been gradually increasing (see table 6.1). During the last decade, the structure of that tradehas remained relatively unchanged. Russian exports consist of cereals, petrochemical products, precious stones and metals, ferrous metals and metallurgical products, wood, pulp and paper, fuel and energy resources, machinery and fertilizers. The volume of the Gulf countries exports to Russia is extremely small ($0.6 billion in 2014). The GCC countries mostly sell to Russia chemical and petrochemical products. They also re-export some consumer goods and luxury products.

In spite of existing positive trends, trade relations between Russia and the Gulf countries remain underdeveloped. By 2015, the GCC share in Russian trade was less than 0.5% (see Table 6.2). The Russian share in the GCC trade was also minimal. In terms of value, Russia was not only left far behind by the U.S., EU and the leading Asian economies (such as China, South Korea and Japan), but is challenged by the less economically powerful Indonesia, Malaysia and Thailand.

The low level of economic relations with the Gulf could be partly explained by the fact that until recently the Middle Eastern region was generally of little interest to Russian business circles. The latter were mainly oriented towards European and East Asian markets. Moreover, the Gulf countries were not seen by Moscow as a priority market for Russian goods, even within the Middle East (see Table 6.3). Consequently, by 2015, the value of trade between Russia and the members of the GCC stood at less than $3.5 billion versus $5.5 billion of Russian-Egyptian trade or $31 billion of Russo-Turkish trade (see Table 6.2).

Table 6.1: Volume of Russian Trade with the Countries of the Gulf, 2006–2014 ($ million)

Year Country	2006	2007	2008	2009	2010	2011	2012	2013	2014
Saudi Arabia	273	427	466	265 (Jan.–Sept.)	366	852	1359	1078	1164
Kuwait	n/a	n/a	n/a	n/a	80	357	83	34	46
Bahrain	11	15	3.6	1.9	2.4	5	13.9	15.8	14.8
UAE	648	821	846	671	950	1489	1487	2516	1997
Oman	n/a	n/a	n/a	24	13	39.3	42.1	59.4	25
Qatar	n/a	n/a	n/a	8.7	14.6	54.6	40	41.4	51

Source: Ministry of Economic Development of the Russian Federation, Russian Customs data.

Table 6.2: Russian Trade with Main Partners in the Middle East in 2014 ($billion)

	Volume	Export	Import	Share in Russian trade (%)
Egypt	5.5	4.9	0.5	0.7
Israel	3.4	2.3	1.1	0.4
Iran	1.7	1.3	0.4	0.2
Turkey	31	24.4	6.7	4
GCC	3.3	2.7	0.6	0.4

Source: Ministry of Economic Development of the Russian Federation, Russian Customs data.

Table 6.3: Russian Trade with Selected Countries of the Middle East in 2010–2013 ($ million)

	2010	2011	2012	2013
Algeria	1337	2486	2785	1589.6
Bahrain	**2.5**	**5**	**13.9**	**15.8**
Egypt	2191	2820	3555	2946
Iran	3651	3755	2329	1602
Iraq	-	99.6	286	379
Israel	2588	2857	2917	3578
Jordan	148	350	426	181
Kuwait	**132**	**357**	**83**	**34**
Lebanon	239	406	202	530
Libya	171	124	260	386
Mauritania	37.8	54.4	33.1	31.7
Morocco	932	1810	1848	1426
Oman	**13.3**	**39.3**	**42.1**	**59.4**
Qatar	**14.6**	**54.6**	**40**	**41.4**
Saudi Arabia	**366**	**852**	**1359**	**1078**
Sudan	-	172	154	129
Syria	1158	1991	656	376
Tunisia	530	1155	594	361
United Arab Emirates	**1019**	**1489**	**1487**	**2516**
Yemen	168	163	234	218
Total	39882.2	52823.9	53583.1	50226.9

Source: Ministry of Economic Development of the Russian Federation, Russian Customs data.

However, the situation has recently begun to change. By the beginning of 2015, the Russian economy was sustaining heavy losses from Western sanctions and the drop in oil prices. The high cost of the Crimea annexation and general structural problems put additional pressure on the country's budget. Under these circumstances, every existing source of income became important for both the Russian authorities and the business elite. Thisaffected their perception of business opportunities in the Gulf area. If, previously, Russian companies never hid the fact that the region had a secondary importance for them, since 2014–2015 they have demonstrated much more interest in dealing with the region.

Economic cooperation with the GCC has certain advantages to Russian businesses. As has been mentioned, since the early-2000s trade relations between Russia and the GCC states have witnessed a positive trend. The fact that the trade balance was (and still is) in favour of Moscow made the Arab countries of the Persian Gulf an appealing consumer market for Russian goods. The share of the Russian exports in trade with the majority of the GCC countries is close to 90%. There is also a wide variety in items exported by the Russian corporations to the region. This, in turn, offers opportunities to a wide range of Russian producers in trade with the GCC. Moreover, the share of oil and gas in Russian exports to the region is not big. From this point of view, trade with the Gulf could support the development of the Russian non-oil sector, and this is important for the implementation of Moscow's economic diversification strategy.

In spite of the fact that the GCC has a small share in Russian trade, the region still represents a source of considerable interest to selected Russian industries, including those of the agricultural and military-industrial complexes, mining, petrochemicals, space and oil and gas industries. Thus, the UAE is one of the main buyers of Russian precious stones and metals, while Saudi Arabia is the largest buyer of Russian barley.[27] Apart from Saudi Arabia, Qatar and the UAE also import Russian cereals.

Moscow has been promoting the interests of the Russian space industry in the GCC. Currently, the Kremlin is actively supporting the Russian GLONASS satellite navigation system in the region. In February 2007, Russia successfully launched the first Emirates' satellite, the distance-sensing Dubaisat-1, from Baykonur. Over the 2000–2012 period, the Russian federal space agency Roscosmos launched 14 telecommunication and distance sensing satellites for Saudi Arabia. In 2015, the UAE expressed its interest in purchasing the sea-based spacecraft launch facility Space Launch, 95 per cent of whose shares are owned by the Russian Energia Overseas Limited company. Its purchase will possibly strengthen the capacity of the Emirates space agency (established in 2013) and facilitate its plans to send a spacecraft to Mars in 2021.[28]

5.2. Perspectives for Military-Industrial Cooperation

Traditionally, the Kremlin has tried hard to penetrate the arms market of the GCC region. Russian weapons remain known for their relative reliability (as opposed to the Chinese equivalents) and reasonable pricing (compared with the products of Western companies). Russian experts are currently acknowledging the substantial growth in the volume of Russian arms trade with the Middle East.[29] The events of the Arab spring clearly demonstrated to Middle Eastern countries the necessity to diversify their sources of arms imports. Even the GCC states expressed interest in purchasing Russian weapons.

The real volume of the Russian arms trade with the Middle East is unknown. The Russian customs, in their statistical reports, usually put arms deals in a so-called "Secret Code" category, which covers all the imports and exports that the country's authorities prefer not to declare. The official data confirms experts' statements regarding the growing numbers of Russian weapons consumers in the Middle East. In recent years this has included the GCC members (see Table 6.4).

Table 6.4: Exports of Products under the "Secret Code" Category to the GCC Countries inthe 2010–2014 Period ($ million)

Country	2010	2011	2012	2013	2014
Bahrain	-	-	0.039	3.7	0.005
Kuwait	-	147	-	-	0.234
Oman	-	-	-	15	3.1
UAE	329	242.4	205	300	113
Saudi Arabia	-	12,8	0.018	0.041	0.095

Source: Ministry of Economic Development of the Russian Federation, Russian Customs data.

So far, the volume of Russian arms exports to the GCC remains minimal (see Table 6.4): Moscow is still testing the water, and the heavy presence of Western weapon producers in the region makes access to the Gulf market extremely difficult for the Russians. However, Russian arms sellers have expresseda certain optimism.[30] They believe that, now, the GCC authorities are more serious in their intention to buy Russian weapons than they were before.

Several years ago, the Saudis were, indeed, discussing the possibility of signing a $ 4 billion contract for the purchase of T-90C main battle tanks, BMP-3 IFVs, strike and transport helicopters, as well as anti-aircraft and anti-missile systems. Howeverthe talks ended with no results at that stage. Russian experts believed that promises to buy Russian weapons were nothing but a Saudi catch to make Moscow stop its support for Tehran and to trade additional concessions in the field of security from the U.S.[31] According to one of the leading Russian arms experts, Viktor Murakhovskiy the situation is different today. The GCC interest in buying Russian weapons is determined by practical needs rather than by political games. The military operation in Yemen demonstrated the unreliability of some Western weapons whereas their Russian/Soviet equivalents have been quite effectively used by the Iraqi government against the IS. As a result, Murakhovskiy acknowledged the increase in the intensity of visits by GCC officials (including Saudis) to discuss the possibility to buy Russian military equipment. He referred to the recent intention of the GCC authorities to upgrade BMP-3 Infantry Fighting Vehicles (IFV) previously bought from Moscow.[32]

According to the TASS news agency, arms exhibition IDEX-2015 that took place in the UAE in late February 2015 proved very successful for Moscow's weapon exporters.[33] The Russian state corporation Rostekh brought about 700 items to demonstrate at the exhibition, including a Khrizantema-S tank destroyer and Ratnik combat gear. This made the Russian exhibition stand very popular among visitors. On the sidelines of IDEX-2015, Rosoboron export signed a memorandum of understanding with an Emirates company regarding the purchase of a AU-200M battle module[34] for APCs and IFVs.[35]

Earlier on, in 2014, Bahrain ordered from Rosoboron export a consignment of Kornet-E anti-tank guided missile (ATGM) complexes. There is little information about this deal. However, as stated by the director general of Rosoboron export, Anatoly Isaykin, the contract "was not only big, but symbolic" for Moscow as Bahrain became the first foreign country to buy modern ATGMs from Russia.[36]

5.3. Investment Perspectives

The volume of accumulated Russian investments in the economy of the GCC countries is, for Russia, relatively substantial. By 2012 it had reached about $4.5 billion. The oil, gas, petrochemicals and high-tech (primarily, space and nuclear energy) sectors as well as banking are considered to be the most appealing for Russian investors.[37]

During the period 2008–2009, Gazprom was active in establishing contacts with Bahrain. The Russian company signed a memorandum of understanding with the National Oil and Gas Authority of Bahrain and studied the options for participation in geological studies of the Awali field. In the latter part of the first decade of the century and the early 2010s, the management of Gazprom was also discussing with Qataripartners the possibilities for undertaking joint projects in the field of LNG production and the organisation of swap operations. Gazprom and its Qatari partners also studied options for cooperation on the regional level within the framework of existing and perspective hydrocarbon exploration and extraction projects in Russia (project Yamal LNG) and the Middle East.

In 2004, Lukoil Overseas signed the above-mentioned contract with Saudi Arabia. Under this contract, the company was granted a 40-year long concession on the exploration and development of a gas field in the Rub-al-Khali desert. For the implementation of this project, Lukoil Overseas and Saudi Aramco established a joint company, Lukoil Saudi Arabia Energy Ltd. (LUKSAR). The share of the Russian company in this is 80%. In 2006, the exploration works of LUKSAR resulted in the discovery of a new hydrocarbon field whose estimated resources were 85 million tons in fuel-equivalent. After that LUKSAR began making an assessment of the nature of the discovered reserves in order to begin the development of the field. By August 2011 the accumulated investments of the Russian company had reached $300 million.[38] However, in 2015, the drop in oil prices put the further participation of Lukoil in the development of the discovered gas field in question.[39] As of late-June 2015, Moscow was looking for options to raise the ARAMCO share in LUKSAR from 20% to 50%.[40]

Oil, gas and petrochemical companies are not the only Russian firms trying to penetrate the Gulf. Nuclear and electric energy corporations, such as Rosatom State Corporation and its subsidiary company Atomstroy export also keep an eye on the GCC. In 2010, Rosatom and the UAE authorities were in discussion over options for cooperation. Although Rosatom failed to win the bid on the construction of the first Emirates nuclear power plant, in 2012 the Russian company Technoprom export and Canadian Uranium One Inc. (which is believed to be controlled by Russian interests) took an obligation to supply four nuclear power plants which are planned for construction in the UAE, using low-enriched fuel.[41] In 2015, Russia and Saudi Arabia also reached preliminary agreements on cooperation in the nuclear field.

The GCC region is also important as a product and investment market for some medium and small Russian companies, from different sector of the Russian economy. For them, trade with the countries of the region often represents the main (and, in some cases, the only) export market for their produce.[42] In this, the UAE has seen the most activity. According to Russian economist Ludmila Shkvarya, by 2015 there were about 50 representative offices of Russian companies in the Emirates. Out of these only 8 belonged to Russian business majors (such as Rosneft, Lukoil Overseas, Amtel, Alrosa, MMK, Sovkomflot, Inter RAO UES, KamAZ and Metalloinvest). Meanwhile, there were about 400 joint ventures with Russian capital registered in the UAE. Most of the latter were in the field of trade, tourism, real estate and the hotel business. About 100 companies were registered in the Emirates' free trade zones.[43]

The GCC countries are considered by the Kremlin not only as an appealing investment market for Russian companies, but, most importantly, as a potential source of investments for the Russian economy. Thus, in 2010, the Russian government corporation Rostekhnologii signed a 0,5 billion dollars contract with the Emirati Gulftainer Company Ltd on the joint implementation of infrastructural projects in Russia. In 2011, the above-mentioned UAEcompany became one of the owners of the Russian port of Ust-Luga on the Baltic Sea.[44] Russian experts have argued that the UAE company Masdar could be of significant interest as a potential participant in Russian projects related to the research on alternative sources of energy.[45] The Kuwaiti Alshaya Group now holds franchise rights to such brands in Russia as Starbucks, H&M, Mother care and The Body Shop. In 2015, the Jumeirah group was considering options for buying a new hotel in St.Petersburg. This would allow it to enter the Russian market.[46] Separately, the GCC countries have demonstrated their interest in investing their funds in the development of Russian transport infrastructure. Thus, the UAE-based Mubadala Development Company is also actively investing money in the infrastructure of the Ust-Lugaport.[47]

At the government level, GCC investments are channelled to different sectors of the Russian economy through the Russian Direct Investments Fund (RDIF). By 2015, the RDIF had already received $5 billion from Abu Dhabi, $2 billion from Mubadala Development, $2 billion from Qatar and $0.5 billion from Kuwait. In 2014, the RDIF and Mubadala Development signed seven contracts on the implementation of joint projects in such fields as mining, telecommunication and financial services.[48] According to some sources, the GCC money forms the largest (if not the main) part of RDIF investment capital.[49] Given preliminary agreements between the Russian authorities, Saudi Arabia and the UAE in 2015, the volume of Gulf investments in the Russian economy may soon increase even more. The Russian economy has been experiencing difficult times and the government is very interested in foreign investments to develop its economic infrastructure.

Russia also needs GCC money to finance its economic projects abroad. In 2014–2015, Moscow substantially intensified its relations with Egypt. It has ambitious plans regarding the development of economic cooperation with Cairo in such fields as nuclear energy, arms trade, and the hi-tech, automobile and space industries. The Egyptian authorities are unable to invest significant sums of money in the majority of these joint projects without external sponsors. Russia also does not have enough funds for the projects. As a result, the Kremlin actively has negotiated with the UAE (and, allegedly, Saudi Arabia) possibilities for creating a joint trilateral fund (with Egypt) to invest in infrastructural projects in Egypt. So far, the negotiation process has moved slowly. Yet, according to some sources, Saudi Arabia and the UAE have already stated their intention to help Cairo with financing the Russian-Egyptian projects (at least, some of them) and have even encouraged their private companies to look into possible investment opportunities.

5.4. Russia and GCC Hydrocarbon Resources

By 2015, the dropping oil prices and growing expenses incurred by the Russian budget (including those related to the annexation of Crimea) made Moscow look cautiously at the situation in the oil and gas sector of the Middle Eastern countries. Regional reserves in other parts of the world can create both challenges and opportunities for Moscow and its interests on the international energy markets. The Kremlin has traditionally been concerned with Saudi influence on international oil prices and Qatar's role in the global gas market (especially its influence on the GECF). Doha's periodic offers to sell LNG gas to Pakistan are definitely not in the interests of Moscow as Islamabad's consent would mean the end of the Iran-Pakistan gas pipeline project and subsequently the failure of the Kremlin's hope to channel Iran's natural gas to the South Asian market, away from Europe. Finally, in 2014, Algeria ratified amemorandum on all-embracing cooperation in the energy sphere with Qatar. This was believed to be the beginning of the formation of an Arab LNG producers' alliance against Gazprom and Moscow's interests in the European energy market.

The document *The Energy Strategy of Russia until 2030,* which was adopted by the Russian authorities in 2009, implies that Russia's strategy is aimed at securing the safety and profitability of governmental and semi-governmental oil and gas corporations. This suggest a relatively aggressive and expansionist approach. The document states that Moscow's ultimate goal should be the preservation of the necessary level of supplies of energy resources to the European market and the manifold increase in exports to the East. These aims were expected to be achieved not only by raising the output of domestic gas and oil fields, but also through active intervention in the energy sectors of other countries (both hydrocarbon producers and consumers) and the establishment of Russian control over most of Eurasia's gas and oil transportation infrastructure.

Russia's 2009 Energy Strategy had controversial outcomes for the Gulf. On the one hand, the Russian government was interested in negotiating with the Gulf countries a common market policy for the international arena, within the framework of established economic organisations (such as the Gas Exporting Countries

Forum). On the other hand, the periodic attempts of some GCC members (first of all, Qatar) to position themselves as an alternative to the Russian supply of gas to the European market made Moscow consider them as potential rivals.[50] However, this perception of the GCC countries as possible opponents in the international oil and gas markets leads to closer Russian cooperation with them: Moscow would like to intensify its interaction with the Gulf countries in international projects so as to acquire a stake in the Gulf energy market.[51]

Under these circumstances, Moscow is ultimately interested in close dialogue with the Middle East countries on oil and gas markets issues. The strategy of coordinating Russia's efforts with those of the other main gas producers such as Algeria, Qatar and Iran, has been cherished by the Russian authorities for years. The Kremlin tried to approach the countries of the region both at the bilateral level and by offering to establish regional OPEC-like organisations. Thus, in different years, Moscow was promoting the idea to creating a Gas Exporting Countries Forum (GECF) (initially proposed by Iran), a Gas Troyka (regular trilateral consultations between Russia, Iran and Qatar) and an International Organization of Non commercial Oil and Gas Associations (MANGO). Yet, in none of these cases has Moscow been successful. MANGO has never been created. The Gas Troika was established in 2008 but did not survive for long due to growing sanctions pressure on Iran and political contradictions between Doha, Moscow and Tehran. In 2007–2008, the Russians managed to finalize the process of creating an institutional base for the GECF, but they lost their bid to establish St. Petersburg as the GECF's new headquarters and, thus, failed to acquire the desired influence over the organisation. Nevertheless, Moscow tries to use the forum as a ground for the dialogue with Qatar.

5.5. Limits of Russian Economic Presence in the GCC

In 2014–2015, the Russian authorities were very persistent in promoting the interests of their businesses in the Middle East and the GCC. On 3–4 March 2015, Russia and Qatar held the first meeting of their joint trade and economic commission. By the end of 2015, it was intended that Moscow would open a trade mission in the UAE to support the growth of bilateral economic ties. Given that this decision was taken when the Russian budget was tight on money as a result of domestic economic troubles, the plans to open a trade mission in the UAE emphasised the growing importance of the region for the Kremlin.

However, Russian economic relations with the Gulf face a number of serious problems. First, Russian economic cooperation with the GCC is developing in unfavourable political conditions. In 2011–2014, the growing confrontation between

Moscow and the Gulf Arabs caused by the Russian position on Syria tangibly limited Russian options to strengthen cooperation with the members of the GCC. For instance, during 2010–2011, Moscow offered Qatar a number of investment projects costing$10–12 billion in different fields of the Russian economy, primarily in the oil and gas, construction, and gold mining sectors. However, these proposals were ignored by Doha. As argued by some analysts, political factors were partly responsible for the Qatari position. [52] Even the UAE where the Russian presence in the Arab part of the Gulf is probably the strongest, has been considered an unreliable partner since the beginning of the Arab Spring.

There is, as noted earlier, an additional problem stemming from Qatar's position as one of Russia's main rivals in the gas market. After the beginning of the Arab spring, this unofficial rivalry was complemented by an ideological dimension. The interaction of these two factors poses a significant challenge to the emergence of a wider economic relationship. political differences and economic competition creates a significant challenge to the emergence of a workable relationship between the two countries.

A number of practical economic factors also negatively affect the development of Russia-GCC trade. These include huge trade misbalances (Russian exports to the GCC greatly exceed imports from there), lack of information about the Russian market in the GCC (and vice versa), the absence of long-term trade contracts (Russian companies still prefer single supply contracts), and the dominance of raw and semi-processed materials in Russian exports.[53] Russian domestic realities are also not very favourable for the development of Russian-GCC economic ties.

Russian statism, moreover, seriously restrains options for cooperation between the two countries. In modern Russia, government support constitutes one of the main (if not the only) factors boosting the penetration of Russian business in foreign markets. In spite of the above-mentioned advantages provided by state protection of government and semi-government corporations, the state patronage also has substantial disadvantages. Firstly, it limits the initiative of the Russian corporations which often act upon the direct orders of Moscow. Secondly, the excessive protectionism leads to the artificial closure of the Russian domestic market for Iranian producers. Thirdly, the existing government support is selective and provided only to business connected with the political elite of Russia. As a result, medium and small business, as well as private corporations with insufficiently close connections with the state, usually face difficulties in dealing with the Gulf by themselves. The lack of government support in certain areas, in turn, weakens the Russian position in a number of fields and creates serious problems for the development of Russo-Gulf economic ties.

Problems with the development of Russian economic relations with the Gulf are also related to the specifics of the economy of the Russian Federation. In spite of the proclaimed attempts of the Russian authorities to accelerate economic growth, Russia is still heavily dependent on the export of raw materials (minerals, hydrocarbons and wood). The policy of diversification and modernisation declared by president Medvedev has been implemented at a slow pace, and it has obviously failed to reach the initial projected goals. The Russian Federation demonstrates aspects of a country with a rentier economy, and the increasing technological backwardness as compared to the West in certain fields makes these aspects more obvious. As a result, Moscow has a very limited range of products to offer the Gulf, and this range is gradually shrinking.[54]

6. Conclusion

The events of the Arab Spring and their aftermath formed a serious stress-test for Russian foreign policy towardsthe GCC. The initial results of this test, however, suggest that Russia has managed to transcend it. By the end of 2015, it became obvious that in spite of existing contradictions over a variety of political issues, neither Moscow nor the GCC intend to cross the red lines that would deprive them of the option of rapprochement. The events of the Arab spring clearly demonstrated to Moscow that it should recognise Saudi Arabia and Qatar as regional leaders. At the same time, Moscow's determination in defending its interests in Syria while at the same time being ready to continue the dialogue with the GCC proved that Russiawas an important player in the region which should not be either neglected or underestimated.

Although economic relations between the countries of the Gulf and Russia remain still underdeveloped, they have a certain potential. Moscow is unable to challenge the West's economic presence in the region, nor the growing influence of China (and other Asian countries). Yet, Russia is probably capable of finding its own niche in the Gulf system of economic relations. Currently, in its economic efforts the Kremlin puts its main stake inthose areas where it has market advantages: nuclear energy, oil and gas, petro-chemistry, space, weapons and grain. At the same time, the main principle of Russian business in the Middle East is based on the maxim of supplying goods at a "Chinese price for European quality".

This maxim may become the guarantee of future Russian success in developing economic cooperation with the GCC countries if Moscow succeeds in its own economic diversification. Price and reliability are among the main reasons for Middle Eastern countries to become interested in Russian technologies. The Russian government also needs to demonstrate considerable patience, vigilance and courtesy in developing its relations with the Gulf. The established ties with the GCC members are still young and fragileand they are exposed to the negative influence of external factors such as the unstable situation in the Middle East.

Notes

1 Aleksandr Potserob, "K Voprosu Obespecheniya Bezopasnosti v Zone Persidskogo Zaliva," Institute of the Middle East, accessed April 25, 2012 <http://www.iimes.ru/rus/stat/2010/31-10-10b.htm>.
2 Ibid.
3 Ibid.
4 Vladimir Isaev and Aleksandr Filonik, "Rossiya – Arabskiye Strany: Politicheskiye Imperativy i EkonomicheskoyeSotrudnichestvo," *NovoyeVostochnoyeObozreniye*, September 3, 2010, accessed April 25, 2012, <http://journal-neo.com/?q=ru/node/1154>.
5 EldarKasaev, "Rossiya i Katar: PrichinyEkonomicheskoyStagnatcii," Institute of the Middle East, accessed October 4, 2013, <http://www.iimes.ru/?p=17847>.
6 EldarKasaev, "EkonomicheskoyePartnerstvoRossii i OAE: TekushcheeSostoyaniye i PoliticheskiyeRiski," Institute of the Middle East, accessed October 4, 2013, <http://www.iimes.ru/?p=18069>.
7 Kasaev, "Rossiya i Katar".
8 *VoA*, "Medvedev PodpsalUkaz o SanktcsiyahprotivLivii," *VoA*, August 12, 2011, accessed October 5, 2013, <http://www.golos-ameriki.ru/content/russia-lybia-medvedev-sanctions-2011-08-12-127578108/241893.html>; *ZhenminZhibao*, "RossiyaSklonyaetsya k Uzhestocheniyu SanktcsiyprotivLivii," *ZhenminZhibao*, August 15, 2011, accessed October 5, 2013, <http://russian.people.com.cn/31519/7568885.html>; *Nakanune*, "BastrykinaPoprosiliProveriDeyatelnostMedvedevanaFaktIzmeny," *Nakanune*, February 4, 2013, accessed October 5, 2013, <http://www.nakanune.ru/news/2013/2/4/22299398/>.
9 Kasaev, "Ekonomicheskoye Partnerstvo Rossii i OAE".
10 Ibid.
11 DmitriyNechitaylo, "Severokavkaztcsy v Grazhdanskoy Voyne v Sirii," Institute of the Middle East, accessed October 4, 2013, <http://www.iimes.ru/?p=18111>.
12 Yuri Shcheglov in, "O RazvitiiSituatscii v Sirii," Institute of the Middle East, accessed May 31, 2013, <http://www.iimes.ru/?p=17029>.
13 Ibid.
14 *NewsRu*, "SinChechenskogo "Chernogo Angela" bilUbit v SiriiVovse ne v Boyu, RasskazaliRodstvenniki' in *NewsRu*, August 23, 2012, accessed on 31 May 2013, <http://www.newsru.com/russia/23aug2012/blackangelson.html>.
15 Shcheglov in, "Razmyshleniya o vozmozhnostekspansiiislamistov v Rossiyu".
16 Chechen communities of different sizes are scattered around the Middle East.
17 Nechitaylo, "Severokavkaztcsy v GrazhdanskoyVoyne v Sirii".
18 Interview with a Russian diplomat. Moscow, January 2013.
19 MinisterstvoInostrannikh del RossiyskoyFederatcsii, "IntervyuMinisraInostrannikh Del RossiiS.V.Lavrova v Programme "Voskresniyvecher s VladimiromSolovevim" na Telekanale "Rossiya-1", Moskva, 10 Fevralya 2013 goda" Russian Ministry of Foreign Affairs, accessed May 31, 2013, <http://mid.ru/bdomp/brp_4.nsf/2fee282eb6df40e643256999005e6e8c/02ebc66354ef10e544257b0e0045ad41!Open Document>.
20 Ibid.
21 Eldar Kasaev, "Ob OtnosheniyakhRossii i KataranaSovremennomEtape," Institute of the Middle East, accessed October 27, 2014, <http://www.iimes.ru/?p=19895>.
22 GrigoriyKosach, "PozitcsiyaRossiipoSiriiskomuKrizisu v ArabskoyPresseposle Vstrechi G8," Institute of the Middle East, accessed October 5, 2013, <http://www.iimes.ru/?p=17779>.

23 Naser al-Tamimi, "Saudi-Russian Relations: Between Assad and Sisi," *Al-Arabiya*, August 18, 2013, accessed October 5, 2013, <http://english.alarabiya.net/en/views/news/middle-east/2013/08/18/Saudi-Russian-relations-between-Assad-and-Sisi.html>.

24 LudmilaShkvarya, "Rossiya i StranyZaliva: InvestitsionnoyeSotrudnichestvo," *Aziya i Afrika Segodnya*, 5 (2011): 18 – 23.

25 *Vesti*, "SaudovskayaAraviyaObeshchayet i UgrozhayetRossiipoSirii," *Vesti*, August 27, 2013, accessed on October 5, 2013, <http://www.vestifinance.ru/articles/31671>.

26 Ekaterina Kudashkina, "Qatar scandal still a "family matter" for GCC countries," *The Voice of Russia*, accessed October 27, 2014, <http://voiceofrussia.com/radio_broadcast/25298789/269002772/>.

27 See <http://stat.customs.ru/>. Accessed July 13, 2015.

28 *Argumenty i Fakty*, "OAE PokupayutRossiyskiyPlavuchiyKosmodrom 'Morskoy Start', " *Argumenty i Fakty*, March 24, 2015, accessed July 13, 2015, <http://www.aif.ru/society/science/1473836>.

29 Interview with the expert on Russian arms sales. Chatham House, London, the UK, February 27, 2015.

30 Anton Mardasov, "RossiyskiyePushkiUderzhivayutSvoyPlatcdarm," *Araf News*, August 28, 2015, accessed August 30, 2015, <http://www.arafnews.ru/news/rossijskie-pushki-uderzhivajut-svoj-platsdarm-.html>.

31 Ibid.

32 Anton Mardasov, "RossiyskiyePushkiUderzhivayutSvoyPlatcdarm. Kakiye Persoektivy u NasheyStranynaRynkeVooruzheniy i Voennoy Tekhniki," *SvobodnayaPressa*, August 28, 2015, accessed August 30, 2015, <http://svpressa.ru/war21/article/130499/>.

33 *TASS*, "Proverenniy Tovar: KakiyeStranyPokupayut u Rossii Vooruzheniye i VoyennuyuTekhniku," *TASS*, February 26, 2015, accessed August 30, 2015, <http://tass.ru/armiya-i-opk/1792767>.

34 Battle module AU-200M consists of a 57 mm gun and a 7.62 machinegun.

35 *TASS*, 'Proverenniy Tovar'.

36 Ibid.

37 Shkvarya, "Rossiya I Strany Zaliva: Investitsionnoye Sotrudnichestvo", 21.

38 Ibid, 18 – 23.

39 ReemShamseddine and Olesya Astakhova, "Russia's Lukoil Last to Leave Saudi Arabia's Search for Gas," *Reuters*, April 13, 2015, accessed August 30, 2015, <http://www.reuters.com/article/2015/04/13/lukoil-saudi-gas-idUSL6N0X30HB20150413>.

40 OlesyaAstakhova, "Russia's Lukoil Says Saudi Aramco Wants to Raise Stake in Luksar," *RIGZONE*, June 24, 2015, accessed August 30, 2015, <http://www.rigzone.com/news/oil_gas/a/139290/Russias_Lukoil_Says_Saudi_Aramco_Wants_to_Raise_Stake_in_Luksar>.

41 *ITAR-TASS*, "Rossiya i OAEZalozhiliPravovuyuOsnovuSotrudnichestva v OblastiIspolzovaniya Atomnoy-Energii v MirnykhTscelyakh," *ITAR-TASS*, December 17, 2012, accessed October 4, 2013, <http://news.rambler.ru/16829418/>.

42 Igor Naumov, "RossiyskiyeUbytkiotArabskoyVesny," *NezavisimayaGazeta*, February 29, 2012, accessed October 4, 2013, <http://www.ng.ru/economics/2012-02-29/1_arab_vesna.html>.

43 LudmilaShkvarya and VasiliyRusakovich, "VzaimnayaTorgovlya Rossii i OAE: Neobkhodimost i VozmozhnostRazvitiya", *UpravleniyeEkonomicheskimiSistemami*, March 2015, accessed August 30, 2015, <http://uecs.ru/uecs-75-752015/item/3412-2015-03-24-12-27-40>.

44 VladislavSenkovich, "PochemuArabskiyeStranyPotentscialnoVazhnydlyaEkonomikiRossii," Russian International Affairs Council, accessed October, 4, 2013, <http://russiancouncil.ru/inner/?id_4=1465#top>.

45 Ibid.

46 *ArafNews*, "Torgovye i InvestitsionnyePotokiStran SSAGPZ i SNG," *ArafNews*, December 15, 2015, accessed 30 August 2015, <http://www.arafnews.ru/news/torgovye-i-investitsionnye-potoki-stran-ssagpz-i-sng.html>.

47 AllaGalanova, "KonsortciumRossiyskikh i ArabskikhKompaniyPriobrelGazoviy Terminal 'SIBU-Ra' v PortuUst-Luga," *Gudok*, August 27, 2015, accessed August 30, 2015, <http://www.gudok.ru/freighttrans/?ID=1302538>.

48 Ibid.

49 *ArafNews*, 'Torgovye i Investitsionnye Potoki'.

50 Nikolay Kozhanov, *EkonomicheskiyeSanktsiiProtivIrana: Tseli, Masshtabi, Vozmozhniye PosledstviyaVvedeniya* (Moscow: InstitutBlizhnego Vostoka, 2011)

51 Interview with a Russian expert on Iran and the Persian Gulf. Moscow, 17 October 2011.

52 Kasaev, "Rossiya i Katar".
53 Shkvarya and Rusakovich, "VzaimnayaTorgovlyaRossii i OAE".
54 Interview with an expert of the Chamber of Commerce and Industry of the Russian Federation. Moscow, 11 December 2011.

References

Isaev, Vladimir, AleksandrFilonik, "Rossiya – ArabskiyeStrany: Politicheskiye Imperativy i Ekonomi cheskoyeSotrudnichestvo,"*NovoyeVostochnoyeObozreniye*, September 3, 2010, accessed April 25, 2012 <http://journal-neo.com/?q=ru/node/1154>.

Kasaev, Eldar, "EkonomicheskoyePartnerstvoRossii i OAE: TekushcheeSostoyaniye i PoliticheskiyeRiski," Institute of the Middle East, accessed October 4, 2013<http://www.iimes.ru/?p=18069>.

Kasaev, Eldar, "Ob OtnosheniyakhRossii i KataranaSovremennomEtape," Institute of the Middle East, accessed October 27, 2014, <http://www.iimes.ru/?p=19895>.

Kasaev, Eldar,"Rossiya i Katar: PrichinyEkonomicheskoyStagnatcii," Institute of the Middle East, accessed on October 4, 2013, <http://www.iimes.ru/?p=17847>.

Kosach, Grigoriy,"PozitcsiyaRossiipoSiriiskomuKrizisu v ArabskoyPresseposleVstrechi G8," accessed October 5, 2013, <http://www.iimes.ru/?p=17779>.

Mardasov, Anton,"RossiyskiyePushkiUderzhivayutSvoyPlatcdarm,"*ArafNews*, August 28, 2015, accessed August 30, 2015, <http://www.arafnews.ru/news/rossijskie-pushki-uderzhivajut-svoj-platsdarm-.html>.

Naumov, Igor,"RossiyskiyeUbytkiotArabskoyVesny,"*NezavisimayaGazeta*, February 29, 2012, accessed October 4, 2013, <http://www.ng.ru/economics/2012-02-29/1_arab_vesna.html>.

Potserob, Aleksandr, "K VoprosuObespecheniyaBezopasnosti v Zone PersidskogoZaliva," Institute of the Middle East, accessed April 25, 2012, <http://www.iimes.ru/rus/stat/2010/31-10-10b.htm>.

Shkvarya, Ludmila,"Rossiya i StranyZaliva: InvestitsionnoyeSotrudnichestvo,"*Aziya i Afrika Segodnya*,5(2011).

Shkvarya, Ludmila, andVasiliyRusakovich, "VzaimnayaTorgovlyaRossii i OAE: Neobkhodimost i VozmozhnostRazvitiya", *UpravleniyeEkonomicheskimiSistemami*, March 2015, accessed August 30, 2015, <http://uecs.ru/uecs-75-752015/item/3412-2015-03-24-12-27-40>.

Tamimi, Naser, "Saudi-Russian Relations: Between Assad and Sisi,"*Al-Arabiya*, August 18, 2013, accessed October 5, 2013, <http://english.alarabiya.net/en/views/news/middle-east/2013/08/18/Saudi-Russian-relations-between-Assad-and-Sisi.html>.

TASS, "Proverenniy Tovar: KakiyeStranyPokupayut u RossiiVooruzheniye i VoyennuyuTekhniku,"*TASS*, February 26, 2015, accessed August 30, 2015, <http://tass.ru/armiya-i-opk/1792767>.

7

India in BRICS and Indo-GCC Relations: Assessing Conflicts and Complementarities

Shanthie Mariet DSouza and Bibhu Prasad Routray

1. Introduction

India's rise as a major economic power coincides with the narrative of the rise of the developing world. A range of measures was initiated following the liberalisation of its economy in the early 1990s ending decades of protectionism and autarky since independence. The attractiveness of India as home to a vast as pirational middle class made it an attractive investment destination. The impressive economic growth the country has registered since then, albeit with periodic slowdowns and an element of downturn, poses a challenge and provides an alternative to the long-held notion of the invincibility of the developed countries in the world economy. India constitutes a paradigm for the economic aspirations of the developing world and its ability to shape the debate over development and global trade. The BRICS organisation, hailed as a collective success story, perhaps coheres with this perspective better than does any other organisation. And yet there are challenges. Contrary to the hyper projections, BRICS' success has not always been convincing. India's impressive growth stands out in comparison to that of some other members of the organisation.

India's trade and economic relations with the members of the Gulf Cooperation Council (GCC) are healtle, marked by continuous growth. Although dominated by oil imports by India from the GCC member states, both India and the GCC countries are increasingly developing as stakeholders in each other's economic development. And yet, political and strategic relations between the two have not as yet developed fully into a robust partnership. Several irritants continue to affect the growth of a mutually beneficial relationship. There are, however, signs of change.

This chapter argues, in two broad parts, that India's relations with the GCC remain important and key to its rise as an economic power – just as BRICS itself is. The first part examines India's role in BRICS, while also assessing the performance of BRICS as a multilateral organisation of the developing world. In the second part of the chapter, India's relations with the GCC are examined with a view to assessing the challenges and complementarities between the two geographically important regions. India's economic ties, the irritants in the bilateral ties and the prospects of cooperation are examined in detail.

2. The Rise of BRICS: A Brief History

In 2001, the then Goldman Sachs Group economist Jim O'Neill coined the term BRIC to describe the growing prominence of Brazil, Russia, India and China in the global economy and to convey "the fact that much of the world's economic growth would soon come from these four countries."[1] Not yet considered developed countries, the four were grouped together for being at the same stage of economic development.[2] Whether O'Neill's coining of the term has anything to do with the emergence of BRIC, and whether political-economic (rather than purely economic) factors played a role in BRIC's formation can be argued. There was indeed much debate about whether the grouping made sense. Nevertheless, the 'catchiness' of the label in some way influenced the holding of a summit by the BRIC foreign ministers in New York in 2006 on the margins of the United Nations General Assembly (UNGA)[3]. It was followed by an informal meeting of the BRIC leaders in Tokyo in Japan in July 2008, on the sidelines of the G-8 Outreach Summit. With the first standalone Yekaterinburg Summit in Russia in July 2009, arguably what began as a hook for an investment bank's research note became a real political institution.

And there were sound economic and political reasons for setting up this organisation. The BRICS countries account for a third of the world's land mass and for more than 43 percent of the world's population. In addition, their economies now "add up in output to about the same as that of the United States and are well on course to overtake the entire G-7 before 2050"[4]. They together account for18 percent of global trade and 20 percent of the world's Gross Domestic Product (GDP). This significant level of economic importance constituted a key factor in the establishment of the group and over time this meant that the dismissive analyses which some gave of the grouping (referring to it being the only world body "invented by a merchant bank"[5]) were discounted.

In 2009, with the Yekaterinburg summit, the BRIC country leaders started meeting as a bloc. When South Africa joined the organisation, following a decision made by the BRIC Foreign Ministers at their meeting in New York in September 2010, BRIC became BRICS. There was some skepticism about South Africa's inclusion, on the grounds that a country of less than 50 million people was too small to join the group. However, South Africa's presence addressed the criticism that the African continent had been overlooked while forming the new bloc - reinforcing the notion of Africa being a supplier of raw materials, and not a key player in global economics. South Africa's inclusion also meant that BRICS could portray itself as representing the entire emerging world.

Table 7.1: BRICS Summits

1st Summit	July 2009	Yekaterinburg, Russia
2nd Summit	April 2010	Brasilia, Brazil
3rd Summit	April 2011	Sanya, China
4th Summit	March 2012	New Delhi, India
5th Summit	March 2013	Durban, South Africa
6th Summit	July 2014	Fortaleza , Brazil
7th Summit	July 2015	Ufa, Russia
8th Summit (Scheduled)	October 2016	Goa, India

BRICS was, thus, established with an agenda of not only providing an alternative to Western domination, but also to erect a flagpole for emerging multi-polarity. Western failures, economic downturn and a difficult relationship with the West spurred the formation of this grouping, and propelled the countries towards much greater cooperation than they may have initially intended. BRICS defied large-scale skepticism and demonstrated steady development, outperforming many developed countries. In 2009, for example, while the economies of Japan and Germany declined by six percent, Brazil sustained its growth, India's economy showed a near six percent growth rate and China's rose by more than eight percent. Prof. Ingo Walter and Prof. Roy C. Smith of the New York University, wrote,

> For the past 15 years, the BRICS have been seen as the world's best hope for sustainable growth. These five countries, representing 40 per cent of the world's population and 25 per cent of its GDP in 2013, recorded growth rates 4 to 5 times greater than those of the US, Europe and Japan, and threatened to displace them as the world's most important economic powers in another 20 years or so.[6]

In July 2014, at the BRICS Summit at Fortaleza, the heads of the member countries signed an agreement on establishing a New Development Bank (NDB), "with the purpose of mobilizing resources for infrastructure and sustainable development projects in BRICS and other emerging and developing economies". The purpose of the $100 billion BRICS Bank, with contributions coming from China ($41 billion), India, Brazil and Russia ($18 billion each), and South Africa ($5 billion)[7], was to "mobilise resources for infrastructure and sustainable development projects" not just in BRICS countries but also in other emerging economies. It seeks to do so by supporting public and private projects through loans, guarantees and equity. The BRICS Bank does not ignore the presence of existing financial organisations like the International Monetary Fund (IMF) and the World Bank. The articles of the BRICS bank say that its creation is to complement "the existing efforts or multilateral and regional financial institutions."[8] But, in a sense, "the BRICS bank was born because the countries that represent this have long realised they need an alternative system to IMF/World Bank, one in which they have greater say."[9] In May 2015, ahead of the 7th BRICS Summit in Russia, the Indian government announced the appointment of Indian banker Kundapur Vaman Kamath as president of the BRICS Bank.

The setting up of the BRICS Bank is also an expression of frustration at the lack of reforms in the IMF. On the occasion of the founding of the BRICS Bank, the committee announced its impatience with failed reform within the International Monetary Fund and said, "We remain disappointed and seriously concerned with the current non-implementation of the 2010 International Monetary Fund reforms, which negatively impacts on the IMF's legitimacy, credibility and effectiveness."[10] Leaders of Brazil, Russia, India, China and South Africa have drafted amendments to the IMF's voting policy and only received a sufficient number of votes for this to be implemented in January 2016. At the BRICS Summit in Brazil, Brazilian President Dilma Rousseff stated that the BRICS nations "are among the largest in the world and cannot content themselves in the middle of the 21st century with any kind of dependency."[11] Similarly, one of President Putin's economic advisers in Russia, not necessarily with abundant influence on the BRICS, has also called advocated setting up an "international anti-dollar alliance"[12] and called upon Russia's allies to eliminate the dollar from international trade. Sergey Glazyev, another of President Putin's economic aides, published an article outlining a plan for 'undermining the economic strength of the United States' in order to force Washington to stop the civil war in Ukraine. Glazyev believes that the only way to make the US give up its plans for starting a new cold war is to crash the dollar system.

It must be stressed that Glazyev's extreme confrontational views would not have many supporters within the BRICS system. Nonetheless, recent dollar-less BRICS energy deals, currency swaps and foreign direct investment indicate that the trend away from the dollar is already evident. The anti-United States stance of some of the BRICS members has indeed led some commentators to term the organisation an anti-dollar alliance.[13] By 2020, about 50 percent of China's cross-border trade will be settled in yuan, rather than US dollars.[14] China launched an initiative in 2009 encouraging five Chinese cities initially to settle cross-border trade in yuan. The trend has grown rapidly, with yuan settlement of trade debts rising from 1 percent of transactions in 2010 to 22 percent in 2014. China has proceeded, with support from several Asia-Pacific nations as well as others, to set up the Asian Infrastructure Investment Bank (AIIB) - an open and inclusive platform that focuses on infrastructure.

3. India in BRICS

India does not share much of the anti-West sentiment mentioned above, and it remains committed to engagement with the West. Its intention to maintain its strategic autonomy co-exists with an increasing tilt towards the United States. BRICS in fact serves India as a balancing association, providing a forum for cooperative relative relations with Russia and China. Prime Minister Narendra Modi of the new Bharatiya Janata Party-led government has focused on improving India's relations with both the United States and China. Given the popular view that the BRICS countries are opposed to the West, India finds itself in the unique position of being a part of the BRICS collective while maintaining overtly friendly relations with the US, a relationship that has further improved following President Obama's January 2015 visit to India and the signing of a slew of agreements in the defence, nuclear, and economic domains.

India's policy of maintaining strategic autonomy has much to do with the less than smooth Sino-Indian bilateral relationship. The two countries have struggled to arrive at a solution to their boundary issue. In the words of one commentator," Booming bilateral trade, far from helping to turn the page on old rifts, has been accompanied by increasing border incidents, military tensions, and geopolitical rivalry, as well as disagreements on riparian and maritime issues."[15] China and India have one of the world's most lopsided trading relationships, marked by a mounting trade deficit to the tune of $50 billion.[16] Similarly, among BRICS member countries, Russia and China have at times had a difficult relationship in the past.

Some have suggested that the obvious clout of China and Russia within the BRICS organisation results in a less prominent role for India, despite the latter's efforts to spread its influence through the $100 billion BRICS Bank. India's approach and positioning between competing economic and security interests in Asia, thus, constitute a complex and interesting case.

Among the differences India has with non-democracies like China and Russia, apart from their anti-US stand, is their attitude towards liberal values. Sashi Tharoor, India's former state minister for External Affairs has written, citing the example of attitude towards internet governance:

> China and Russia are suspicious of liberal ideas, wary of information technology and decidedly unsympathetic to democratic dissent; India, Brazil and South Africa are lively democracies. It is unlikely, for example, that the five would see eye to eye on issues of Internet governance. China and Russia wish to legitimize greater government control over the Internet; India is an energetic advocate of multi-stakeholderism.[17]

It can be projected that the issue of internet governance will emerge in the long-run a key issue for BRICS as an organisation.

4. Challenges and Underperformance

Attitudes towards democracy, freedom and liberal values are not the only issues which divide the BRICS members. In terms of economic growth, poverty eradication, and long term economic vision they can be very different from one another.

In the year 2001, Goldman Sachs predicted that Brazil, Russia, India and China would increasingly drive global growth, filling a void left by the West. However, by 2015, this did not seem plausible. BRICS's sub-par performance could become the source of immense worry for the rest of the world and might even drag down the rest of the world. In 2015, for example, the Chinese economy became subject to weak demand abroad and a sluggish economy at home. A stock bubble has severely affected its financial system. Its exports have declined and imports slumped.[18] Similarly, at the time of writing imports are declining in Brazil, India and especially Russia, which makes the BRICS responsible for a drop in annual world trade of about 1.3 percentage points, the most pronounced deceleration since the 2008-2009 global financial crisis.

The state of Brazil's economy is particularly parlous, with its commodities-dependent economy estimated to have shrunk by3.8 per cent in 2015 and forecast to shrink by another 3.5 per cent in 2016. The country's government, moreover, has its job cut out in controlling inflation which has rising to the upper end of its comfort zone since mid-2014, after the government imposed several tax increases aiming at balancing the overall budget. In 2014, Brazil posted an inflation rate of 6.41 percent, against an upper limit ceiling set by its central bank of 6.5percent.[19] By August 2015, inflation had risen to 9.53 percent, before easing marginally to 9.49 percent in September. In order to control inflation, its central bank for the first time since 2003 raised its base rate to 11.75percent. The industrial growth rate is in negative territory. Dependence on commodities, all of which are in a down cycle, has led to sluggish growth in the country.[20] In relation to Russia, the World Bank has downgraded its economy on account of a sharp fall in oil prices. Russia's GDP is estimated to have shrunk by 3.7 percent in 2015 and is forecast to shrink by a further 1.0 percent in 2016. The Russian government, in order to prevent the outflow of foreign currency, has sharply increased interest rates to 17 percent, increasing it by 6.5 percent - the highest since Russia's 1998 crisis. Russia's inflation rate is estimated as having reached 15.8 per cent in.[21]

The Chinese economy, after growing at more than 10 percent for a decade and contributing significantly to global growth, slowed down to 6.9 percent in 2015. The World Bank has termed this 'managed slowing', and even the Chinese leaders project the slowdown as normal and apparently policy-driven.[22] According to a World Bank report released in April 2015, China's growth will continue to moderate, "reflecting continued policy efforts to address financial vulnerabilities and gradually shift the economy to a more sustainable growth path"[23]. There are, however, predictions, by Jeffrey Kleintop, chief global investment strategist at Charles Schwab, that China's growth will go down to 5 percent or below over the coming decade. Lack of demand is visible in China's inflation rate, which is at a five year low of 1.5 percent.

In South Africa, inflation is on a downward path from 6.6 percent in mid-2014 to 5.8 percent towards the end of 2014. However, a slump in commodity markets has affected growth rates in the country. The country has marginally escaped recession, but Morgan Stanley has downgraded the country's growth estimate to 1.3 percent from an earlier forecast of 1.8 percent. In 2016 the country's GDP is expected to grow by 2.5 percent.

This leaves India as the only BRICS country which the Organisation for Economic Cooperation and Development (OECD) predicted in September 2015 would maintain its existing fast rate of growth, making it the fastest growing major economy over the coming two years. India is pegged to grow at 7.2 per cent in 2016 and 7.3 per cent in 2017.[24] The OECD report ascribes this in part to the country having a strong and stable government with commitment to market reforms. Other factors are India's lesser exposure to China, "which is now facing mounting deflation fears, a collapsing housing market, and an economy growing at its slowest rate in decades"[25]; its import substitution and domestic demand-led growth plans; and its favorable demographics. The report states: "India's dependency ratio is declining and almost 30 percent of the population is under the age of 14. Those people will make up the country's consumers, employers, workers, and taxpayers in the decades to come."[26]

However, it does not augur well for BRICS if India is the only BRICS country whose economy is forecast to grow fast and consistently. Pitched as an alternative to the West, BRICS no longer looks so convincing. In recent times, some non-BRICS countries have in fact fared better than BRICS. Experts believe that the reason for this is the delivery capacity of these non-BRIC nations. Economic growth, fuelled by domestic factors such as favourable demographics and consumption growth, have led to superior corporate profitability, and this drives higher returns for investors. Non-BRIC countries like Philippines, Peru, Indonesia, and Thailand have delivered on this potential over the past decade.[27]

Notwithstanding India's growth, in the realm of development and poverty eradication it (along with South Africa and Brazil) lags behind China. While China has largely eliminated mass poverty, a significant proportion of the populations in India, South Africa, and Brazil still struggle with existential questions of survival. With this backdrop, it is questionable what sort of common view BRICS could adopt on development aid, global macro-economics, and international resource transfers. Similarly, China's prioritisation of the AIIB conflicts with the BRICS bank. Trade divides the BRICS countries, and so does global geopolitics. Commercial ties between them continue to be marked by disharmony. In order to find its collective feet, therefore, BRICS will have to base itself on key compromises, which may not add to the organisation's strength in the long run.

5. India and GCC

India and the GCC have a wide complementarity of interests. The Gulf constitutes the immediate neighborhood of India, making India a vital stakeholder 'in the stability, security and economic well-being of the Gulf.[28]

Trade linkages between India and the Gulf countries can be traced back to ancient times when people across the Arabian Sea established bilateral economic contacts. In the narratives of the past, Indian and Arab traders would sail across the Arabian Sea, and buy and sell different commodities. Such historical interactions continued and have played a part in deepening the trade linkages in the age of globalisation. Both the volume and nature of trade expanded. Large number of Indians started working in the Gulf after the discovery of oil and the numbers continue to increase. India's dependence on Gulf oil, furthermore, became an important aspect of the economic relationship between the two regions. Even though the political and diplomatic relationship between India and the Gulf region remained tense during the Cold War period, owing to polarised political rhetoric, trade and business between the two continued to grow and flourish.

Table 7.2: India–GCC Total Trade (including oil and gas)

(Figures in $ billion)

Country	2008-09	2009-10	2010-11	2011-12	2012-13	2013-14	2014-15
Bahrain	1.72	0.75	1.29	1.34	1.32	1.20	0.92
Kuwait	10.39	9.03	12.16	17.62	17.63	18.22	14.58
Oman	1.98	4.53	5.08	4.66	4.54	5.77	4.13
Qatar	4.17	5.18	7.1	13.72	16.3	16.67	15.66
Saudi Arabia	25.08	21	25.06	37.5	43.91	48.62	39.27
UAE	48.26	43.46	66.57	72.68	75.45	59.54	59.17
TOTAL	91.6	83.95	117.35	147.52	159.45	150.02	133.73

Source: Department of Commerce, Ministry of Commerce and Industry, Government of India.

The GCC has become a major trade partner for India as bilateral trade has grown tremendously. The total trade between India and the GCC has risen from about $ 5.55 billion in 2000–01 to $ 133.73 billion in 2014–15. Such a massive growth during the brief period of a decade can be attributed mainly to the higher commodity prices, especially oil prices, over those years, but it also reflects the increased efforts made by both sides to enhance their trade relationship. Today, the United Arab Emirates (UAE) and Saudi

Arabia are both among the top five trading partners of India. The high volume of trade and commerce between the two indicates a high degree of economic complementarity.

The GCC countries, with large hydrocarbon reserves are crucial for India's energy requirements While India's demand for energy is increasing rapidly, its domestic energy output is too low to cater to the growing needs of the country. According to India's Petroleum Ministry, while crude oil production in India was a mere 37.8 million metric tonnes (MMT) in 2013-14, the total consumption of petroleum products was a huge 158.2 MMT, accounting thereby for an import dependency of 77.6 percent.[29] India Hydrocarbon Vision 2015 projects that by the year 2024–25, the demand for petroleum products in India would reach 368 MMT. The estimate of the International Energy Agency for that same year is not quite so large, putting it at 230 MMT. The Power and Energy Division of India's Planning Commission of India projects that by 2024–25, demand will be 240 MMT. Whichever estimate is correct, the growth of demand is substantial and such huge demand can only be met by increasing the imports of petroleum. The Gulf region has been the primary source of oil imports for India. The geographical proximity between India and the region makes the transportation cost of importing crude oil lower than importing from any other part of the world. Traditionally, India has been dependent upon Gulf oil and it will continue to be so in the near future.

Table 7.3: India's Oil Imports from GCC Countries: 2008–2009 to 2014–15

($ millions)

Country	2008 09	2009 10	2010 11	2011 12	2012 13	2013-14	2014-15
Bahrain	0.03	NA	NA	NA	56.33	183.34	NA
Kuwait	7,914.95	7,310.90	8,759.29	14,196.17	14,450.94	15,150.28	11,478.90
Oman	261.01	2,762.69	3096.86	1,835.42	344.54	1339.36	561.98
Qatar	1,412.94	2,398.23	3075.73	5,224.51	6,668.78	4315.40	2301.40
Saudi Arabia	15,827.31	14,049.15	16,294.82	26,311.67	28,384.08	30,964.24	21,803.40
UAE	9,208.67	5,448.84	7,861.38	12,564.31	12,641.64	11,011.98	11,057.33
TOTAL	34,624.91	31,969.81	39,088.08	60,131.91	62,546.31	62,964.6	47203.01

Source: Ministry of Commerce and Industry, Government of India.

India's expatriate workers in the GCC countries will continue to form an important link between the two regions. The expatriate workers from India not only constitute the largest workforce in the region, but the GCC has in recent years been the largest source of remittances to India. According to a study, in the 2012-13 financial year they accounted for 37 per cent of the total remitted amount. Remittances from the GCC to India rose from $16.431bn in 2010-11 and $24.382bn in 2011-12, to $24.93 billion in 2012-13.[30] Migration of Indians to the GCC countries for work has occurred mainly since the oil-boom of 1973, as a result of the increased demands for skilled, semi-skilled and unskilled workers increased in the oil sector and other related infrastructure development projects. The trading, transport, fishing and security sectors also became heavily dependent on expatriates. With the growth of the Gulf economies over the decades, multinational companies that undertook extensive development in the infrastructural sector recruited labour from the cheapest sources in Asian countries, and in particular this involved India. According to a report of the Arab Labour Organization on the GCC labour force in 2012, "Egyptians and other Arab workers accounted for only 11 percent, while Indian workers dominated the work force by 52 percent followed by 10 percent Pakistanis."[31] The following figures substantiate the movement of such workforce from India to the GCC countries: in 1975, the total number of Indian migrant workers in the GCC countries was 257,655, rising to 721,000 in 1987; at present, the Indian workforce there is estimated to be around 8 million

6. Weak Political and Strategic Partnership

The success of the bilateral economic relationship, however, has not been translated into a stronger political and strategic partnership. Several factors have hindered the growth of a strong political relationship between India and GCC members, in spite of the strong and growing economic and trade linkages.

India's relationship with Shia-dominant Iran has continued to raise an element of apprehension among the GCC countries. According to a Carnegie study, the GCC governments

> see Iran as a great threat to their regional autonomy, their political stability, and the management of the Israeli- Palestinian struggle. Wariness toward Iran reflects deep historical tensions between Shiites and Sunnis, between Persians and Arabs, and between the revolutionary Iranian republic and the Gulf monarchies.[32]

India's attempt to re-engage Iran is based on its energy security needs, and is also intended to enhance its bilateral trade and help secure connectivity to Afghanistan and Central Asia. Iran's nuclear ambition is deeply frowned upon in the region and, notwithstanding India's opposition to the Iranian nuclear programme at the United Nations, India's desire to build a strong political and economic relationship with Iran has remained a source of irritation for the GCC countries.

Pakistan's religious affinity and close relationship with the GCC countries has also created a divide between India and the GCC. Due to Pakistan's lobbying, India, in spite of being home to 176 million Muslims (the second largest Muslim population in the world behind Indonesia), is largely depicted as an anti-Muslim country. Communal clashes between Hindus and Muslims in India have been exaggerated by Pakistan and put before the GCC countries as a proof. Similarly, on Pakistan's bidding, the GCC has viewed the Kashmir issue through a narrow sectarian prism. Nevertheless, in recent years, there has been a growing realisation among the GCC countries that India is a liberal, secular and progressive country in which Muslims enjoy equal rights and opportunities. They have also realised that whereas India is emerging as a big political, economic and military power in the region and beyond, Pakistan is descending into chaos day by day. Notwithstanding this realisation, Pakistan remains an irritant in the relationship as it still enjoys a close filial relationship with some countries in the Gulf region.

The GCC countries remain excessively dependent on the United States for political and security matters and this has limited their interaction with other powers. Though some countries of the region have started looking towards the Asian powers, such a policy is still in evolution. India has made its mark in the Gulf, but there is still along way to go before it could even be considered as a suitable replacement for the US.

India's close ties with Israel, particularly the Indo-Israeli defence cooperation which began in the1990s, have been resented by the GCC countries - albeit to a much lesser extent. The GCC countries do not recognise Israel as a state and have no diplomatic or economic relations with it, a policy borne out of stated Arab solidarity with the plight of Palestinians living under Israeli occupation. India's toning down of the Palestinian cause has generally been attributed to the growing Indo-Israeli ties. Though India has reiterated its continued and undiluted stand over the issue, skepticism continues among the Gulf countries. However, of late, the Arab states themselves have not taken so strongan anti-Israel stand as before, and Qatar has a record of interaction with Israel. In addition, there are unconfirmed reports of Israeli surveillance equipment reaching the UAE.[33]

7. Areas of Cooperation

In August 2015, Prime Minister Narendra Modi undertook an official visit to the UAE. The visit was hailed as the first to that country by an Indian prime minister in 30 years. During the visit, in a significant development, Modi and the UAE prime minister called on all countries to dismantle terrorist infrastructure where it existed and to bring the perpetrators of terrorism to justice. The significance of this was that it indirectly referred to Pakistan, which India alleges has used terrorism as an instrument of state policy. The two governments also announced that they would institute a security dialogue between their national security advisors so as to buttress cooperation against terrorism, money-laundering and drug trafficking. The visit and the declaration cohere with a range of cooperative measures which India has managed to agree with from the GCC member states over the past couple of years. There is still, however, a wide area where the two countries still need to establish workable cooperative mechanisms.

During the last decade, the strategic environment in the Gulf region has undergone considerable change. Events like the 9/11 terrorist attack, the US offensive in Iraq, the continuing stand-off between the US and Iran over the Iranian nuclear issue, and the Israeli threat to attack Iran, have raised new security issues and shaped the whole strategic environment. It is on such issues that cooperation is now needed.

Terrorism is an important concern, and this is an area where India could engage the GCC. As far as India is concerned, there is evidence that a number of Pakistani and Kashmiri terrorist groups have gained financial support from unofficial sources in the Gulf countries. Militant groups such as Lashkar-e-Toiba (LeT) have obtained financial support from some quarters in Saudi Arabia and from several charity organisations in the wider Gulf. India, being a victim of Islamist terrorism, can work in close cooperation with the GCC in terms of intelligence-sharing and tracking the movement of terrorists, money, arms, etc. In recent years, both the UAE and Saudi Arabia have extradited a number of terrorists to India boosting bilateral counter-terrorism cooperation. Some of these extraditions have indeed taken place amid attempts by Pakistan to declare those terrorists as its own nationals in a bid to prevent them from being sent to India. For example, the 2012 extradition of Syed Zabiuddin Ansari alias Abu Zundal, the LeT terrorist who was one of the plotters of the 2008 Mumbai attack, was delayed by several months after Pakistan pressured the Saudi authorities to stop the process.[34] Such counter-terrorism cooperation between the GCC and India is especially meaningful to India, given India's commitment to controlling the spread of radicalisation among its Muslim youth. The Islamic State phenomenon makes this particularly pertinent today.

Countering maritime terrorism is another area for possible cooperation between India and GCC. Though terrorists have been attacking India mainly by land, the November 2008 Mumbai attacks clearly exposed the weakness of India's maritime security and the possibility of terrorist threat semerging from the sea. Similarly, securing the sea-lanes from pirates is an area of concern for both India and the GCC. In recent years, India and the GCC countries have both been victims of piracy off the Somali coast. A joint effort on the part of the navies of India and the GCC countries to check piracy in the region would be beneficial for both. The primary concerns of India lie in the safety of the oil tankers in the Arabian Sea, the Strait of Hormuz and the Gulf of Aden. India has expressed its interest in undertaking naval exercises with the GCC, both bilaterally and in the wider context of multinational level. Since 2008, the Indian navy has been partnering GCC navies in anti-piracy duties, and it has also played an important role in supporting and training the region's maritime forces. A report states:

> Through defence cooperation MoUs and joint committees on defence cooperation, India has substantially enhanced its exchanges in maritime training, operational exercises, and information sharing with Arab Gulf navies – many of them members of the Indian Ocean Naval Symposium (IONS), an initiative pioneered by the Indian Navy.[35]

Naval exercises have been held with Oman, Saudi Arabia, Bahrain and Kuwait. The fact that piracy concerns most of the BRICS countries could form the starting point for a comprehensive cooperative mechanism between the two organisations.

Narco-trafficking has been a major concern for both India and the GCC. Narcotics produced in Afghanistan make their way to both India and the GCC countries. Even though strict laws and security measures have been in place, drug-trafficking nonetheless takes place in the GCC region. Narcotics are supplied from Afghanistan to India via Pakistan, and to the Gulf via Pakistan, Iran and Iraq. Dubai is the major port of transit for these illicit drugs while Saudi Arabia is emerging as a potential consumer in the region. According to the 2009 International Narcotics Control Strategy Report(INCSR) of the US State Department, Dubai serves as a major regional transportation, financial, and shipping hub for narcotics.[36] Hashish, heroin, and opium shipments originating in Afghanistan, Pakistan and Iran are smuggled in cargo containers via small vessels and powerboats, and/or sent overland via Oman. Most of the cocaine landing in Qatar comes from Latin American countries such as Argentina and Brazil, which criminal groups see as a potentially lucrative drug route.[37] In recent times, the UAE, Oman, Qatar have introduced measures to check and regulate the flow of narcotics into their territories and are devising ways to prohibit their land being used in transit or as a destination for the narcotics. India and the GCC need to undertake a joint effort in this regard to check the flow of drugs into their territories.

Illicit supply of small arms has been another source of concern for both India and the GCC with terrorists and criminal gangs operating in these countries. Identifying the supply routes, breaking into the arms supply networks and finally identifying the receiving groups requires close cooperation, intelligence-sharing and a joint effort at preventing the flow. Money laundering is another concern. This is a problem for a long time and success has eluded both India and the GCC in regulating and putting curbs on it. It has been estimated that the amount of money laundered in the Arab world is about $100 billlion a year, most of it in the Gulf states.[38] The GCC is attractive to money launderers because it is close to both Asia, a narcotics producing region, and to consuming countries in Europe. International airports link it to the US and other regions, and there is a large labour force that can be used to transfer money.

India seeks to be a major world power, thereby making it necessary for it to engage with its extended neighbourhood more productively. The active support of these neighbours would provide India not only the much needed political and diplomatic standing in the world, but also positively change India's image in the rest of the Muslim world. Building a cordial relationship with the GCC would constitute a very useful platform to begin that process. The growing insecurity in the area surrounding India, the Middle East, and the Arabian Sea and Indian Ocean requires a much higher level of cooperation on important issues pertaining to both traditional and non-traditional security threats. An Indian presence that emphasizes stability, economic and military cooperation is of relevance to the GCC. Moreover, India, both on its own as well as a part of BRICS grouping, can act as a "bridging power" in bringing about a constructive dialogue with Iran. The GCC can and should use to its advantage the shared interests between India and the US to further strengthen stability in the region and secure oil transit routes. While India's non-intrusive policy makes it a welcome partner to the GCC, the presence of a huge Indian diaspora which has a favourable reputation for being law-abiding, and the benefits of remittances to the Indian economy, continue to be critical push factors for India's engagement with the GCC.

8. Conclusion

As India rises on the global stage, and as the international power dynamics change, the pattern of alignment it chooses to adopt relative to the West, BRICS and the GCC will be critical to the future of the economies of these regions. Whether India will adopt a cooperative, competitive or bargaining strategy in the formation of its alliances and counter-alliances to secure its interests in Asia, will have a telling effect on its own economy and will also affect and shape its standing in the world.

Notes

1 "Why is South Africa included in the BRICS?", *Economist*, March 29, 2013, accessed June 14, 2015, <http://www.economist.com/blogs/economist-explains/2013/03/economist-explains-why-south-africa-brics>.
2 Sanjay Vijaykumar, "The building of the BRICS bank", *The Hindu*, May 8, 2015, accessed May 10, 2015, <http://www.thehindu.com/business/the-building-of-the-brics-bank/article7214558.ece>.
3 Government of India, "BRICS-A Snapshot", August 2011, accessed December 1, 2015, <http://www.mea.gov.in/Portal/ForeignRelation/brics-august-2011.pdf>.
4 Sashi Tharoor, "The BRICS Summit: A Look at Some of the Issues", *Diplomat*, July 13, 2015, accessed December 12, 2015, <http://www.huffingtonpost.com/shashi-tharoor/brics-summit_b_7769914.html?ir=India&adsSiteOverride=in>.
5 Ibid.
6 BRICS, "India announces first BRICS Bank President", May 11, 2015, accessed May 14, 2015, <http://thebricspost.com/india-announces-first-brics-bank-president/#.VX3TPvmqqko>.
7 BRICS, "BRICS Central Bank experts meet in Turkey to finalise joint Monetary Fund", June 14, 2015, accessed June 14, 2015, <http://thebricspost.com/brics-central-bank-experts-meet-in-turkey-to-finalise-joint-monetary-fund/#.VX7Fp_mqqko>.
8 Government of India, "Agreement on the New Development Bank and the BRICS Contingent Reserve Agreement", February 25, 2015, accessed December 1, 2015, <http://pib.nic.in/newsite/PrintRelease.aspx?relid=115907>.
9 "India announces first BRICS Bank President", op.cit.
10 Jordan Totten, "BRICS New Development Bank Threatens Hegemony Of U.S. Dollar", *Forbes*, December 22, 2014, accessed June 15, 2015, <http://www.forbes.com/sites/realspin/2014/12/22/brics-new-development-bank-threatens-hegemony-of-u-s-dollar/>.
11 "BRICS Summit Opens In Brazil", *Radio Free Europe Radio Library*, July 15, 2014, accessed June 12, 2015, http://www.rferl.org/content/brazil-russia-india-china-south-africa-summit-/25457016.html>.
12 Mark Leibovit, "Putin's Economic Adviser proposes anti-dollar alliance", *WND Weekly*, June 26, 2014, accessed June 12, 2015,<http://www.wnd.com/2014/06/putins-economic-adviser-proposes-anti-dollar-alliance/>.
13 Kevin D. Freeman, "Voice of Russia: BRICS morphing into anti-dollar alliance", *Global Economic Warfare*, July 3, 2014, accessed June 12, 2015, <http://globaleconomicwarfare.com/2014/07/voice-of-russia-brics-morphing-into-anti-dollar-alliance/>:
14 "Half of China's total trade to be settled in yuan by 2020 - HSBC CEO", *Reuters*, March 26, 2015, accessed December 12, 2015, <http://uk.reuters.com/article/uk-china-yuan-offshore-idUKKBN0MM0EL20150326>.
15 Brahma Chellaney, "Sino-India mutual trust deficit continues", *Gulf News*, May 25, 2015, accessed June 15, 2015,<http://gulfnews.com/opinion/thinkers/sino-india-mutual-trust-deficit-continues-1.1521553>.
16 "Sino-Indian trade deficit up 34% to $48 bn in FY15", *Millennium Post*, May 14, 2015, accessed June 12, 2015, <http://www.milleniumpost.in/NewsContent.aspx?NID=114499>.
17 Sashi Tharoor, "The BRICS Summit: A Look at Some of the Issues", op.cit.

18 William Pesek, "BRICs hit a wall", *Live Mint*, June 9, 2015, accessed June 12, 2015, <http://www.livemint.com/Opinion/3spgZixQJx9BG4JfbwjfjK/BRICs-hit-a-wall.html>.

19 "Brazil's inflation rises 6.41 pct in 2014, within official target range", *Reuters*, January 9, 2015, accessed December 2, 2015, http://www.reuters.com/article/brazil-economy-inflation-idUSE6N0QL01920150109.

20 Shishir Asthana, "India's fundamentals best among BRICS nations", *Business Standard*, January 15, 2015, accessed June 16, 2015, <http://www.business-standard.com/article/economy-policy/india-s-fundamentals-best-among-brics-nations-115011500573_1.html>.

21 "Inflation Expected to Reach 11.8-11.9% in Russia for 2015", *Sputnik News*, June 10, 2015, accessed June 14, 2015, <http://sputniknews.com/russia/20150610/1023167765.html>.

22 Shyam Saran, "The perils of China's slowing economy", *Business Standard*, February 10, 2015, accessed December 11, 2015, <http://www.business-standard.com/article/opinion/shyam-saran-the-perils-of-china-s-slowing-economy-115021001664_1.html>.

23 Amy He, "Chinese economy to slow more: World Bank report", *China Daily*, April 14, 2015, accessed June 14, 2015, <http://usa.chinadaily.com.cn/world/2015-04/14/content_20434441.htm>.

24 "Indian economy an 'exception'; to grow 7.2% this fiscal: OECD", *Economic Times*, September 17, 2015, accessed 12 December 2015, <http://articles.economictimes.indiatimes.com/2015-09-17/news/66642293_1_advanced-economies-oecd-global-growth>.

25 Portia Crowe, "India Is The Last BRIC Standing", *Business Insider*, November 28, 2014, accessed December 12, 2015, <http://www.businessinsider.in/India-Is-The-Last-BRIC-Standing/articleshow/45311326.cms>.

26 Ibid.

27 Scott Berg, "Why have the BRICs underperformed?", June 9, 2015, accessed June 13, 2015, <http://www.morningstar.in/posts/33399/why-have-the-brics-underperformed.aspx>.

28 Government of India , 'Gulf Cooperation Council', February 2013, accessed June 12, 2015, <http://www.mea.gov.in/Portal/ForeignRelation/Gulf_Cooperation_Council_MEA_Website.pdf>.

29 Government of India, "Ready Reckoner: Snapshot of India's Oil & Gas data", May 2014, accessed December 12, 2015, <http://petroleum.nic.in/docs/readyrecknor_May14.pdf>.

30 Rebecca Bundhun, "GCC again India's top remittance source", *The National*, December 11, 2013, accessed 12 December 2015, <http://www.thenational.ae/business/industry-insights/economics/gcc-again-indias-top-remittance-source>.

31 "Expat population 'could threaten' GCC security", *Arab News*, October 7, 2012, accessed December 10, 2015, <http://www.arabnews.com/expat-population-%E2%80%98could-threaten%E2%80%99-gcc-security>.

32 George Perkovich, Brian Radzinsky, Jaclyn Tandler, "The Iranian Nuclear Challenge and the GCC", Carnegie Endowment for International Peace, May 31, 2012, accessed June 2, 2015, <http://carnegieendowment.org/2012/05/31/iranian-nuclear-challenge-and-gcc>.

33 Rori Donaghy, "Falcon Eye: The Israeli-installed mass civil surveillance system of Abu Dhabi", *Middle East Eye*, February 28, 2015, accessed June 11, 2015, <http://www.middleeasteye.net/news/uae-israel-surveillance-2104952769>.

34 "Abu Jundal arrest: US squeeze on Pak, Saudis nets gain for India", *Firstpost*, June 26, 2012, accessed December 11, 2015, <http://www.firstpost.com/world/abu-jindal-arrest-us-squeeze-on-pak-saudis-nets-big-gain-for-india-356987.html>.

35 Abhijit Singh, "The Indian Navy's Arabian Gulf Diplomacy", *IDSA*, September 24, 2015, accessed December 9, 2015, <http://www.idsa.in/idsacomments/TheIndianNavysArabianGulfDiplomacy_asingh_240915>. Accessed on 12 December 2015.

36 U.S. Department of State, "International Narcotics Control Strategy Report: Volume 1: Drug and Chemical 0Control", March 2006, accessed December 9, 2015, http://2001-2009.state.gov/p/nea/ci/79192.htm.

37 Salman Siddiqui, "New regional plan sought to curb drug trafficking", *Gulf Times*, September 17, 2013, accessed December 1, 2015, <http://www.gulf-times.com/qatar/178/details/365989/new-regional-plan-sought-to-curb-drug-trafficking>.

38 Ismail A. Odeh, *Anti-Money Laundering and Combating Terrorist Financing for Financial Institutions, (Pennsylvania: Dorrance Publishing, 2010)*,5.

0BRICS, "BRICS Central Bank experts meet in Turkey to finalise joint Monetary Fund", June 14, 2015, <http://thebricspost.com/brics-central-bank-experts-meet-in-turkey-to-finalise-joint-monetary-fund/#.VX7Fp_mqqko>. Accessed June 2015.

Crowe, Portia, "India Is The Last BRIC Standing", *Business Insider*, November 28, 2014, <http://www.businessinsider.in/India-Is-The-Last-BRIC-Standing/articleshow/45311326.cms>. Accessed December 2015.

Government of India, "Agreement on the New Development Bank and the BRICS Contingent Reserve Agreement", February 25, 2015, <http://pib.nic.in/newsite/PrintRelease.aspx?relid=115907>. Accessed December 2015.

Government of India, "BRICS-A Snapshot", August 2011, <http://www.mea.gov.in/Portal/ForeignRelation/brics-august-2011.pdf>. Accessed December 2015.

Government of India , 'Gulf Cooperation Council', February 2013, <http://www.mea.gov.in/Portal/ForeignRelation/Gulf_Cooperation_Council_MEA_Website.pdf>. Accessed June 2015.

Government of India, "Ready Reckoner: Snapshot of India's Oil & Gas data", May 2014, <http://petroleum.nic.in/docs/readyrecknor_May14.pdf>. Accessed December 2015.

Perkovich, George, et al, "The Iranian Nuclear Challenge and the GCC", Carnegie Endowment for International Peace, May 31, 2012, <http://carnegieendowment.org/2012/05/31/iranian-nuclear-challenge-and-gcc>. Accessed June 2015.

Tharoor, Sashi, "The BRICS Summit: A Look at Some of the Issues", *Diplomat*, July 13, 2015,<http://www.huffingtonpost.com/shashi-tharoor/brics-summit_b_7769914.html?ir=India&adsSiteOverride=in>. Accessed December 2015.

Totten, Jordan, "BRICS New Development Bank Threatens Hegemony Of U.S. Dollar", *Forbes*, December 22, 2014, <http://www.forbes.com/sites/realspin/2014/12/22/brics-new-development-bank-threatens-hegemony-of-u-s-dollar/>. Accessed June 2015.

Kevin D., "Voice of Russia: BRICS morphing into anti-dollar alliance", *Global Economic Warfare*, July 3, 2014, accessed June 12, 2015, <http://globaleconomicwarfare.com/2014/07/voice-of-russia-brics-morphing-into-anti-dollar-alliance/>.

8

China's One Belt One Road Initiative and its Strategic Connections with Arab Countries in the Gulf

Tingyi Wang

1. Introduction

This chapter will begin by discussing the purpose, blueprint, visions and development of China's One Belt One Road initiative. The Silk Road Economic Belt and the 21st Century Maritime Silk Road, called the One Belt One Road initiative (OBOR) in short, was initiated by Chinese President Xi Jinping in 2013, accompanied with a Silk Road fund with $ 40 billion and further funding from the Asian Infrastructure Investment Bank (AIIB) to support infrastructural investments in the countries involved in this plan. The idea of One Belt One Road is more than an updated version of the ancient Silk Road strategy of the Han Dynasty or an imitation of Zheng He's fleet of the Ming Dynasty in China's history. It is a geopolitical initiative based on a Eurasian perspective - an Asian-European economic cooperation zone, with Europe at one end and China at the other end. Africa is added into this plan due to its tremendous resources, substantial population, wide market and promising future. The plan remains a somewhat unclear and unspecific conception without an authoritative definition. Considerable debate and discussion about this new Silk Road are still going on inside and outside China.

The chapter will then discuss the challenges that the OBOR plan faces in the Middle East, listing religious and ethnic issues in the area, historical and political challenges, traditional geopolitical alignments, and the lack of experience of Chinese companies. Further it will give supportive information to explain why the Middle East is important to the OBOR.

For the Gulf region, energy cooperation is the dominant aspect of expanding relations between China and the Gulf countries. Based on energy reliance, Sino-Gulf economic relations have broadened dramatically over the past decade, and there is no reason to expect that these fast-growing energy demands and economic connections will reverse in the near future. Even in 2008, some experts predicted that a "New Silk Road" could emerge as a force to be reckoned with economically and perhaps also politically. Some have questioned whether the Gulf region and especially the Arab states in the Gulf (the GCC countries, plus Iraq and Yemen) will be an essential part of this new project, or just an inconsequential fringe area of it. This chapter will explain why these states are important to the plan and how China's connection with the region will extend far beyond the energy trade in the future.

According to the OBOR plan, China intends to link the Gulf to the OBOR network. However with so many competitors and players in this area, questions can be raised about how China will guarantee its interests in the region and at the same time cooperate with the other powers which have interests there. The project may constitute a good opportunity for both China and the Gulf, but it also carries with it many challenges. In seeking to balance its geopolitical and economic interests in the Gulf, China has proceeded cautiously and pragmatically. This is wise, given that China has not been deeply involved with the regions' complicated and muddled politics before. But China can not ignore the unstable situations that may threaten its energy security and leave such a strategic area in turbulence. Many questions arise from this. Without the military strength like US, and still unable to provide security guarantees, by what methods could China protect its New Silk Road project and its growing interests in this region? Is this New Silk Road project a strategic tool which China can use to dominate the region? While the Gulf region will inevitably be part of the plan, based on its geostrategic position in Eurasia and its connections to Africa, does it necessarily follow that China will be more involved in the region as a result? Will Sino-Gulf relations, on the basis of their growing interdependence, go beyond the realm of the purely economic? This chapter will try to answer these questions.

2. What is China's New Silk Road?

The Silk Road Economic Belt (SREB) concept was first introduced by Chinese President Xi Jinping during his visit to Kazakhstan in September 2013. In a speech delivered at Nazarbayev University, Xi proposed that China and Central Asia should cooperate to build a Silk Road Economic Belt[1], in order to make economic ties closer, mutual cooperation deeper, and the development space broader between Eurasian countries.[2] It was the first time the Chinese leadership had mentioned this strategic vision.[3]

In October 2013 President Xi, in a speech to the Indonesian parliament, proposed building a close-knit China-ASEAN community and constructing a 21st Century Maritime Silk Road. Xi also proposed on this occasion the establishment of an Asian Infrastructure Investment Bank (AIIB) to finance infrastructure construction and promote regional interconnectivity and economic integration. The AIIB was set up in 2015 and is believed to have a registered capital of $ 100 billion[45]. In January 2014, when president Xi met with a GCC delegation, he proposed building a Silk Road Economic Belt with West Asian states – including the GCC countries.[6] In November 2014, Xi announced that China would contribute $40 billion to a Silk Road Fund. Xi explained that this fund would focus on the investment and financial support for infrastructure, resources, industrial cooperation, financial cooperation and other projects in countries along the Belt and Road.[7]

Zhao Xijun, professor of Renmin University of China, has described the OBOR as a "long-term macroscopic program of strategic development for the entire state",[8] while Zheng Yongnian, Director of the East Asian Institute of the National University of Singapore, has contended that it will probably make a difference on the geopolitical landscape.[9] Many people, however, still have doubts, remaining skeptical of the real intentions behind the initiative and wondering about its political and security implications. A distinctive element in the project is its intention to "break the connectivity bottleneck" which has seriously hindered development in Asia and many developing countries.

The One Belt One Road Initiative has now become China's major foreign policy goal. Beijing is committed to promoting the initiative economically, politically, militarily and culturally over the next eight to ten years.[10] The Chinese Foreign Minister Wang Yi has stated that the One Belt One Road Initiative is a "public good provided by China".[11]

3. The Blueprint of the New Silk Road

The state-owned news agency Xinhua has published a clear overview of China's vision of the new Silk Road. Just like the ancient Silk Road, this new Silk Road has both land and maritime routes.[12] The land route, the so-called Belt, will start from Xi'an, in central China, stretching to Xinjiang and Central Asia, then heading southwest to Iran, Iraq and Turkey, crossing South Europe and ending at Rotterdam in the Netherlands. The land route will also spread to Russia and the Gulf region according to the plan. The maritime route, the so-called Road, begins in Quanzhou, one of the biggest cities in southeast China, goes through Southeast Asia via the Malacca Strait, crosses the Indian Ocean, goes around the Gulf region, then heads to East Africa in one direction and in another goes into the Mediterranean – with a final stop in Greece before reaching Italy.[13] Some may doubt whether the plan should take in such a vast area, from East Asia to Europe and Africa. The truth is, considering the size of China's current economy (the world's second largest economy by GDP and largest by purchasing power parity, valued at $12.98 trillion and $19.51 trillion respectively)[14], only a broad Eurasia and Africa together could serve the needs of China's economy and enable it to maintain its 7% growth per annum. With Europe's advanced technology and large market from Europe, and Africa's abundant resources and labour power, China may be able to achieve its development goals and build a win-win model for people living along the "New Silk Road".

President Xi paid a state visit to the UK in October 2015[15] and then visited in December of that year.[16] Before Xi's visit to Britain, Chancellor of the Exchequer George Osborne made a noteworthy visit to China. He even embarked on a trip to Xinjiang in northwest China, which no other senior Western politician had done before, with a view to securing construction contracts for British firms. The context for this is clearly the One Belt, One Road initiative and the projects which arise from it.[17] In Xi's foreign visits and action, we see evidence that China is committed to strengthening its relations with Europe and Africa. The OBOR is clearly inherent in China's global ambitions.

Besides taking diplomatic actions, China has also made use of institutional frameworks in moving its ambitious plan forward. The meetings of APEC, the Conference on Interaction and Confidence-Building Measures in Asia (CICA), the China-Arab States Cooperation Forum (CASCF) and many other international fora have been used to explain the meaning and content of the One Belt One Road Initiative.[18]

Economically, Beijing has launched and advanced a number of related economic corridors, and has at the same time committed itself further to the China-ASEAN free zone, the Asia-Pacific free trade zone, and the China-Gulf free trade zones.[19] These measures indicate that China is undergoing a strategic foreign policy transformation, away from the policy of 'keeping a low profile' and towards being 'proactive and enterprising'.[20]

Professor Yan Xuetong, one of the leading international relations scholars in China, has stressed that China's diplomatic policy should not be limited to creating a peaceful environment for economic development. It needs to pay attention to improving its image and expanding friendly relationships. Effectively implementing diplomatic policies to create a harmonious world is critical to China improving its international political role. '[21] In Yan Xuetong's opinion, China's new diplomatic approach should focus on its neighbourhood, such that neighbourhood diplomacy comes to be more important in its overall strategy than the traditional diplomatic emphasis on China-US relations.[22]

Clearly, China's foreign policy is changing: it will in future be more pro-active than over the last three decades and will pay more attention to regional issues. The One Belt and One Road initiative brings China's global ambitions and its regional economic and secure concerns together. But the adjustment of China's foreign policy is not completed yet. It will need a longer time-span to make the plan a reality on the ground, and it remains to be seen whether this movement will make more mistakes than record achievements in the future.

4. What is Behind the Plan?

There are many driving factors and forces behind the OBOR plan. These are covered in the sections which follow.

4.1. Geographic Vision

A greater Eurasian idea seems to be one of the driven factors behind this plan. Eurasia has traditionally been the centre of world power, and a power that dominates "Eurasia" would control two of the world's three main economically productive regions. As Brzezinski has said: once the Eurasia connection was set up, it would automatically attract Africa's attention.[23] However, Brzezinski may only be half-correct. Africa, as the second largest and second most populous continent, would be a vital partner and not simply a follower in this strategic triangle.

The ancient Silk Road symbolized trade and cultural exchange linking Eurasian cultures through history. About 2000 years ago, a Chinese envoy, Zhang Qian, twice traveled to Central Asia.[24] Over the hundreds of years which followed, the trade corridor connecting the different parts of Eurasia extended and expanded. Businessmen brought silk, porcelain, tea and other goods from the eastern end of Eurasia via Central and West Asia to the western end of Eurasia and to Africa. At the same time spices, gold, jewelry and other products were transported through this corridor from West to East. People along the route, of different colours, regions and cultures, traded with and benefited from each other. The Silk Road is in fact a good model of economic and cultural integration and common prosperity.

But in more recent centuries, maritime trade replaced many of the functions of the ancient land corridor. As a proportion of international trade and communications, Eurasian economic and cultural exchanges shrank.[25] Turbulent geopolitical developments in the Middle East, inadequate infrastructure construction along the route, challenges from radical religious movements, deficient government funding and unbalanced economic development were among the negative factors which limited transregional cooperation along what had been the Silk Road.

The One Belt One Road initiative aims to break these barriers, enhance Eurasian land trade, and strengthen economic and cultural integration in the wider region. Whereas the ancient Silk Road emerged as a natural outcome of large- or small-scale market conditions, in the needs of people residing along the Silk Road, the new Road is a planned project undertaken by a political authority.[26]

China's is not the only Silk Road project to have been conceived. The US government launched its new Silk Road Strategy in 2011, aiming to advance the liberalisation of trade, foster economic cooperation, increase trade volume, and establish people-to-people connections between and within South and Central Asia.[27] US Secretary of State Hillary Clinton called for the revitalization of the ancient Silk Road:

> [Let's build] an international web and network of economic and transit connections That means building more rail lines, highways, [and] energy infrastructure, like the proposed pipeline to run from Turkmenistan through Afghanistan through Pakistan into India (TAPI). It means upgrading the facilities at border crossings. And it certainly means removing the bureaucratic barriers and other impediments to the free flow of goods and people. [28]

In 2012 the Minister of Customs and Trade of Turkey, Hayati Yazici, put forward a Turkish "Silk Road Project". This aimed at simplifying and unifying customs formalities and reconstructing the historical Silk Road as a link between European and Asian markets. Yazici stated: "The trade volume of the Silk Road countries has quadrupled in the last decade and there is a noticeable shift in the growth of these countries in contrast to Europe and other regions".[29]

These two other new Silk Road Initiatives, however, can not be compared with China's proposal. The latter is both more ambitious and more pragmatic, given the accompanying AIIB and Silk Fund support. China's new Silk Road carries a diverse range of geopolitical meanings for the Eurasian region. As Xi said, in a speech on November 28, 2014:

> We have advocated the building of a new type of international relations underpinned by win-win cooperation, put forward and followed a policy of upholding justice and pursuing shared interests, and championed a new vision featuring common, comprehensive, cooperative and sustainable security.[30]

4.2. Economic Vision

In proposing this giant new plan, Xi intended to outline a new direction for Chinese trade and investment in the coming few years.[31] Under the depressed conditions in much of the global economy, it is natural for China to turn its attention to the large area to the west of it, where many opportunities exist for Chinese companies to invest and which constitute at the same time a large market for Chinese imports. Countries along the Belt and Road have a significant share of world international trade and cross-border capital flows. They accounts for 23.9% of the world's total exports of goods and services, 22.1% of global imports of goods and services, and 25.7% of FDI inflows.[32] Economies covered by the new Silk Road also have a highly complementary industrial structure and resource endowment. There are economies in the very early stage of industrialisation, such as the Central Asian countries, but also manufacturing economies like Germany and China. As for natural endowment, some countries are rich in oil and gas, especially in the Gulf area.

Some scholars have seen the new Silk Road as an "Iron Silk Road" or an East-West High-Speed Railway Project",[33] in the light of the transportation infrastructure required for the Economic Belt: railways, roads, air transportation and pipelines, etc. The engineering projects pose considerable challenges for China, but also a good opportunity for investment. The New Silk Road, however, is not just intended to be an economic trade route, but the basis for a community with "common interests, fate, and responsibilities." It represents China's visions for an interdependent economic and political community stretching from East Asia to Western Europe. This community will not be a formal political or economic alliance, but rather a collection of states that have common interests and would like to cooperate together.

4.3. Security Vision

Another driver for the new Silk Road project is energy security. In the last three decades, China has enjoyed an average economic growth rate of 10% per year, and its energy needs have grown accordingly.

In the early 2000s, China increased its energy imports from Russia, Central Asia and South America in an attempt to limit its dependency on the Middle East and sub-Saharan Africa This was done for two reasons:. First, the transport of energy stemming from the two latter regions relied on maritime routes, which were sometimes subject to attacks by pirates or administrative delays in the delivery of the supplies. Second, both regions suffer from chronic political instability, which can lead to shortages in provision or the outright cessation of supply. [34] The new Silk Road project would allow China to lock in supply from its new Central Asian energy partners. It would also allow the country to secure and improve supply routes for its energy imports from these states and to mitigate the potential effects of supply cuts from the Middle East, Africa or Russia.

Terrorism is the enemy of all governments and peoples around the world, and the lives, safety and economic conditions of people in the Central and Western Asia regions have long been threatened by terrorism and extremism.[35] The Economic Belt could facilitate arrangements for the countries of the region to join together in anti-terrorism cooperation and information-sharing to fight against the violence of the terrorists. The OBOR may also, in the future, help China build a security framework with the western Asia countries.

5. Challenges of the New Silk Road in the Middle East

The One Belt One Road Initiative is ambitious, and it carries with it considerable challenges.. Four of the main challenges are covered below:

i. Religious and Ethnic Issues: Central Asia, West Asia, North Africa and other regions covered by the Silk Road Economic Belt are cradles of ancient civilisations, where a variety of religious such as Islam and Christianity were born.[36] The countries concerned are faced with complex religious and ethnic issues. China also faces terrorism and extremism in its western provinces, which makes the Chinese government particularly sensitive to these issues. It has to take into account the impact which conflicts between different religions, factions, races and nations may have on the economic development of the area. The ISIS phenomenon – located in the core area of the ancient

Silk Road on the borders of Turkey – provides a bitter example of what can happen. How China will deal with such challenges remains unknown.

ii. Historical Problems and Political Challenges: The Middle East is suffering turbulence in the wake of the 2011 Arab Spring, with the collapse of political systems in several states (Syria, Iraq, Libya and Afghanistan in particular) This has led to external military intervention. There is, moreover, the historical legacy of conflicts in Palestine-Israel and Iraq. The great differences in levels of economic development, social system, religion and culture between these countries create tension, as also do the differences between political systems. For now, China is a friend to almost every state in this region, but for how long will China maintain its friendship with all of them when the geopolitical conflicts between them are so intense? The tensions between Iran and Saudi Arabia pose particular problems for China. China, moreover, gives support to the Bashar al-Assad regime in Syria, which rankles with many countries. If China can not face up to these problems and seek appropriate forms of cooperation (while respecting the differences), the prospects for the Silk Road Economic Belt will not be positive.

iii. Traditional Geopolitics: Significant parts of the New Silk Road are located in areas where three continents border each other. Their inherent strategic importance is complemented by huge reserves of oil and gas.[37] The US, Russia and European countries all have interests in this region. Since World War II, this area has had more wars than any other part of the world. Conflicts stoked by geopolitics pose problems for regional governments. The proposal to build the new Silk Road in this region will inevitably raise the concerns of the powers with established influence there. The Chinese government needs to make clear that the Silk Road Economic Belt aims primarily to promote the economic development and achieve mutual benefits and win-win results along the Road. Enhancing mutual trust among all states with interests in the region is important.

iv. Lack of Experience of Chinese Companies: Although China has one of the largest economies in the world, this does not mean that Chinese companies have the experience needed for successful investment overseas. China's economic take-off started in the 1980s, and most Chinese companies are focused on domestic business. Some Hong Kong and Taiwan corporations do have substantial international business operations, but in general mainland Chinese companies do not. Professor Huang Yiping of Peking University

> warned that "China has become the third-largest direct investing country, but more than half of its deals do not provide financial returns."[38]

Compared to western and Japanese companies, Chinese companies have few connections or experienced employees in the Middle East. They sometimes recruit employees who can speak local languages (such as Arabic, Persian or Turkish) but the number of such people still can not satisfy the expanding demand. It is even harder to find people who are both familiar with the local market and with Chinese business culture. Chinese companies desperately need people who can help introduce them to the local market and build connections with local society and governments.[39]

6. The Importance of the Middle East to the New Silk Road

Trade is central to the growing ties between China and the Middle East. It has increased by more than 600% in the past decade (see the statistics provided in chapter one of this book). Bahrain, Egypt, Iran and Saudi Arabia all import more from China than from any other country. China is also the top destination for exports from a number of countries in this region, principally Iran, Oman and Saudi Arabia. In April 2015, Qatar announced the opening of a clearing bank for transactions in yuan.[40] Nonetheless, the Gulf trade (and in fact, the Middle Eastern trade overall) does not constitute a major part of China's overall global trade. This would change if the New Silk Road is established. The Middle East would then play a bigger role in China's international trade. Middle Eastern countries would effectively constitute a bridge connecting China, Europe and Africa.

With regard to strategic objectives, Zhuang Jianzhong, vice director of Shanghai Jiao Tong University's Center for National Strategy Studies, has stated: "The idea of one belt and one road is based mainly on the economy, but has political and strategic components and implications. It aims for joint development, common prosperity and for energy security, too."[41] Ben Simpfendorfer, chief China economist for the Royal Bank of Scotland, has contended that the Sino-Arab relationship is largely commercial in scope, and that China would continue to defer to the United States if it believed its activities in the Middle East were harming Sino-American relations.[42] It is important to recognize, however, that this region has significance in China's geographic and security visions, as well as its economic vision. China's engagement in the Middle East will nonetheless take a different form than the military-oriented involvement of the US. China will emphasise non-interference in internal affairs and win-win cooperation - principles it has consistently followed in the past decades. As stated by the Chinese Foreign Minister Wang Yi, China will "further enhance policy communication with other countries and expand the convergence of our shared interests and explore possible areas of win-win cooperation," with a principle of "wide consultation, joint contribution and shared benefits."[43] Such an approach requires cooperation and understanding from the Middle Eastern side, without which it would be almost impossible for China to pursue its objectives successfully.

7. The Arab Countries in the Gulf and the OBOR

As China looks west, Arab countries turn east. Currently, China has strategic partnerships with four Arab countries. Two of these are GCC countries, Saudi Arabia and the UAE. [44]

In March 2014, Salman Bin Abdulaziz Al Saud, Saudi Arabia's Defense Minister and Crown Prince at that time, visited Beijing. He was given a warm welcome by Chinese President Xi Jinping, who called Saudi Arabia "China's good friend, brother and partner in the Middle East and Gulf region." The two leaders pledged to "strengthen strategic partnership" between China and Saudi Arabia.[45] Xi Jinping told Salman, "Both sides should take energy cooperation as a pillar and expand partnership in aerospace and new energy to forge closer ties." He also invited Saudi Arabia to join the Silk Road Economic Belt and the Maritime Silk Road.[46] In response, Salman said that "Saudi Arabia is ready to enhance cooperation with China to protect peace, security and stability in the region." According to a statement from the Saudi Press Agency, Salman also stated that "We look forward to China as an international magnet with great political and economic weight to play a prominent role in achieving peace and security in the region".

Another important official visit to China was that of Sheikh Mohammed Bin Zayed Al-Nahyan, crown prince of Abu Dhabi in the United Arab Emirates (UAE) in December 2015. While the visit was taking place, Sultan Ahmed Al Jaber, UAE Minister of State and Chairman of the National Media Council, participated in a press conference where he described China as a country with important influence in the world, saying that the UAE attached great importance to its relations with the country. China and the UAE, he said, are strategic partners whose relationship is built upon the foundations of mutual respect, equality and trust. He welcomed China's Belt and Road initiative and that of the Asian Infrastructure Investment Bank (AIIB). Thanks to the

Beijing International Book Fair and Dubai Week in Beijing, the UAE has had a growing profile in China, and Chinese tourists are expected to visit the UAE in increasing numbers.[47]

China has, furthermore, established a number of "strategic dialogue" mechanisms with the GCC countries, such as the China-GCC Countries Forum on Economic and Trade Cooperation, based in Ningxia. The trade between China and the GCC countries is driven by China's thirst for oil, although it is not limited to this. In 2015 China became the world's biggest importer of crude, half of it—more than 3m barrels a day—from the Middle East.[48] By 2035 China's imports from the region will roughly double again, according to the International Energy Agency,[49] far exceeding those of any other country. Chaoling Feng of Cornell University sees this as "a big shift rather than incremental change."

8. Moving from Energy to the New Silk Road

From the above, the value of connecting the Gulf region to China's One Belt One Road is clear. The Gulf region can play an important role in China's Belt and Road initiative due to its strategic connections with the wider Middle Asia, South Asia, North Africa and the Indian Ocean. The Arab States in the Gulf region, indeed, could form a "crossing point" for the Economic Belt and the Maritime Road. It should be noted that in the Horn of Africa China may be developing a military presence. The Chinese government has confirmed that it has started negotiations with the government of Djibouti for the construction of a new military base there. It will be China's first military installation in Africa. The Chinese Foreign Ministry has said that the base would be used to provide supplies for Chinese warships on escort missions in the Gulf of Aden. [50] As this base will face the Red Sea and the Gulf of Aden, it is believed that it could have many functions in the future. China has already used the port in Djibouti when it withdrew its citizens from Yemen during the Yemen Civil War in 2012 and again in 2015.[51]

On the other side of the Gulf China is, furthermore, developing the China Pakistan Economic Corridor. The corridor is to be integrated into the One Belt One Road initiative, with Gwadar Port constituting an outlet to the Indian Ocean. [52] The strategic location of the port has caught the attention of regional and world powers. Complementing it, Iran's Navy Commander Habibollah Sayyari has said that his country would establish a new naval base in Pasabandar, about 30 kilometers west of Gwadar port, according to reports in the Iranian media.[53] Clearly Gwadar and Djibouti will play vital roles in China's foreign policy and its global strategy in the future. They could be seen as guarantees for China's interests in the region. The Arabian Peninsula, located between these two strategic ports, gains further significance for China in this perspective.

As Africa is far from China, the Gulf is a perfect transportation hub between the two sides for passengers and goods. A country like the UAE is an ideal place for signing business contracts between Chinese and African companies. The legal system of the UAE is well accepted by both sides. Some Chinese businessmen feel that it is too risky to follow the local laws in African countries, believing that local governments would not protect their interests effectively. Substantial quantities of Chinese goods exported to Africa transit via the UAE and other Gulf countries.[54] For the emerging African economies, the GCC and especially the UAE has been a natural hub for trade with Asia and China.

Dragon City in Dubai is a significant symbol of China's tight economic ties with the UAE, providing a focus for more than 200,000 Chinese who live and work in the UAE. Thousands of Chinese work in Dragon City, living in the International City close to it. Those areas resemble a small Chinese town, with elderly Chinese taking care of their grandchildren, and people conversing only in Chinese. Chinese supermarkets and restaurants are everywhere, giving people the feeling that they are living inside China. [55] There are more than 3,000 Chinese companies registered in the UAE, mainly in Dubai but also in Abu Dhabi, Ajman and other emirates.

Since China and the UAE eased bilateral visa regulations in September 2009 and the UAE obtained the Chinese government's "approved destination status", the number of Chinese travellers pouring into the Gulf state mushroomed to over 300,000.[56] Several thousand Chinese students study in the UAE, from the kindergarten level to university. These Chinese students will have unique advantages in fostering linkages between the two sides in the future.

Although energy has been the main driving force in the development of Chinese-GCC economic relations, the future is likely to be fundamentally different. China and the GCC countries are all diversifying their economies and it may be expected that Chinese goods, products and services will gradually challenge those of their Western counterparts. Car brands such as Geely, Cherry, Great Wall and Lifan may become household names, perhaps taking precedence over GM, Chevrolet, Fiat, Opel and Peugeot.[57] China's trade with the GCC countries currently accounts for almost 70 percent of overall Sino-Arab trade and 3 percent of China's global trade. McKinsey forecasts that by 2020, total trade flows between China and the Middle East will mushroom to between $350 billion and $500 billion, with China-

GCC trade accounting for the majority share. Given their energy natural resources, the Middle East in general and the Gulf countries in particular are strategic trade and investment partners for an energy-hungry China.[58]

9. Cooperation between the GCC Countries and China

With China launching its One Belt One Road initiative and indicating that it is seeking to establish strategic relationships with the Gulf states, the GCC countries need to take the opportunity to build a more solid relationship with China. Four main lines of action could be pursued:

i. Taking part in the OBOR plan. By participating in this initiative the GCC states could make use of Chinese capital and experience so as to improve their infrastructural facilities and their connectivity to global trading networks – especially those which open up closer links with the BRICS countries.

ii. Completing the negotiation for the China-GCC Free Trade Agreement. In July 2004, China and the Gulf Cooperation Council (GCC) announced the launch of China-GCC Free Trade Agreement negotiations. The China-GCC Free Trade Agreement has been under discussion ever since then. The two parties have held five rounds of negotiations and have reached agreement on the majority of issues concerning trade in goods, and negotiations on trade in services have been initiated.[59] In the meantime, China has concluded free trade agreements with Korea, Australia and several other countries. In 2014, when Xi met with a delegation from the GCC countries in Beijing, he called for the early signing of the agreement with the GCC, but as yet it remains unsigned.[60] Among other fields, the China-GCC negotiations have looked towards cooperation and joint investment between the Sovereign Wealth Funds of the two sides. Given that together they hold liquid assets in excess of $ 7 trillion mainly invested in Western markets and government securities, cooperative ventures between them could be of great value – leading to wiser investment in financing economic development in Asia/China, the BRICS countries, the Middle East, Africa and other emerging markets where the real returns are promising.[61]

iii. Cooperating in renewable energy. China has emerged as the world's clean energy and clean technology powerhouse. There is the opportunity to develop an industrial partnership between GCC countries and to undertake joint renewable energy research, cooperate in the field of water resource management and build solar power technology and energy capacity.[62] The MENA region has significant potential for the development of solar and wind energy, as also for carbon capture and storage. The GCC countries, moreover, have plentiful resources which they can invest in renewable technology and energy research. China is also developing renewable technology and exploiting sources of renewable energy in the vast territories of its western provinces. Given its geographic and climatic comparative advantage, the GCC could become a global powerhouse in solar energy, based on shared GCC-Chinese technology.

iv. Establishing a regional security framework. Obama's "pivot to Asia" strategy has aimed to balance China's influence in the Asia-Pacific region. There are two key pillars to the strategy which the US is pursuing in this regard: the deployment of more US forces in the Asia-Pacific region, and the implementation of the Trans-Pacific Partnership (TTIP). This means that China will now confront both military and economic challenges from the United States in East Asia. At the same time China has to take account of ongoing conflicts in the Middle East – the region which provides half of its oil imports. China's One Belt One Road initiative may partially balance the impact of the US pivot to Asia, but the security of communications would remain a problem. The GCC may have similar concerns.

With a naval presence in Gwadar and Djibouti, and enjoying good relations with Iran and Pakistan, China could cooperate with the GCC countries in creating a new security framework for the Gulf. While this would be led by the Gulf states themselves, it could bring in (as interested states) not only China but also Pakistan and India, and perhaps Japan and Korea. All these countries have a common security interest in the Gulf, based on their energy needs.

10. The Role of India

India and China are partners in BRICS, but at the same time they have a competitive relationship with each other.[63] The relationship is both complex and dynamic, alternating between periods of tension and times of robust cooperation.[64]

The two countries, nonetheless, are committed as BRICS members to building a multipolar world order.

India is important both to the new Silk Road and to the Arab States in the Gulf. Chinese officials have highlighted the special importance of India, describing it as at the intersection of the overland silk roads and maritime silk routes.[65] India has substantial influence in the Gulf region, both at a governmental level and through the presence of some 8 million India expatriates in the GCC labour force.[66] More than 50% of all the oil consumed by India comes from the Gulf. [67] Like China, India inevitably has security concerns in this region, and it has maritime security arrangement with Oman and Qatar. [68]

The OBOR has clearly raised some apprehensions in India, especially in the light of it being linked to the China-Pakistan Economic Corridor which leads down to the potential naval port of Gwadar. OBOR is seen by some as an appendage to Beijing's supposed "String of Pearls" strategy, which some Indian observers see as an attempt to expand China's influence over an area traditionally dominated by India. It seems unlikely, however, that China, facing challenges from the US and coping with energy security threats emanating from instability in the Middle East, would wish or feel able to contain India.

India, for its part, needs infrastructural investment and financial support. It could, moreover, benefit from the development experience of China. These two countries, the largest developing countries in the world with so many interests in common and so much to lose from conflict, can greatly benefit from cooperation. There is already, in fact, a record of cooperation in the evacuation of their nationals from conflict areas. China rescued more than 600 people from Yemen in 2015, some of whom were Indian. For both China and India, with significant populations living abroad, extricating compatriots from zones of conflict or natural disasters has become a recurring challenge.[69] Between 2006 to 2010, over 6000 Chinese nationals were rescued from areas of unrest, largely in the Middle East. In 2011, nearly 50,000 Chinese had to be evacuated, most of them from Libya.[70] India had to repatriate some 17,000 people from Libya in 2011.

As a member of the BRICS and now a formal member of the Shanghai Cooperation Organization[71], India can both cooperate and compete with China in the Gulf, in the fields of energy security, economic relations, and in helping to shape the regional security framework. This new form of coordination may help to unfold a wider geo-economic transformation in Asia and the Indo-Pacific region.

11. Conclusion

The concept of "One Belt and One Road" was put forward by China in 2013, accompanied with the Asian Infrastructure Investment Bank and $40 billion Silk Road Fund to finance infrastructure construction and promote regional interconnectivity and economic integration. It has become China's national policy and major foreign policy goal since then. One Belt and One Road initiative is a plan that could combine China's global ambition and its regional economic and secure concerns together. It still needs more time to consult with the countries of interest to develop further plans and programs of action.

The former Chinese Middle East envoy, Wu Sike, has stated that:

> ...the Sino-Arab friendship in half a century is just like towering trees with deep roots. The proposal of "One Belt and One Road" has added a nutritional agent for this tree, and makes it to thrive. The Chinese side will always consider the promotion of peace, stability and development in the Middle East as the starting point and foothold of China's Middle East policy.[72]

To give practical effect in the Gulf region to these good intentions, the GCC countries and China need to examine the possibilities for GCC participation in constructing the OBOR project, complete the negotiation of the China-GCC Free Trade Agreement, undertake joint research in renewable energy and high-technology, and work towards developing a regional security framework for the Gulf. India, Pakistan and perhaps other states with strong Gulf interests could also provide support for this new regional security framework. After all, these countries have common energy security interests in the Gulf, hundreds of thousands of expatriates in the area, and growing economic ties with Gulf States. None of them can deal alone with the challenges to come.

Notes

1 "Chronology of China's Belt and Road Initiative", Xinhua Net, March 28, 2015. Accessed May 30, 2015. <http://news.xinhuanet.com/english/2015-03/28/c_134105435.htm>.

2 Silk Road Economic Belt: Prospects and Policy Recommendations, Center for China in the World Economy, Tsinghua University China Economic Net. May 20, 2014.

3 Yang Fuchang, Invigorating Sino-Arab Relations by "One Belt and One Road" Strategy.

4 *Ibid.*

5 "Fifty Countries Sign the Articles of Agreement for the Asian Infrastructure Investment Bank", the website of AIIB, June 29, 2015. Accessed July 28, 2015. <http://www.aiibank.org/html/2015/NEWS_0629/11.html>.

6 *Ibid.*

7 *Ibid.*

8 "One Belt One Road pushes forward China's economy abroad", Xinhua Net, Oct.18, 2014, <http://news.xinhuanet.com/fortune/2014-12/18/c_127314569.htm>. Accessed May 30, 2015.

9 Zheng Yongnian: The 'One Belt and One Road' Policy Will Change the Geopolitical Landscape. March 29, 2015, <http://english.boaoforum.org/hynew/19361.jhtml>. the website of boao forum for 2015 Asia Annual conference.

10 Xue Li and Xu Yanzhou, "How China Can Perfect Its 'Silk Road' Strategy", The Diplomat, April 09, 2015. Accessed May 30, 2015. <http://thediplomat.com/2015/04/how-china-can-perfect-its-silk-road-strategy/>.

11 Wang Yi: 'One Belt and One Road' is public goods provided by China, the website of the Chinese Foreign Ministry, March 23,2015. Accessed May 30, 2015. <http://www.mfa.gov.cn/mfa_chn/zyxw_602251/t1247712.shtml>.

12 "China Focus: Trans-regional customs cooperation furthers Belt and Road Initiative", May 28,2015. Accessed May 30, 2015. <http://news.xinhuanet.com/english/2015-05/28/c_134278782.htm>.

13 *Ibid.*

14 "Report for Selected Countries and Subjects". World Economic Outlook Database, International Monetary Fund. October 2015. Retrieved 20 November 2015.

15 'London set to benefit after rolling out the red carpet for Xi", Roger Blitz, Financial Times, November 30, 2015. Accessed November 30. <http://www.ft.com/intl/cms/s/2/ee7d4fe2-7f14-11e5 -98fb-5a6d4728f74e.html # slide0>.

16 Africa: Chinese President Xi Jinping to Visit Zimbabwe and South Africa, Phyllis Johnson, All Africa, 30 November 2015, <http://allafrica.com/stories/201512020397.html>. Accessed Nov. 30, 2015.

17 Xi Jinping UK visit highlights changing times for Britain, Andrew Jones, 2015/10/20, <http: //gbtimes.com/china/xi-jinpings-uk-visit-highlights-changing-times-britain-us>. Accessed Nov. 30, 2015.

18 Wang Yi: President Xi Jinping's Proposal to Jointly Build the "One Belt One Road" Is a Historic Opportunity Leading the Development of the China-Arab Relations, <http://www.fmprc.gov.cn/mfa_eng/zxxx_662805/t1163558.shtml> 2014/06/05, The Website of Ministry of Foreign Affairs, the People's Republic of China. Accessed May 30, 2015.

19 China Focus: China to advance free trade talks with Arabs, Israel amid Silk Road initiatives March -5-2015 <http://www.npc.gov.cn/englishnpc/Special_12_3/2015-03/05/content_1910012.htm>. The Website of the National People's Congress (NPC) of the People's Republic of China.

20 2014 in Review: A Successful Year for China's Diplomacy Wang Yi No.50, January / February 2015 China International Studies.

21 Yan Xuetong, "The Path for China to Increase its 'Soft Power'", <http://www.thinkinchina.asia/wp-content/uploads/3-ThePathforChinatoIncreaseitsSoftPower.pdf>.

22 Xue Li and Xu Yanzhou, "How China Can Perfect Its 'Silk Road' Strategy, The Diplomat. <http://thediplomat.com/2015/04/how-china-can-perfect-its-silk-road-strategy>.

23 Brzezinski, Zbigniew (2006) The grand chessboard: American primacy and its geostrategic imperatives ([. Repr] ed) New York, NY: Basic Books . p. 31. ISBN 0465027261.

24 Xinru Liu , The Silk Road in World History, Page 7,8,10, 2010 Oxford Express, Inc.

25 *Ibid.*

26 Vladimir Fedorenko,"The new silk road initiatives in Central Aisa", Rethink Paper, August 2013. p. 1

27 "US Support for the New Silk Road", The Website of U.S. Department of State, Accessed May 30, 2015. <http://www.state.gov/p/sca/ci/af/newsilkroad/>.

28 Hillary Clinton," Progress Noted, but Questions Remain Over 'New Silk Road' Initiative, "US Department of State, July 2011. Accessed May 30, 2015. <http://www.state.gov/secretary/rm/2011/07/168840.htm>.

29 Abdullah Bozkurt, "Turkish minister says reviving Silk Road trade route remains Turkey's goal," Today's Zaman, December 2012. Accessed May 30, 2015. <http://www.todayszaman.com/newsDetail_getNewsById.action?newsId=299947>.

30 Michael D. Swaine, "Xi Jinping's Address to the Central Conference on Work Relating to Foreign Affairs: Assessing and Advancing Major Power Diplomacy with Chinese Characteristics", Swaine, China Leadership Monitor, no 46.

31 CKGSB Knowledge, Mapping China's New Silk Road Initiative, APR 8, 2015, <http//www.forbes.com/sites/ckgsb/2015/04/08/mapping-chinas-new-silk-road-initiative/>.

32 Silk Road Economic Belt: Prospects and Policy Recommendations, Center for China in the World Economy, Tsinghua University, China Economic Net May 20, 2014. Accessed May 30,2015.
33 'Iron Silk Road':? Dream Or Reality Selçuk Çolakoğlu and Emre Tunç Sakaoğlu <http://www.eurasiareview.com/27052015-iron-silk-road-dream-or-reality-analysis/>.
34 China's way: the new Silk Road by Camille Brugier, European Union Institute for Security Studies May 2014.
35 *Ibid.*
36 *Ibid.*
37 *Ibid.*
38 Half of China's investment abroad do not provide financial returns. Huang Yiping, Xinlang Net, Dec 21, 2014. <http://news.cnfol.com/huiyihuodong/20141221/19748895.shtml>. Accessed Sep 30, 2015.
39 According to my interviews with managers from branches of Chinese companies and Chinese businessmen in the UAE, Bahrain, Oman, Egypt from Dec 2014 to Jun 2015. And interviews with Businessmen in China in July 2015.
40 *Ibid.*
41 China's 'One Belt, One Road' Strategy, Wendell Minnick, Defence News, April 12, 2015. <http://www.defensenews.com/story/defense/2015/04/11/taiwan-china-one-belt-one-road-strategy/25353561/>.
42 The New Silk Road: The Arab Rediscovery of China, Center for Strategic and International Studies, Middle East Program, September 21, 2009.
43 'One Belt and One Road' to Further Boost the Rise of China, Xu Qinduo, Sohu Net, <http://mt.sohu.com/20150310/n409572016.shtml>.
44 *Ibid.*
45 Saudi Arabia, China's 'Good Friend', by Shannon Tiezzi, the Diplomat, March 14, 2014. <http://thediplomat.com/2014/03/saudi-arabia-chinas-good-friend/>. Accessed May 30, 2015.
46 *Ibid.*
47 This is based on the news and my talks with scholars and diplomats with from China and UAE. I also helped to build connections between Chinese universities and UAE institutes, like the Tsinghua-Masdar Institute cooperation during this visit. See Tsinghua- Masdar cooperation, <https://news.masdar.ac.ae/explore-news/in-the-media/item/8876-masdar-institute-chinese-tsinghua-university-to-research-sustainability-zawya-registration.html>.
48 Sources: EIA, <http://www.eia.gov/beta/international/analysis.cfm?iso=CHN>.
49 *Ibid.*
50 China, Djibouti negotiate over military base, Xinhua Net, Dec 27, 2015. <http://news.xinhuanet.com/english/video/2015-11/27/c_134860423.htm>.
51 *Ibid*
52 "China Pakistan Economic Corridor: Gwadar Port", by Admin, the London Post, September 13, 2015. <http://thelondonpost.net/china-pakistan-economic-corridor-gwadar-port/>.
53 China takes over Gwadar Port, By Xu Tianran, Global Times, Feb 19 2013, <http://www.globaltimes.cn/content/762444.shtml>.
54 Interviews with Chinese businessmen and companies in UAE and Oman. Dec 2014 to May 2015.
55 This is based on the talks with local Chinese in Dubai from Dec 2014 to May 2015.
56 *Ibid.*
57 *Ibid.*
58 *Ibid.*
59 China FTA network, http://fta.mofcom.gov.cn/topic/engcc.shtml.
60 Xi calls for early signing of China-Gulf FTA, By Li Xiaokun and Zhang Fan, China Daily, Jua.18,2014, <http://www.chinadaily.com.cn/china/2014-01/18/content_17242935.htm2014-01-18>.
61 *Ibid.*
62 *Ibid.*
63 China's One Belt One Road Strategy: The New Financial Institutions and India's Options, Ajay Chhibber, National Institute of Public Finance and Policy.
64 India's Perception and Response to China's "One Belt, One Road" Initiative: Views From Indian Mainstream Media, Lucio Blanco Pitlo III, Asian Politics and Policy, <http://xueshu.baidu.com/s?wd=paperuri%3A%281a6faf2c0272b54c579ee7a498c70a61%29&filter=sc_long_sign&tn=SE_xueshusource_2kduw22v&sc_vurl=http%3A%2F%2Fonlinelibrary.wiley.com%2Fdoi%2F10.1111%2Faspp.12214%2Fpdf&ie=utf-8>.

65 Chinese Takeaway: One Belt, One Road, C. Raja Mohan, Indian Express, Aug 13, 2014, <http://indianexpress.com/article/opinion/columns/chinese-takeaway-one-belt-one-road/>.

66 "Saudi Arabia Woos China and India: Middle East Quarterly". Meforum.org. Retrieved 21 November 2009.

67 "India, Gulf share special relationship-Indicators-Economy-News-The Economic Times". <economictimes.indiatimes.com.> 15 January 2008. Retrieved 21 November 2009.

68 "Front Page: Navy foils bid to hijack Indian ship in Gulf of Aden". The Hindu (Chennai, India). 12 November 2008. Retrieved 21 November 2009.

69 Chinese Takeaway: Yemen Evacuation, C. Raja Mohan, April 7, 2015 Indian Express, <http://carnegieendowment.org/2015/04/07/chinese-takeaway-yemen-evacuation>.

70 China impresses with Yemen evacuation, Tim Collard China.org.cn, April 9, 2015.

71 Shanghai Cooperation Organization Admits India and Pakistan. China Briefing, July 11, 2015. <http://www.china-briefing.com/news/2015/07/11/shanghai-cooperation-organization-admits-india-pakistan.html>.

72 China's Special Envoy on the Middle East Issue Wu Sike Gives Exclusive Interview to Al-Arabiya Television, Chinese Embassy in Egypt, July 22, 2014.

References

Davidson, Christopher, "Persian Gulf- Pacific Asia linkages in the 21st century: A marriage of convenience?" (The Centre for the Study of Global Governance), January 2010, Number 7. <http://www.lse.ac.uk/middleEastCentre/kuwait/documents/Davidson%20paper.pdf>. Accessed 30 May 2015.

International Monetary Fund, "Report for Selected Countries and Subjects", in *World Economic Outlook Database 2015*, Accessed 20 November 2015.

Niblock, Tim, "Gulf-Asia Economic Relations: Pan-Gulf and Pan-Asia Perspectives", in Tim Niblock (ed) with Monica Malik, *Asia-Gulf Economic Relations in the 21st Century* (Berlin: Gerlach, 2013).

Pitlo, Lucio Blanco, "India's Perception and Response to China's 'One Belt, One Road' Initiative: Views From Indian Mainstream Media, Asian Politics and Policy", <http://xueshu.baidu.com/s?wd=paperuri%3A%281a6faf2c0272b54c579ee7a498c70a61%29&filter=sc_long_sign&tn=SE_xueshusource_2kduw22v&sc_vurl=http%3A%2F%2Fonlinelibrary.wiley.com%2Fdoi%2F10.1111%2Faspp.12214%2Fpdf&ie=utf-8>. Accessed 30 December, 2015.

Sun, Degang, "Building a New Silk Road: China and the Middle East in the 21st Century", in Degang Sun (ed) with Yahia H. Zoubia (Shanghai: World Affairs Press, 2014).

Yan, Xuetong, *China's National Interest*, (Tianjin: Tianjin Renmin Chubanshe,1997), pp 105-111 and 154-160.

9

In Search of a Strategic Partnership: China-Qatar Energy Cooperation, from 1988 to 2015

Gafar K. Ahmed

1. Introduction

China has clearly become a major force in the international relations arena. With the geopolitical changes at international and regional level, China's foreign policy has expanded from consolidating relations with the established powers such as the US, to strengthening relations with the BRICS, and now to other "emerging powers" such as the GCC countries. This chapter discusses China-Qatar relations in the energy sector from 1988 to 2015, a crucial period when the two countries worked towards establishing a strategic partnership and lifting their bilateral cooperation to a higher level. The process, however, was not always easy. Bilateral relations in fact passed through three distinctive phases. The first phase (1988-2002) featured intensive efforts made by the Qatari side. Energy was the main focus. The Qatar-led initiatives, however, failed to translate over a decade of efforts into a meaningful cooperation. The second phase was from 2002 to 2008, when bilateral relations experienced a major setback as a result of Qatar's failure in the bid to build a liquefied natural gas (LNG) terminal and trunk line project in Guangdong. The main factor accounting for the setback was Qatar's rejection of China's reasons for failing to accept the Qatari bid, namely the instability in the Middle East and the possibility of sabotage in the Malacca Straits. The third phase was from 2008 to 2015 and was characterized by increasing engagement between the two countries' energy companies. Mutual confidence was restored with strong initiatives pursued by the Qatari diplomats in China. China's growing demand for LNG, changes in its assessment of the geopolitical balance in the Gulf, and domestic policies allowing private companies to import LNG from the international market, have all contributed to the establishment of the China-Qatar strategic relationship. Finally, the paper concludes by examining challenges and opportunities facing the development of the relationship today.

It is suggested that Qatar's experience holds lessons for other GCC countries, in terms both of their relations with China specifically and with other BRICS countries generally. The material presented here is based on documents which were accessed at the Qatari embassy in Beijing, as well as some other sources.

2. Exploring the Potential for Cooperation in the Energy Sector (1988-2000)

The year 1993, when China's Deputy Premier Li Lanqing visited the GCC states, has been considered as the beginning of China's efforts towards energy cooperation with these states. At the China-Qatari level, Abdurrahman Al-Attiyah, the Qatari ambassador to France, made contact with his Chinese counterpart in Paris with the aim of exploring the possibility of forging closer relations between the two countries. Diplomatic relations had been established in 1988. The Qatari ambassador observed that his Chinese counterpart enquired closely about the nature of Qatar's exports to the world, the size of its external investments and its oil production.[1]

To demonstrate Qatar's interest in cooperating with China in energy, the Qatar Petroleum Corporation (QP) had already sent a delegation headed by the Director-General to China in 1991. Energy cooperation was duly discussed with Chinese officials.[2] However, the first serious bilateral dialogue on energy at the ministerial levels took place in 1993, when the Qatar foreign minister Sheikh Hamad Al-Thani, made his first visit to China. During the latter's meeting with the Chinese foreign minister, Qian Qichen, the potential for cooperation in energy and investment was discussed.[3] The dialogue continued when China's deputy-premier Li Lanqing visited Qatar in July 1993 to explore energy cooperation opportunities.[4] As a result of these visits, the volume of Qatar's fertilizer and petrochemical exports to China increased.[5] Yet no real breakthrough in overall bilateral cooperation occurred.

Not until the beginning of 1994 did the two countries begin to explore the possibility of cooperation in the gas sector. This was done during the visit of Dr. Jabir Al-Mirri to China in 1994.[6] In October 1994, the two countries signed a memorandum of understanding (MoU), whereby the Qatari Ras Laffan Liquid

Natural Gas Company and the American Wing Group would supply China with 2.5 million tons of LNG every year.[7]

The visit of Qatar's Minister of Energy and Industry Abdullah Bin Hamad Al-Attiyah to China in March 1995 pushed forward the China-Qatar talks on energy cooperation. According to the documents, Al-Attiyah recognized China's future dependence on oil and gas imports and encouraged the Chinese government to explore cooperation possibilities with Qatar in LNG, and the potential for joint investment in the wider energy field. He told the Chinese minister of electrical energy that, "the State of Qatar can supply China with its future needs of LNG." The Chinese Minister responded that,

> At the present, China does not have the capacity to import LNG due to the lack of terminals and other facilities. Yet, importing gas from abroad in the future is a matter of time and Qatar will be one of the states with which we are going to work in this respect.[8]

As a result, a joint China-Qatar committee was established to study China's LNG demands.[9]

Al-Attiyah's visit to China laid the foundations for China-Qatar in the energy cooperation in general, but especially in LNG. Qatari energy companies had recognized the importance of the Chinese LNG market. They believed that the biggest LNG consumption market in history would soon be open for competition. Hence, the Qatari companies accelerated their efforts to enter this promising market, and were successful in obtaining a clear assurance from the Chinese officials that Qatar would be one of its future choices in energy cooperation. Qatar established a joint cooperation mechanism, which was mandated to monitor closely the developments in China's gas market and the growing demand.

Following this visit, the Qatari diplomats in Beijing held intensive efforts in meetings with the Chinese oil and gas companies, as well as with the relevant Chinese government officials, aiming to encourage them to take concrete steps in energy cooperation. The Qatari ambassador to China, Mohammed Abdullah Abdul-Ghani, called upon both the Chinese and Qatari governments to "seek joint investment recipes in the fields of oil and gas."[10] Furthermore, the Qatari diplomat proposed to his home authorities that Qatar should open Consulates-General in Hong Kong and Shanghai as Qatar required more centres in China to monitor oil and gas developments and consumption, as well as to assess the nature and size of petrochemical markets in China and the South-East Asian region.[11]

In April 1999, the state visit to China of the Qatari emir, Sheikh Hamad Bin Khalifa Al Thani, marked the peak of Qatar's interest in cooperating with China in energy at this time. During his visit, important negotiations took place on the possible export of Qatari LNG to China. When meeting with President Jiang Zemin, the emir stressed Qatar's keen interest in reinforcing the energy cooperation and indicated his personal backing for the cooperation and special treatment that China would enjoy. In return, China suggested that Qatar should invest in the LNG terminals needed to prepare for receiving Qatari LNG in the future. The joint statement released at the end of the visit reiterated their recommendation that the relevant bodies in the respective countries should explore cooperation possibilities and achieve consensus and mutual understanding in the LNG sector.[12] Thus, the Qatar emir personally led the diplomatic efforts aimed at reaching a gas cooperation agreement with China.

This was repeated in a message from the emir to President Jiang when the new Qatari ambassador to China, Saleh Abdullah Saleh Al-Bouanin, presented his letter of accreditation to President Jiang. The message stated, "We in the State of Qatar are willing to make the issue of cooperation in the gas sector a tangible reality."[13] In March 2000, the Chinese company SINOPEC and the Qatar Petroleum Company (QAPCO) signed an agreement in which the Qatari company would supply China with 15,000 barrel of crude oil per day, effective from July 2000. This was the first formal contract signed by state-owned companies of the two countries in the energy sector, and was seen as an important and symbolic step.[14]

3. The Guangdong Tender and the Road to Crisis (2000 - 2002)

In September 2000, China made its first official call for bids for the construction of the country's first LNG terminal and the import of around 3,000,000 tons of LNG from abroad. Australia, Iran, Indonesia and Qatar all launched vigorous diplomatic campaigns, which were led by presidents, prime ministers and ministers of energy.[15] Encouraged by the message during the visit of the Qatari Emir to China in 1999, Qatar exerted every effort to win the tender.[16]

Between 2000 and 2002, the Qatari Ambassador met with nearly all the Chinese officials in the energy sector, including Chinese President Jiang Zemin and Premier Zhu Rongji, to express Qatar's strong interest in gas cooperation and its readiness to provide China's LNG demands.[17] The minister of energy also presented several invitations to the relevant Chinese officials, including Deputy-

Premier Zeng Peiyan, who was in charge of the energy sector, and Zhou Shouwei, head of the China National Offshore Oil Corporation (CNOOC). In addition, exporting LNG to China was one of the most important items on the agenda at the first meeting of the Qatar-China joint committee for economic, commercial and technical cooperation.[18][19]

The visit to China of the Qatari prime minister, Sheikh Abdullah Bin Khalifa Al Thani, in April 2001 marked the peak of Qatari diplomacy in securing the bid. Sheikh Abdullah, in discussion with the Chinese president, the prime minister and the president of the Permanent Committee of the National Council of the Chinese People's Conference on Energy Cooperation, conveyed Qatar's hopes of winning the Guandong Tender. When meeting with the Chinese prime minister, Sheikh Abdullah welcomed "a full swing competition between Qatar, Australia and Indonesia", expressing confidence that the Ras Gas Company of Qatar would present the best offer. He hoped that China would "deal with this tender in a transparent manner". Qatar would "do its best to win this tender."[20] The Chinese prime minister promised that China would act transparently, indicating that the winning of the contract by the Qatari company would be based on its competence.[21]

When visiting China in 2001, the Qatari minister of finance, Yusuf Hussein Kamal, also carried a message from the Qatar emir to the Chinese president.[22] In addition to assuring the Chinese side of the Qatari company's readiness for undertaking the contract, it was noted that the company was proposing to purchase four LNG carriers manufactured in China if they won the tender. This would lift China into a new position in manufacturing huge LNG carriers, putting it on a par with South Korea.[23] Qatar would invest about $1.6 billion dollars in manufacturing these LNG carriers in China.[24]

Despite the intensive efforts by the Qatari senior leadership in winning this tender, Qatar did not win it. In August 2002, China officially announced that the Australian Wood Side Petroleum and BHP Billiton Group had won the Guangdong contract, the first gas deal in Chinese history. According to the official newspaper, the Australian companies had granted CNOOC a stake in an Australian gas field. That was achieved by establishing a company for developing the North West Shell gas field.[25]

After the bid, Deputy-Minister of Foreign Affairs Yang Wenzhang met with Abdel Aziz Al-Rumaihi, the Qatari charge d'affaires at the Qatari embassy in Beijing. According to Qatari documents, the Chinese minister explained the rejection of the Qatari bid as follows:

> The distance between Qatar and China. If Qatar was selected, 4 LNG carriers would be needed for transporting the LNGs from Qatar to China. The Middle East region is a hot-spot region full of disturbances. Imports of LNG from Qatar must pass through the Straits of Malacca where continuous events occur. It is also a very crowded channel of ships. As this project is the first of its type, in China, no risks should be taken. The Qatari company presented an offer which is less than what Australia and Indonesia did.[26]

Mr. Yang concluded by hoping that the result would not lead to disappointment in Qatar over its future gas cooperation with China. He assured the Qatari side that bilateral cooperation in this field was a matter of time only[27], and requested the Qatari diplomat to inform the Qatari leadership, especially the emir, of the strong desire of the Chinese leadership to develop gas relations. He also mentioned that thirty Chinese provinces were preparing to act by themselves in importing LNG from abroad.[28]

Despite the assurances of the Chinese officials, Qatari officials were not convinced by the reasons offered after seven years of efforts. This was clearly expressed in a press conference statement by Ibrahim Al-Ibrahimi, the Deputy Chairman of the Board of Directors of the Ras Gas Company and the Chairman of the Gas Marketing Committee:

> We have a bad experience with the Peoples' Republic of China. We applied for two tenders and have complained to the Chinese authorities clearly about the absence of transparency. Based on this experience, we will not apply for any gas tenders unless reforms are made in China's bidding system. This is our policy, not only with China, but with any other countries.[29]

The Qatari leadership sent a letter to Premier Zhu Rongji stating that they were not convinced by the reasons offered by the Chinese side, and that there had been no transparency in the bidding process.

The Qatari side was further discomfited when China compensated Indonesia, which had also lost the bid, by granting an Indonesian company a tender to supply LNG valued at $8.5 billion to Fujian Province. Qatari officials believed that China was compensating all parties which had applied for the tender except for Qatar.

Qatar seems to have decided after this unsuccessful experience to stop cooperating with China in energy. It turned towards Europe and also other East

Asian countries such as Taiwan. In July 2003,[30] the Taiwan Power Company, a Taiwanese state-owned utility, was awarded a contract to supply US$ 8.7 billion worth of Qatari LNG to the island over the next 25 years. Based on the media report, "CPC will supply 1.7 million metric tons a year of LNG from the Ras Laffan ventures."[31]

4. Qatari Diplomacy and the Dismantling of the Crisis

Despite this background, Qatari diplomatic circles in Beijing often said, "cooperation between the two countries, in this sector, is a matter of time." In 2003, the Qatari ambassador to Beijing, Saleh Abdullah Saleh Al-Bouanin, reported to his home authorities that there were several reasons why doors should remain open. First, he said, China's growing demands in the LNG could not be covered by one or two suppliers. Second, China could not ignore a major LNG supplier, like Qatar. Third, China's deputy-minister of foreign affairs had confirmed that it was intended that China would consider Qatar as a priority to work with in the gas sector. Fourth, it was not right to abandon the largest LNG market in history, when Qatar was increasing its gas production and exports. Fifth, based on the ambassador's understanding of China's decision-makers, China was willing where possible to please all its friends. Sixth, China would endeavor to obtain the confidence of Qatar by signing purchase contracts in future, as it did with the other parties. Finally, Qatar could aim to create links of direct bilateral cooperation in the future, avoiding any entry into a tender in the gas sector.[32] However, the authorities and companies in Doha did not respond favourably to the diplomat's call and continued to refuse meeting with Chinese oil delegations between 2002 and 2006.

The Qatari ambassador nonetheless persisted in his attempts at reconciliation. He held more than thirteen meetings in 2003-5 with experts and officials of the Chinese oil companies. He called for the Chinese side to conduct a dialogue and understand the reasons behind the Qatari situation. He did, however, continue to assert that his country's failure to win the bid had no relation to the terms and conditions of free competition over prices and quality. He maintained that China needed to correct the mistake in real terms.

The Chinese also made efforts to resume the dialogue. In February 2004, Zhai Jun, assistant to the Chinese minister of foreign affairs, delivered a written message from Premier Wen Jiabao to Qatari Prime Minister Sheikh Abdullah Al Thani, dealing with gas cooperation.[33] Moreover, a written massage from Chinese

President Hu Jintao to the Qatari emir stated that China would support Qatar's membership of the WTO, and that China would consider LNG and related products as environmental commodities.[34] Chinese oil companies were clearly having some influence on the decision-makers.

In response to a proposal by the Qatari ambassador in Beijing, the president of CNOOC, Fu Chengyu, visited Qatar in July 2004 to resume the bilateral energy cooperation dialogue. The Chinese side made proposals for the import of Qatari gas but, despite support from the Qatari ambassador, no formal response came from Qatar at this stage The ambassador almost lost hope in March 2005 in finding a solution. In a letter to his ministry, he stated: "Despite the continuous dialogue with the Chinese officials regarding the bilateral cooperation in the gas sector, no progress has been made in this sector. During the same period, China had signed a new agreement with Indonesia."[35] The crisis continued.

In the course of 2005, however, the Chinese oil companies began putting forward draft agreements, to be concluded through bilateral dialogue and not through the bids and tenders system. There was, moreover, competition between the companies in seeking such agreements.

In December 2005, the crisis began to come to an end. The Qatari ministry of energy and industry directed the ministry of foreign affairs to deliver a message to the Chinese National Development and Reform Commission (NDRC), stating that Qatar had a strong interest in supplying China with clean energy and oil exports.[36] It seems that Qatar was now prepared to look into the possibility of transferring to China some shipments of LNG which had previously been directed to North American markets.[37] The Qatari minister of energy was therefore giving a green light to the officials concerned to resume the dialogue with China.

5. Road to a Strategic Partnership in the Energy Sector (2008 - 2015)

All the relevant officials and departments on both sides now started to prepare a new round of confidence-building between the two countries. Encouraged by the new development, the Chinese Petro-Chemical International Company (PIC) in April 2006 presented the draft of a heads of agreement (HoA) to the Qatar Liquid Gas Company (QLGC). It covered the purchase of 5-8 million tons of LNG per year from 2010. QLGC would be invited to cooperate with PIC in exploring marketing opportunities in China. Equally significant was the provision that Qatar Petroleum (the majority shareholder in QLGC) would welcome PIC's participation in bids to explore and subsequently develop oil and gas in Qatar.[38]

It was envisaged that the two companies would work together in opening up an exploration area (block 3 offshore) in the north of Qatar.[39] This was the first time that Qatar had invited Chinese companies to bid for the exploration and production of oil in Qatar.

Qatar's First Deputy Prime Minister and the Minister of Foreign Affairs, Sheikh Hamad Bin Jasim Bin Gabr Al Thani, visited China in February 2007. This visit was perceived by the Chinese side as ending the crisis for good.. The Qatari delegation met with nearly all the executive leaders of the Chinese oil companies, and relevant officials in the NDRC and in investment and financial institutions. Sheikh Hamad urged the Chinese leaders to look to the future, calling for strategic bilateral cooperation in the energy sector, at home and abroad. Thus all the Chinese officials Sheikh Hamad met with were made aware that the issue of establishing strategic energy cooperation was on the agenda. Agreements were also inked with CNOOC and CNPC in the gas sector. This was the first time that Qatar had shown a desire for close collaboration with CNOOC.[40]

Consequently, a significant number of agreements were signed between the two countries following Sheikh Hamad's visit. They can be seen as steps towards establishing a strategic partnership in the energy sector.[41] Sheikh Hamad visited China again in April 2008 and some important sales and purchase agreements for millions of tons of Qatari LNG were signed. There was also a memorandum of understanding between Qatar Petroleum International (QPI) and CNPC to enhance and enlarge strategic cooperation.[42]

For the first time since the establishment of diplomatic relations in 1988, the leaders of the two countries were now describing the relations between Qatar and China as strategic. The Qatari prime minister confirmed that it aimed to develop China-Qatar relation to a new high level when he met with President Hu Jintao during his April 2008 visit. He stated: "We are intending to establish and build strategic relations between the two countries." He also said that the two countries had established an action plan towards creating a strategic partnership.

China had called for a long-term bilateral partnership in energy between the two countries since 2005.[43] It is significant that the two countries were beginning to discuss the possibility of Chinese-Qatari investments in the energy sector outside of China, such as in building transcontinental cooperation between Russia, Qatar and Iran if the international conditions permitted.[44] Meanwhile, the Qatari prime minister confirmed that Qatar was studying prospects for investing $50 billion in China over the coming decade.[45] The visit had clearly laid the basis for a lucrative strategic partnership in energy between the world's largest LNG producing country and the world's largest LNG consuming market.

Against this background, the then Chinese Vice-President, Xi Jinping, visited Qatar in June 2008. Once again, he called for building "a long-term partnership in the energy sector to enhance (our) direction and build comprehensive strategic relations."[46] A number of new MoUs and HoAs were signed.[47]

The years 2009 and 2010 saw further progress in bilateral cooperation. Both sides were committed to establishing a strategic energy partnership and finding solutions to outstanding difficulties.[48] CNOOC established its first office in the Middle East in Doha in March 2009, and Qatar Gas opened an office in Beijing in November of that year.[49] Qatar's first LNG shipment finally arrived at Shenzhen's Dapping terminal on 19 October 2009. Abdulla Abdulrahman Al-Muftah, then ambassador of Qatar to China, described this as "a crucial moment in the history of trade and economic exchange between the two countries, and an important turning point in the nature of bilateral relations.[50] Less than one month later, Abdullah Bin Hamad Al-Attiyah, the Qatari deputy prime minister and minister of energy and industry visited China. On this occasion Qatar Gas signed two MOUs with CNOOC and the Petro-China Company (a subsidiary of the China National Petroleum Corporation) for the supply of an addition 7 million tons of LNG in November 2009.[51] Despite all the encouraging signs, the MoUs signed with CNOOC and Petro-China for supplying the Chinese companies with an additional 7 million tons of LNG have never been effected. The Chinese companies have continued to push the Qatari companies to offer lower prices for LNG imports, and have asked the Qataris to be more flexible.[52]

In May 2010 the two countries signed an MoU on investment and energy, to the effect that they would jointly invest $20 billion in energy and related infrastructural projects.[53] Furthermore, the emerging strategic partnership in energy was beginning to enter a new core area. Qatar had previously forbidden any international companies to exploit their deep offshore gas reserves. CNOOC became the first foreign firm to explore Qatar's deep offshore gas reserves. In August 2009, CNOOC and QP had inked an exploration production sharing agreement (EPSA) in Doha. According to the agreement, CNOOC would invest about $100 million to drill three wells in Block B/C, which covers 5,649 square km off the east coast of Qatar. The EPSA would be valid for 25 years.[54] A similar agreement was signed with the Petro-China Company for Block D in May 2010.[55]

6. Future of Energy Relations: Private Sector Entering The Gas Import Market

Three important developments since 2014 should be noted. First, when Sheikh Tamim Bin Hamad al-Thani, the Qatari emir, visited China in November 2014, a joint Declaration on the Establishment of a China-Qatar Strategic Partnership was released. During the visit President Xi stated that "China is willing to establish a long-term stable energy partnership with Qatar, and boost cooperation and investment in infrastructure, telecommunications and finance as well as joint investment in third countries". There would be comprehensive strategic cooperation in the LNG sector. He also called on the two militaries to "enhance communication and cooperation in security, law enforcement and counterterrorism measures". He described the outcome of the visit as involving a decision to "upgrade our bilateral ties to a strategic relationship", and said that China supported Qatar's sovereignty and its efforts to safeguard its national security and stability. China would support Qatar in playing a "unique role in regional affairs".[56] In practice, the visit of the Qatari Emir to China made no major breakthrough in new gas deals due to differences in the gas price mentioned earlier. It did, however, demonstrate the full support of the two leaders to bilateral cooperation in gas.

Second, a further significant development has been the shift in Chinese government policy on the private sector's involvement in LNG importing rights. Private operators can now play a part in this. China's NDRC in 2014 issued guidelines encouraging the private sector to invest in LNG and natural gas infrastructure and opening the existing LNG terminals owned by the three state oil companies to use by private companies. It is also possible that the central authorities may delegate the approval rights for LNG imports to the local authorities. This new policy of allowing private companies to import LNG from the spot market has provided new opportunities for Qatar Gas, which in October 2014 sold its first cargo of 64,000 cubic metres of LNG to the Jovo Group, a private energy firm based in Guangdong.[57] Khalid Bin Khalifa Al-Thani, Qatar Gas CEO commented on this development, "(T)his delivery will undoubtedly encourage other potential independent players both in China and across the world to consider Qatar Gas as a reliable source of LNG no matter how big or small their operations are."[58]According to an industry source, Qatar Gas is currently negotiating LNG deals with some other private Chinese companies.

Third, the One Belt One Road Initiative (OBOR) has provided new opportunities, especially in the energy sector. The Qatari authorities signed an

MoU with the NDRC at the time of the November 2014 visit, entitled Qatar-China Joint Promotion of Related Cooperation on the One Belt One Road". Article 2 of the MoU called for the two sides, within the context of the OBOR, to "enhance substantial cooperation of mutual benefits as well as mutual cooperation and exchange of industrial investment, economic and trade cooperation, key project construction, finance, energy, energy conservation and environmental protection."[59]

7. Challenges

Qatar joined the Asian Infrastructure Investment Bank (AIIB) as a founding member in 2014, and the Conference on Interaction and Confidence-Building Measures in Asia (CICA) Conference in the same year, notwithstanding strong US disapproval of both institutions. Qatar has, moreover, established the first RMB clearing centre in the MENA region, enhancing Doha's position as a major regional financial centre.

Despite the positive developments, however, there are three factors which pose challenges to the Qatari energy industry in developing its engagement in China. These are the availability of Russian gas supplies, the development of shale gas in the US, and the return of Iran to the energy market. Chinese scholars also mention the security situation in the Middle East as a possible challenge.

Yet, the major challenge facing China-Qatar relations, as well as GCC-China relations in general, is the impact of China-US relations on the GCC's relations with Beijing. In fact, ever since China started to secure stable energy supplies in the early 1990s, Chinese bureaucrats and researchers have been cautious about over-dependency on the Middle East and the Arab Gulf States. This stems from the Chinese assessment that the US enjoys a monopoly position over decision-making process in the region, and concerns over the increasing US political influence in the Middle East Western companies are seen as having a hegemonic position on energy-related investment in the GCC states.[60] The exclusion of Qatar from the Guangdong tender was deemed by some outside observers to be linked to the strategic cooperation between Doha and Washington. Several Chinese officials made it clear that the instability in the Middle East region weakened Qatar's bid to win the tender. Recently, some Chinese scholars have accused the US and some Arab Gulf countries of supporting the Arab uprisings of 2011 and 2012, leading to instability in the region.

As the tensions between the US and China increase in the Pacific and worldwide, anti-US sentiment is again making itself felt in China's decision-making circles. An increasing number of Chinese scholars are questioning their leaders about the nature and limits of China's relations with some countries in the Gulf region, such as Qatar and Saudi Arabia. The possibility of developing real strategic political and economic cooperation between Qatar and China may be difficult despite strong political will on the Qatari side. The Joint Declaration on the Establishment of a China-Qatar Stratigic Partnersship that Doha has signed with China on November 2014 has demonstrated, however, that Doha is determined to pursue an independent foreign policy.

With regard to the wider field of relations between GCC and BRICS countries, it is suggested that the Qatari experience shows the value of building long-term strategic relations in those economic fields which are significant to both sides. These can then form the basis of a wider strategic relationship or partnership which encompasses a fully-fledged political, economic and perhaps military strategic partnership.

Notes

1 Source: Conversation between the writer and the Undersecretary of the Ministry of Foreign Affairs, Qatar (Former Qatari Ambassador to France – Abdurrahman Bin Hamad Alattiya).

2 Gafar Karar Ahmed (2004), *Oil and Petrochemicals Industries in China and Their Implications for Sino-Arab Relations*, Cairo University, *Asian Monograph*, Issue no. 54, Feb, 2004, p.30.

3 Embassy Archive: Minutes of Meeting between H.E. Hamad Bin Jabr Al-Thani, Minister of Foreign Affairs, Qatar, and H.E. Qian Qichen, Deputy President of the Council of State and Minister of Foreign Affairs of the People Republic of China, Beijing 8 April 1993.

4 See: Gafar Karar Ahmed (2005), 'Relations Between China and the Arab Gulf States in the Oil Sector, the Present situation and the Challenges', in *Journal of Strategic Studies*, Bahrain, Vol, 1 No,2, December 2005.

5 Gafar Karar Ahmed (2004), *Oil and Petrochemicals Industries in China and Their Implications for Sino-Arab Relations*, Cairo University, *Asian Monograph*, Issue no. 54, Feb, 2004, p30.

6 Embassy Archive: Letter No: 2/2113-85 dated 13 April 1995, Subject: The Coming Visit of Minister of Energy and Industry to China 27/3-1-4/1995.

7 Embassy Archive: Letter from Qatari Ambassador Mohamed Abdulla Al Abdul Ghani to the Ministry of the Foreign Affairs of Qatar, Subject: A Comprehensive Report On the Current Economic and Political Situation in the People's Republic of China, and China-Arab Gulf States Relations with Special Emphasis On the Qatar–China Relations, April 1999, p. 21. See also: Embassy Archive: Abdel Razzaq Abdul Jalil Al Abdul Ghani, The Counsellor, Report to Ministry of Foreign Affairs of Qatar, Subject: General Remarks and Recommendations about my period of work in China, 18 December 1993 – 15 September1996, Embassy of The State of Qatar, Beijing.

8 Embassy Archive: dated on 13 April 1995, Subject: The Visit of Minister of Energy and Industry to China.

9 *Ibid.*

10 Embassy Archive: The Final Full Report of the Term of H.E. Ambassador Mohamed Abdulla Al Abdul Ghani, Ambassador of Qatar to China, December 1995-1999.

11 *Ibid.*

12 See: The Joint Press Statement between The People's Republic of China, and The State of Qatar On the Occasion of the Visit of H.H the Emir of The State of Qatar to Beijing on 9 April 1999.

13 Embassy Archive: Letter No 2/2/113-54 dated 6 December1999, Subject: Presenting My Credentials Papers to the Chinese President.

14 Embassy Archive: Letter from Zhang Jixing, Deputy Director General SINOPEC, Foreign Affairs Bureau, Addressed to H.E Saleh Buainien, the Ambassador on 11 July 2000.

15 For more information on the background of the competition of Guangdong gas project, See: Gaafar Karar Ahmed (2005), *Sino-Arab Relations in the Gas Sector*, Bahrain Centre for Studies and Research, published in Manama, January 2005, pp.15-48.

16 *Ibid.*

17 Embassy Archive: The Annual Reports of the Bilateral Relations between Qatar and China, No 2/3/3- 1994 dated 19 February 2001. See also the Annual Report No 2/3/15, dated 8 February 2002.

18 Embassy Archive: Minutes of the First Session Meeting of the Joint Committee for Technical, Economic and Commercial Committee between The State of Qatar and China, Beijing 10-13/7/2000.

19 Embassy Archive: Letter No. 2/3/15-650 dated 20 November 2000. Subject: The Visit of Minister of Energy and Industry to China (29/10-1/11/2000).

20 Embassy Archive: Minutes of The Official Talks between H.H. Sheikh Abdalla Bin Khalifa Al Thani, Prime Minister, and Premier Zhu Rongji on 2 April 2001. See also: Embassy Archive Letter NO. 2/3/15-255 dated 17/4/2001, Subject: the Visit of H.H. Sheikh Abdallah Bin Khalifa Al-Thani, the Qatari Prime Minister to China.

21 *Ibid.*

22 Embassy Archive: The Annual Reports of the Bilateral Relations between Qatar and China, No 2/3/3- 1994 dated 19 Feb 2001.

23 According to an informed source in the gas industry.

24 *Ibid.*

25 *People's Daily*, August 9 2003.

26 For more information, refer to Li Weijian (2000), "Middle East Oil and the Chinese Energy Security". *Al-Arab Magazine*, issued by the Arab League Office, Beijing, issue No (35) November- December 2000 (p.45), and Dong Fang Xiao (2000), "New Millennium Retrospection: Geopolitical Changes in the Western Region and Oil Security of China", a paper presented at the Globalization and the MENA Region Symposium.(November 2000, Beijing) p.10.

27 Embassy Archive: Letter dated 7 August 2002, Subject: Chinese leadership Apologizes for not Choosing Qatar as an Importer of Gas.

28 *Ibid.*

29 *Al-Raya* Daily Newspaper (Qatar), Nov. 6, 2003.

30 For more information on the background of the competition of Guangdong gas project, see: Gaafar Karar Ahmed (2005), *Sino-Arab Relations in the Gas Sector*, Bahrain Centre for Studies and Research, published in Manama, January 2005, pp.15-48.

31 *International Herald Tribune*, 7 July 2003.

32 Embassy Archive: Letter No. 94-15/3/2/ dated 4 March 2003. The Annual Report of the Embassy for the Year 2002 and The Annual Report of the Work of the Embassy for the Year 2003, p.23.

33 *Ibid.* p.4.

34 *Ibid*, p.6

35 Embassy Archive: Letter No. 2/3/15/ - 96 dated 14 March 2005; Subject: The Annual Report for 2004, p.9.

36 Embassy Archive: A Note from the Office of the Second Deputy of the Prime Minister and the Minister of Energy, to the Director of the Asian and African Affairs Department, Ministry of Foreign Affairs. No. 1032/2 3/2005, dated 11 February 2005.

37 According to an informed source in Qatar energy sector.

38 Embassy Archive: Letter No. Qatar / Liu / 20060040, dated 4 April 2006 from Liu Zhang Qiu, Vice President of Petro – China International Company to Mr. Abdulla Al-Muuftah, the Ambassador. See also: Draft of Heads of Agreement (HOA) between Qatar Liquid Gas Company and Petro- China International Company.

39 Embassy Archive: Letter from Nassir K. Jaidah, Director of Oil and Gas Ventures, Qatar Petroleum, to Chen Geng, President of Petro-China International dated 24 May 2006. Subject: Invitation for SPSA on Block 3 Qatar.

40 Embassy Archive: Letter No.5/77100/70/2007/ dated on 28 Jan 2007, Subject: The Visit of the First Deputy of the Prime Minister to China. See also: Embassy Archive: Letter No. 5/510/00510/7/2007 dated on 26 February 2007.

41 Qatar announced, in February 2008, that the French Company Total is in partnership with QP on Qatar Gas 2 project on transferring LNG from other markets to China for CNOOC.
42 Embassy Archive: Minutes of the Meetings of H.E Sheikh Hamad Bin Jasim Bin Jabir Al-Thani, with Premier Wen Jiabao on 10 April 2008, and the President Hu Jintao on 11 April 2008.
43 *Ibid.*
44 *Ibid.*
45 *Ibid.*
46 Embassy Archive: Minutes of The Official Negotiations between H.H. The Crown Prince of the State of Qatar and Mr. Jang Ping, Deputy President of The People's Republic of China at Doha, dated 23 June 2008.
47 Embassy Archive: The Agreements signed between Qatar and China during the Visit of Che Jing, Deputy President of China to Doha, 23-24 June 2008.
48 Documents archived in Embassy of the State of Qatar, Beijing.
49 People's Daily, March 7, 2009, See also, *Al-Sharg* newspaper (Qatar) February 9, 2009.
50 *Al-Watan* Qatar newspaper, 14 November 2009.
51 Press release, Qatar Gas to increase LNG supplies to Petro-China, Beijing / China, 13 November 2009. See also Deputy Prime Minister and Minister of Energy and Industry Qatar Address on 13th November 2009 Penning Ceremony of Qatar Gas- China Representative Office.
52 The writer'sr's interview with a Qatari official in the gas industry at Beijing on 15 April 2015.
53 The Qatar newspaper, *Al-sharag* 13 May 2010. See: also, New China News Agency (Xinhua 12/5/2010, Qatar News Agency on 12 May 2010, and People's Daily Online on 12 May 2010.
54 See Oil Daily Online, 2 September, 2009; *Al-Sharq Al-Awsat* newspaper (Qatar) 2 September 2009 and <http:// press.mofa.gov/news>.
55 <www.shell.com/hom/content /investor/news.Qatar>, Petroleum, Petro-China and Shell signed a new EPSA, on 6 May 2010. See also www.rigzone.com/newsop.Shell.Petro-China join Forces in Qatar Block D.
56 Source: <http://english.peopledaily.com.cn>, accessed on 26 May 2014.
57 <https://www.qatar>, gas.com/English, 26 October 2014.
58 *Ibid.* For more information on the new role of the Chines private firms in energy sector, see: *South China Morning Post* ,19.4.2015, Jing Yang, Opportunities Emerge for Private Firms to Enter China's LNG Market.
59 Embassy Archive: The MOU on Qatar China Joint Promotion of the Related Cooperation of The Silk Road Economic Belt And Maritime Silk Road Between Ministry of Foreign Affairs of The State of Qatar and National Development and Reform Commission of The People's Republic of China, 3 November 2014.
60 Gafar Karar Ahmed (2005), 'China Relations with the Middle East and North Africa', in *International Review*, Shanghai Institutes for International Studies, Autumn 2005, Volume 40, p.98.

Note: There is no bibliography to this chapter, as the materials used are mainly those accessed by the writer at the Qatar Embassy in Beijing, or the writer's other articles based on the same source.

10

A GCC-China Security "Strategic Partnership": Its Potential and Contours[1]

Imad Mansour

1. Introduction

The search for security by Gulf Cooperation Council (GCC) states makes them interested not only in global options with their traditional allies but also in other potential opportunities, such as an engagement with China. Seeking options, of course, does not assume abandoning established ties, nor does it assume major power confrontation over involvement in Gulf politics. Rather, it aims to minimize GCC vulnerabilities that have the potential to emerge from a lack of alliance options. It is timely, therefore, to ponder the potential China has to contribute to the security of the GCC. China-GCC relations have been growing steadily, especially in this decade. Formal relations, which are mostly bilaterally-structured between individual GCC states and China, are mostly focused on the realms of economy and trade. Discussions of military and security relations are underdeveloped; nevertheless, in the past few years, the phrase 'strategic partnership' has been used by both sides to signal interests in something more than the purely economic. Such discussions come at a time when GCC leaders are trying to grasp the full long-term implications of America's global politics vis-à-vis China and other major powers, its 'pivot to Asia', as well as its Gulf policies (especially towards Iran). Moreover, discussions about GCC-China ties are occurring in the midst of an increase in China's global political profile.[2] Questions which arise from this are: Can China be a security partner, and how? And what would a 'strategic partnership' entail? Asking if China is a viable security partner for GCC states has two dimensions: GCC security preferences and perceptions of what could China offer, and Chinese willingness and capacity to be a partner. This chapter is dedicated to interrogating the former.

In trying to think through the potential for GCC-China security ties and the shape they can take, the chapter starts with an investigation of how the relationship has been understood in official communications from the GCC side; it tries to unpack the many meanings of a "strategic partnership." After which it investigates security issues of concern to the GCC and tries to see how GCC decision makers see China's position on them. Building on the understanding that geographic proximity correlates positively with security concerns/threats, the chapter looks at three "geographic dimensions" in identifying such security issues: the GCC neighborhood, the Middle East, and the global system. The writer then examines what China's position has been in regards to these concerns with the aim of understanding where mutual grounds and compatible preferences exist on which further security ties could be built.

Four preliminary findings can be summarized.[3] First, political and security-related coordination lags behind trade and business deals. Second, China and the GCC states have interests in securing energy and trade routes such as in the Indian Ocean, Gulf of Aden, the Arabian Gulf, and the Red Sea; here the GCC seems to be interested in more Chinese initiatives in security-seeking. Third, China and the GCC have incompatibilities on issues such as intra-Gulf relations, Iran, Israel, and overall partisan support. Fourth, the GCC states and China assess their options towards each other on the backdrop of a complex canvas of ties both have with the United States; GCC states see a strategic partnership in the security field as a long-term commitment, not as a transaction. Thus, while tactical changes in China-GCC relations are occurring, a strategic shift does not appear in the making.

2. The Meanings of 'Strategic Partnership'[4]

A buzz phrase is being increasingly used by GCC diplomats: "strategic partnership with China." During a March 14th 2014 visit to Beijing, Saudi Arabia's (then) Crown Prince Salman announced that "we are witnessing the transformation of the relationship with China to one of strategic partnership with broad dimensions to what would serve the benefits of both our countries."[5] Using the term "strategic partner" seems to mean that GCC leaders perceive the relationship with China to merit long-term investments and an upgrading of what it currently is.

2.1. A 'Strategic Partnership' in Trade and Business Exchanges

Trade and business dimensions in GCC-China relations have flourished in the past decade, and promise to continue to expand. Such ties have been largely bilateral between GCC member states and China without elaborate official institutional multilateral frameworks. For example, the First China – GCC Business Forum (an attempt to collectively interact with China) was held in Bahrain on March 23rd 2010, but no second forum has been convened.[6] China is the second largest oil consumer in the world after the United States, and the third importer after the United States and Japan. The GCC states have the largest confirmed oil reserves. GCC trade with China sits at around 166 billion USD in 2015, representing far more than half of the total volume of trade between China and Arab states.[7] China and the GCC states have sought to create a free trade zone for the near future, and proposed plans to build strategic oil stocks and build refineries through business partnerships and political cooperation.[8] Difficulties have faced the forging of a GCC-China free trade agreement, especially with regard to the issue of access for Gulf petrochemicals, and disharmony over the parties' general preferences.[9]

Nevertheless, GCC decision-makers view the potential of closer economic relations with China positively. Abdel Aziz Aluwaisheg, the GCC assistant secretary-general for negotiations and strategic dialogue, notes that:

> over the past few years, China has negotiated free trade agreements with its neighbors and far-away partners, including Japan, Korea, and Australia, in addition to the ASEAN group and Pacific Rim countries. Although China is somewhat of a late believer in free trade, now it appears to be eager to engage in free trade agreements with most of its key partners, recognizing that is the way to the future.[10]

However, GCC states are – in comparison – more vulnerable to China's economic policies than are the other states mentioned. Trade talks stalled in early 2009 mainly due to China's protectionist inclinations. To favour local companies, China refused to end import tariffs on Gulf-produced petrochemicals, and thus the GCC halted the talks until further notice; talks resumed in 2014 with the third round of negotiations.[11] It may be that GCC states were uneasy about a variety of Chinese policies at that time, and it is certainly true that there were tensions between China and the GCC with regard to China's voting on the Syria issue in the Security Council. Nevertheless, a pragmatic approach by the two parties prevented any potential disruption to economic relations. An expression of this pragmatism, and of the interest in pursuing trade and business relations, was the holding of the 2014 Strategic Dialogue.

2.2. A 'Strategic Partnership' in Military and Security Realms

China-GCC political ties have also grown in the past decade, with promise for further development. In a symbolic move, King Abdullah's first overseas visit as a monarch was to China in 2006, and that itself was the first visit by a Saudi monarch to China since diplomatic relations were established in 1990.[12] The GCC's security and military driver has always been Saudi Arabia. Although Saudi Arabia has a long history of ties to China, tangible contacts with the People's Republic started in the mid-1980s when Saudi Arabia negotiated in secret a $1 billion purchase of Chinese intermediate range ballistic missiles (that could hit targets in Iran, Israel, and Iraq). Bilateral relations after that progressed.[13] Although the China-Saudi Arabia missile deal may not have been significant when compared with Saudi weapons deals with the United States, it was nonetheless noteworthy as it was concluded at a time when China and Saudi Arabia did not have diplomatic relations. The deal came after the US Congress had vetoed plans for Saudi Arabia to purchase updated F-15 planes from the US. A later indication of how close Saudi relations with China were to become was when the Kingdom donated $80 million to China after the 2008 earthquake in Sichuan, making Saudi Arabia the largest external donor. Three top-leadership visits between the two countries between 2008 and 2011 provide further evidence of the overall trend.[14]

Other GCC states saw a similar improvement of ties. Qatar's Emir visited China in 2014; discussions included ways to combat terrorism.[15] The Qatari Emir voiced a GCC-agreed upon appreciation of China's "neutrality" position on the international scene and its commitment to security and stability in the region. Kuwait's position has also been similar and was relayed during the Emir's visit to China in 2009, when several trade agreements were signed.[16]

In addition, the present decade has seen an increased Chinese military presence in the Gulf. In March 2010, Chinese naval vessels docked in the United Arab Emirates (UAE). Afterwards Chinese airplanes refueled in Iran (and Pakistan) on their way to Turkey; this was a first time for Iran to host foreign aircraft since 1979. In September 2014, Chinese vessels docked in Iran to partake in counter-piracy operations, salvage and rescue missions, and to improve overall preparedness in the face of regional contingencies.[17]

Until mid-2015, "strategic partnership" in the lexicon of GCC decision makers has mostly meant elevated political coordination – not security or military coordination. In the third round of the China-GCC Strategic Dialogue held in Beijing in January 2014, the parties emphasized improving political, cultural, environmental and other ties without mention of security or military ties. Both parties, however, welcomed a further exploration of what a strategic partnership between them would entail.[18] Such a position rests on the assumption that shared security preferences exist and form a basis on which to build relations. It is important therefore to investigate these preferences, and the next section is dedicated to that end.

3. China-GCC Shared Security Interests

In considering GCC-China security compatibilities, this chapter will first identify the security issues of major interest to the GCC states. Three dimensions are covered: the Gulf neighbourhood, the broader Middle East, and the global political system. China's position in regard to each of the issues will then be examined, and how its policies are perceived by the GCC.

3.1. First Dimension: the Gulf Neighbourhood

GCC leaders (and many scholars) perceive the primary threat in the Gulf as coming from Iran, but they disagree on the magnitude of this threat, as well as its causes and how best to interact with Iran.[19] Qatar and Oman, for example, diverge from Saudi Arabian positions in these latter fields, and the extent of the UAE's economic exchanges with Iran seems to overshadow rivalry over the three islands. Nevertheless, Iran remains a security concern. In addition to decades of hostility that have tarred relations, fears are raised by Iran's possession of a wide range of medium- and long-range missiles with serious destructive capabilities. In concrete terms, the GCC has outspent Iran on purchases of conventional military systems in the past decade at least,[20] but the relevant issue here is the perceptions of threat held by GCC governments. The unfolding US-Iran rapprochement has not quelled GCC concerns, despite US attempts to re-assure the GCC.[21]

Al-Qaeda and recently the Islamic State have also posed threats to the GCC countries by targeting them domestically (demonstrated by the waves of explosions in Saudi Arabia, Kuwait, and Bahrain). As many of the combatants in Iraq, Syria, and Yemen have come from outside the region, the GCC countries need to maintain a high level of coordination with the US and EU intelligence authorities. At the GCC summit in Doha in December 2014 the GCC leaders recognized the need for intra-GCC political agreement as a necessary condition for utilizing external support.[22]

Another important interest for the GCC is in securing Gulf transportation routes for energy and trade with the outside world. With respect to China, the

Chinese and GCC governments have liaised about the New Silk Road Economic Belt and the 21st century maritime Silk Road.[23] These grand plans have security implications in terms of the flow of goods and people. It is estimated that by 2025, the straits of Malacca will be the gateway for about 75% of China's external trade. China is also investing in Pakistan's port of Gwadar as an outlet for its trade. To secure these maritime routes for its trade China would need to undertake more patrolling to keep piracy at bay, including in the region extending from the southern exit of the Straits of Hormuz to Bab el Mandeb.

China has already been involved in trying to protect sea navigation from piracy in the Western Indian Ocean off the Horn of Africa and the coasts of Somalia – where the sea lanes are important for Chinese trade not only with the Gulf but also with Europe.[24] This started in January 2009 when China deployed naval forces in the Gulf of Aden with the express purpose of protecting shipping from Somali pirates. According to the China Daily, China's Ministry of Transport thereafter began accepting escort requests from Chinese vessels for protection by two missile destroyers and a supply vessel in the region.[25] The commander of the Chinese Navy commented on the occasion that "it's the first time we go abroad to protect our strategic interests armed with military force", emphasizing the novelty of such a move by China, given how it was its "first potential combat mission beyond its territorial waters in centuries."[26] China framed its new initiative as consistent with its role as a major power acting under sanctioned international agreements to maintain global stability. Thus its move into the Gulf of Aden came after UNSC Resolution 1851 of December 2008, which specifically targeted piracy and emanating from the collapsed Somali state. A report stated: "According to China's delegation to the United Nations, both UN Secretary-General Ban Ki-moon and the rotating president of the UNSC, Neven Jurica of Croatia, welcomed Beijing's decision to dispatch Chinese naval ships for combating piracy around Somalia."[27] China clearly wanted to legitimate its naval action within an international consensus. The Chinese navy, furthermore, coordinates tactically with existing forces in the region, which work together within the framework of Combined Task Force 150.[28] China's main tactical coordination has been with the Japanese and South Korean navies, which is significant given how these are often seen as competitors and that tensions between them continue in the South China Sea.[29]

3.1.1. GCC Perceptions of Chinese Policies in the Gulf

Many GCC observers believe that Iran is empowered by Chinese regional policy. They regard it as problematic that, on the issue of the security of maritime waterways, China has shown interest in liaising with Iran (and others) without directly approaching the GCC. An observer notes that "China is not even part of the Combined Task Force 150 which monitors the security of the Gulf." When asked what China could do, the observer replied: "perhaps China could start by joining this CTF 150 which includes more than 29 states, most of whom are NATO members".[30]

From a GCC perspective, the Chinese rapprochement and building of relations with Iran are more substantial than what China has been building with the GCC; this is seen as an empowering factor for Iran. A prominent GCC expert communicated to the writer (in a personal correspondence) his belief that Iran has been aggressive in its confrontational positions vis-à-vis Gulf states because it feels that it has the protection of Russia and China. It seems unlikely, however, that China would actually compromise its relations with the US to help Iran, and it has not yet exhibited any sign that it would be willing to do that. China, indeed, has a clear interest in keeping good relations with the Western countries that have orchestrated the sanctions on Iran. China's trade with Iran is of little significance compared to its trade with the US and its closest allies.[31] Given the need to maintain domestic employment and the stability of its society, it would be difficult to see China challenging its largest trading partners.

GCC observers find somewhat disconcerting the feebleness of China's security or military engagement with the region, despite China having much at stake if the security of the sea lanes around the Gulf are threatened. Perhaps this reflects a failing on the GCC side to appreciate the extent to which China has the ability to take on such an engagement, or how much China's approach depends on the position of other actors. Nevertheless, the current reality is that the GCC governments feel most threatened by the rise of the Islamic State, and the US is the major power in the best position to protect them from this threat.

China's "sovereignty first" stance makes it a valuable source of political support, as seen in its tacit support of Saudi Arabia's intervention in Bahrain, but GCC states do not see China providing a security umbrella – or at least not in the next decade or two. Attitudes may change with more interaction and new information, but for today GCC decision-makers in general do not trust China's intentions in the Middle East (mainly because they are unsure of them). Issues of particular mistrust are developments over Syria and Israel, relations with Iran, and measures for safeguarding navigation. GCC states are therefore wary of a stronger Chinese military presence in their immediate backyard. From a GCC perspective, China could act positively by ensuring that Iran works with others to maintain the security of the sea lanes, given that China's massive energy trade is depending on this. So far, while China has the means to pressure Iran, the China-Iran relationship does not seem to be exerted.

Not far from GCC interests, China has been reported to be negotiating with Djibouti the upgrading of a current arrangement (of February 2014) that allows access for Chinese military vessels. A Chinese spokesperson has noted that China is indeed involved in such negotiations, and that they are linked to China's vision for bringing stability to the region.[32] The immediate aim, of course, is to supply China's ships which are involved in anti-piracy operations in the Western Indian Ocean. The connection with the GCC is not very direct, but some observers noted that Djibouti had rescinded a decade-long contract with the World Dubai Ports Authority (DP) to administer the port, explaining its decision in terms of DP having used bribery to win the contract.[33] This came alongside a decision by the Djibouti government to fine the French company Total for environmental violations, leading some to speculate that the timing of the ruling was such that space could be opened up for new actors.[34] These changes were not totally unexpected. In a 2010 interview to the Saudi Arabian *Al-Riyadh* newspaper, Djibouti's foreign minister noted that Arab states (hinting at GCC interests) were not investing in his country, whereas there was an influx of Chinese and Indian investments in productive projects as well as in social infrastructure.[35] It is not suggested here that China was behind these various moves by Djibouti, or that some nefarious scheme is being hatched. But it is important to point out that China is becoming active in the Gulf neighborhood and that GCC states themselves have not been attentive enough to regional changes and how they can involve themselves strategically and constructively in the wider region.

Finally, GCC states are developing an indigenous collective security framework, which has come a long way since 1981 but still needs harmonization. Many see the experience of Desert Shield interventions in Bahrain (against protesters) as a success, but Desert Shield still needs more work, especially in making its operational strategy effective, drawing up a military doctrine, creating command and control centres, developing intelligence facilities, and especially building up troop numbers.[36] The military industry in the GCC states is limited and dependent on Western technology.[37] The problem facing the GCC's armed forces, however, is not local production versus purchases, but personnel. Its military spending is among the highest in the world, but military budgets do not correlate with combat capacity or fighting power because much money is spent on sinecure employment, often politically-motivated.[38] China could play an important role in supplying the GCC with weapons such as long-range missiles, unmanned planes, and satellite and nuclear technology. However, such purchases would need political will, navigation of how the US would be involved (or not involved), and operational effort to integrate different military hardware in existing structures. While GCC states have an interest in expanding arms purchases, many considerations complicate and slow down the process.

3.2. Second Dimension: the Wider Middle East

The war in Syria and internal conflict in Iraq are seen by the GCC as part and parcel of Gulf security, making the GCC attentive to any global participation in that conflict. The concern is both with the expansion of the Islamic State and the magnitude of the Iranian presence there.[39] The GCC states clearly have preferences for supporting some actors over others, thereby clashing with China's supposed "non-involved" position.[40] China's use of veto powers at the Security Council have not been viewed favourably. GCC governments see, in these votes, a coordination of Chinese and Russian positions which have, so far, run counter to GCC positions. This reinforces their view that China is not investing diplomatic energies because it does not want to be part of Middle East politics.[41] At one level, GCC elites appreciate Chinese fears of the Middle East being opened up to deeper NATO involvement, and they understand China's alarm over US policy in Asia. Nonetheless, at another level, GCC states' mistrust and frustration because of China's politics is widely shared.

However, it may be that China's striving towards neutrality and trying to stay out of the conflicts will work in the GCC's favor after all. In 1998 China called for the lifting of the embargo on Iraq, although it did not actively pursue this policy. Talking, from China's perspective, allowed it to take a position that could later be a conduit to more trade with Iraq; not acting meant that China did not alarm other Gulf states (or the US), be they GCC or Iran, about any potential empowerment of Iraq. Today, with the US and Russian engagement in Syria, China's non–intervention may remove a potential source of worry for the GCC – the long-term concern over what the activities of major powers may mean for Syria and Iraq. There is, furthermore, concern over China's relations with Israel. [42] China has historically been an important ally of Arab liberation and a supporter of anti-colonial causes, especially in standing with the Palestinians in their conflict. GCC leaders have observed that after peace treaties between some Arab states and Israel, China's position vis-à-vis Israel changed towards one of forging a solid trading partnership. Given the continued conflict between GCC states with Israel, Chinese-Israeli cooperation is viewed with suspicion by GCC states.[43]

The issue here is that Israel has the military advantage, and GCC elites do not see China as a viable option which can help build Arab military capacities towards parity with Israel.[44] This stems from a combination of factors, among them the fact that China does not want to challenge US dominance in Middle East security. The GCC states have, moreover, sunk vast sums of money in military hardware, training, and operational systems bought from the US government and American contractors and businesses, such that their armed forces are now dependent on those systems.[45]

According to one close observer of Gulf politics, Saudi Arabia's refusal of a UN Security Council seat was mainly (although not exclusively) in protest at China's position on the Syrian conflict. Riyadh apparently relayed this position to the Chinese and Russian governments. China and Russia's veto was seen as favouring the sitting Syrian government, while Saudi Arabia and its allies were standing with the Syrian opposition. Saudi Arabia and other GCC states are, of course, aware of how China's interests are aligned globally; if they GCC are not publicly putting up a fight, this does not mean they are unaware of strategic implications of China's policies.

3.3. Third Dimension: the Global System

It is clear that GCC leaders think of potential security ties with China through the prism of their enduring relationship with the United States. China upholds the current global order with little interest in a systemic conflict with the US.[46] China does not exhibit any interest in producing an alternative to the dominant capitalist global economic order, but is interested in reforms (such as with the Asian Infrastructure Investment Bank).

GCC leaders understand that, in the framework of current power politics, China wants the US to be the supplier of Gulf security and does not want to be burdened with the costs of supplying security. In an important way, this agrees with the GCC states' own interests of having no challenger to the US - at least not in the foreseeable future.[47] That China engages the GCC via its global goals need not deter the GCC from realist strategising on its own side, given that China has economic growth potential, is willing to build relations without political or ideological conditions, and has veto power in the United Nations Security Council.

China can, in this perspective, be part of the solution to certain pertinent issues, and it has in any case been "a historical friend of the Arabs." China's "hands off" policy would actually fit with the reality, from a GCC standpoint, that the "Arabian" Gulf falls within the ambit of NATO. This position was explicit in the Istanbul Cooperation Initiative of 2004.[48] In addition, the presence of bases and facilities for American, British and French military forces, which now stud the Gulf Coast, act as a seal of confidence in the benefit of Western-Gulf cooperation to safeguard regional security.

At the core, and in concrete policy outcomes, China and the US converge in their positions on the security issues which concern the GCC – albeit for very different reasons. On the GCC's most critical security concern, which is Iran, China seems to share the US's strategic preferences even if the sources of these preferences are substantially different.[49] The US position in seeking a rapprochement with Iran is not likely to be transient. Hence, while GCC states pursue a policy of containment and confrontation with Iran, as evidenced in the Decisive Storm operation in Yemen, the US and China both favour the defusing of tensions. Moreover, GCC concerns about Iran's regional politics are closely tied to events in Iraq and Syria, where (in both cases) China has been rather uninvolved. Regarding balances of military capacities, GCC arms procurement is likely to continue to come mostly from the United States and its western allies; China will remain a supplier, but at a more limited level, even if in lesser volumes. What the US and its allies and China share is the hesitation to provide GCC states with qualities and quantities of weapons that would tilt the existing regional power configuration away from Israel. Here again we see policy convergence between China and the US, despite the driving forces being different. The US and its allies start from a pro-Israel position, while China has been acting on a basis of calculated interest.

China does not have any negative historical baggage with the GCC and is generally non-interventionist in the domestic politics of other states. It is clear that China does not care greatly about regime type. However, whether this constitutes a significant difference between the US and China is doubtful. Some suggest that the US has never really pressured GCC states on political reform issues. After the domestic conflict in Bahrain in 2011, the US Congress in September 2011 protested against the selling of a $53 million arms deal with Bahrain, at least until the results of an independent enquiry were out. Bahrain nonetheless managed to obtain a $1 million deal for its immediate needs. China would not necessarily have acted any differently. It is commonly argued that China does not mix business with politics, but it is also true that China can not, and has no intent to, deliver the same security and military services which western states provides – and especially the United States.

GCC concern about the US's Gulf policies reached their peak in early 2015. The US's engagement with the GCC seemed to be positioned for reduction in the light of its planned scaling-back in global security engagements – especially its global military presence.[50] In the midst of the GCC's deep concern about a US-Iran nuclear deal, however, the US held talks with GCC leaders at Camp David in May 2015, and it was agreed that the US would upgrade its ties with the GCC to an alliance. This served to quell GCC fears. Aluwaisheg affirms that GCC states now have confidence in the United States' continued commitment to their security, and that such commitments would not be jeopardized by a US-Iran nuclear-related deal.[51] For the time being and until it is clear what the operational outcomes of this US-GCC alliance would be, the upgraded relationship serves to add another layer of deterrent against Iran, which is needed by the GCC as a comforting mechanism regardless of what Iran is doing or plans to do. This seems to confirm that, for the GCC, a "strategic partnership" in the security realm with China does not (and will not in the foreseeable future) imply that China would become an alternative to the US in terms of providing a military umbrella or in being a central security provider.

4. Conclusion

The meanings of strategic partnership and what it entails in terms of concrete policy outcomes for the GCC as a whole and GCC states individually remain unclear. All the actors involved have vested interests in a dialogue, yet have so far avoided some of the critical issues which might divide them. GCC states and China are at one in upholding a statist logic, which for example prioritizes national sovereignty over minority independence tendencies. GCC states' reactions to domestic contestations in China, therefore, have been predominantly in favour of the Chinese emphasis on "national security" and the necessity of respecting the rights of minorities under the umbrella of Chinese sovereignty. Diplomatic and business links appear to be uninterrupted by issues relating to Chinese Muslims.[52] All in all, then, relations are improving.

As a close observer of the GCC commented in a personal communication to the writer, GCC elites (despite the historic ties with the US which have served well), want to open new doors and seek other foreign policy options worldwide, moving from single-country relationship to multi-country relationships. Another observer noted that a special China-GCC relationship might not be that special. With GCC reliance on the US decreasing (albeit without a break), the GCC may pursue more independent and assertive foreign policies across a range of directions. China can still help with arms supplies or with tactical, logistic, or other forms of support, and the GCC states for their part can still pursue a variety of security-seeking options with China in fields such as securing the routes of expanded trade ties, monitoring the movement of Islamic militant groups, helping to stabilise Pakistan, and securing the Gulf-Indian Ocean waterways. There is no lack of opportunities to explore.[53] However, a gap exists in GCC-China understanding of their strategic security interests vis-à-vis each other. This gap needs time to attend to, and perhaps it will never be closed. In the meantime, it seems that the GCC's security options with China remain limited.

Notes

1 The author thanks Tim Niblock, Talmiz Ahmad, and Nikolay Kozhanov for comments on earlier drafts of the chapter.

2 The GCC states are Bahrain, Kuwait, Oman, Qatar, Saudi Arabia, and the United Arab Emirates. For this chapter, the Gulf includes the GCC plus Iran, Iraq, and Yemen; and the Middle East comprises the Levant, North Africa, and the Gulf.

3 These findings are part of a larger project which aims to understand perceptions of GCC decision makers vis-à-vis security ties with China; it also aims to unpack how these decision makers understand the meanings of a proposed 'strategic partnership'. Such perceptions on security relations are subject to change given global and regional dynamics, and as decision makers further develop better repertoires with Chinese counterparts.

4 For earlier work on this topic see Tim Niblock, "Strategic Economic Relationships and Strategic Openings in the Gulf", in Hook, Steven W. and Tim Niblock, eds, *The United States and the Gulf: Shifting Pressures, Strategies and Alignments* (Berlin: Gerlach Press, 2015), pp. 5-22.

5 See the text of the speech at: <http://www.alriyadh.com/918225> (last accessed November 19, 2015).

6 See <http://www.fgccc.cn/en/fenghao.asp?id=1111>_(last accessed November 19, 2015).

7 See Tim Niblock's chapter in this volume, Table 5.

8 GCC Secretary General Abdel Rahman Al-Atiyya's speech at the 2008 Asian-Middle Eastern Ministerial meeting in Sharm Al-Shaykh (<http://www.gcc-sg.org/index63f5.html?action=News&Sub=ShowOne&ID=806&T=A>) (last accessed November 19, 2015).

9 Jasim Ali, "GCC Focus GCC FTA with China no easy task," Gulf News (March 28, 2010): <http://gulfnews.com/business/analysis/gcc-focus-gcc-fta-with-china-no-easy-task-1.603754> (last accessed November 19, 2015).

10 Abdel Aziz Aluwaisheg, "China-GCC strategic dialogue resumes," *Arab News* (January 19, 2014): <http://www.arabnews.com/news/511401>_(last accessed November 19, 2015).

11 Abdel Aziz Aluwaisheg, "Taqatu' al-Tijara wal-Siyasa fil Hiwar al-Istratiji al-Khaliji al-Sini" (the intersection of trade and politics in the Gulf-China strategic dialogue), *Al-Watan Online* (January 21, 2014): <http://www.alwatan.com.sa/Articles/Detail.aspx?ArticleId=19808> (last accessed November 19, 2015).

12 Al-Tamimi, Naser M., *China-Saudi Arabia Relations, 1990-2012: Marriage of Convenience or Strategic Alliance?* (Oxon: Routledge, 2014), p. 74.

13 Al-Tamimi, pp. 65-173.

14 Naser Al-Tamimi, "China Saudi Arabia relations: economic partnership or strategic alliance?" Discussion Paper no. 2, *HH Sheikh Nasser Al-Sabah Programme*, Durham University (June 2012): p.5.

15 See: <http://www.arabsino.com/articles/14-11-06/11697.htm> (last accessed November 19, 2015).

16 Khizar Niazi, "Kuwait Looks towards the East: Relations with China," *Middle East Institute*, policy brief no. 26 (September 2009).

17 See <http://goo.gl/Ojb4PE> (last accessed October 27, 2015). In addition to these novel military engagements, China has established military relations with Israel, as well as various joint infrastructure projects. See Michael Singh, *China's military presence in the Gulf* (<http://www.washingtoninstitute.org/policy-analysis/view/chinas-military-presence-in-the-gulf>) (last accessed November 19, 2015).

18 Abdel Aziz Aluwaisheg, "China-GCC strategic dialogue resumes," *Arab News* (January 19, 2014): <http://www.arabnews.com/news/511401>. See the speech of China's Minister of Foreign Affairs during the closing ceremony of the Third GCC-China Strategic Dialogue Ministerial Meeting in Beijing (January 17, 2014): <https://www.gcc-sg.org/indexb663.html?action=News&Sub=ShowOne&ID=3174&T=A> (last accessed November 19, 2015).

19 Turki Al Faisal (2013). This was also confirmed in the May 14, 2015 Whitehouse press release after the 2015 Camp David meetings.

20 Cordesman and Peacock (2015): figure II.2.

21 Alajmi (2015).

22 See <http://english.alarabiya.net/en/views/news/middle-east/2014/11/21/Building-a-NATO-GCC-wall-The-time-is-now.html> (last accessed October 27, 2015). See also Al-Tamimi (2012, 10).

23 Abdel Aziz Aluwaisheg, "China, GCC set to walk the new 'Silk Road'," *Arab News* (February 3, 2014): <http://www.arabnews.com/news/518966> (last accessed October 27, 2015).

24 Sager (2010, 17-18).

25 Reported by *United Press International:* "Chinese Naval Fleet Arrives Off Somalia" (January 6, 2009): <http://www.upi.com/Top_News/2009/01/06/Chinese_naval_fleet_arrives_off_Somalia/UPI-96771231248514/> (last accessed October 27, 2015).

26 See <http://www.sinodaily.com/2006/081226114324.rn7y1ndr.html> (last accessed November 19, 2015).

27 Weitz (2009, 31).

28 Ibid.

29 Jason Nicholson, "Japan, South Korea Boost their African Presence: The focus on the South China Sea misses some important, and relevant, strategic developments further west," *The Diplomat* (October 1, 2015).

30 The idea that that China would join a grouping led by NATO states, and headquartered in a US base, is interesting. For its part China's ETG works with CTF 151 (see: <http://combinedmaritimeforces.com/2014/07/31/a-new-era-of-partnership-between-ctf-151-and-chinas-etg-150/>) (last accessed October 27, 2015).

31 Sahriatinia (2011). For an update on trade figures see Iran's Press TV story (<http://www.presstv.com/Detail/2015/06/28/417908/Iran-China-Trade-Drop>) (last accessed November 19, 2015).

32 *Alarabiya* (May 11, 2015): <http://goo.gl/ulX5ey> (last accessed October 27, 2015).

33 Tom Arnold, *The National* (July 9, 2014): <http://goo.gl/GopgeG> (last accessed October 27, 2015).

34 See <http://goo.gl/lRmHHF> (last accessed October 27, 2015).

35 See the interview at: <http://www.alriyadh.com/519228> (last accessed October 27, 2015). For a more recent expose on the booming coastal towns – with heavy Chinese investments, see: <http://elaph.com/Web/News/2015/5/1010338.html> (last accessed October 27, 2015).

36 See interview with Zafer Alajmi (December 9, 2013): <https://www.youtube.com/watch?v=BXcEQK_S2pE> (last accessed October 27, 2015).

37 Personal communication with a regional expert.

38 Gulf Center for Development Policies, *Al-Khaleej 2013: al-Thabit wal-Moutahawel* report (2013): chapter four (<https://www.gulfpolicies.com/index.php?option=com_content&view=category&layout=blog&id=188&Itemid=444>) (last accessed October 27, 2015).

39 Syria and Iraq are places for Iran to act in the Middle East and theatres on which it increases its influence. While it is important to note Iran's role in these societies' politics, I do not ascribe to the banal and ideological - yet widespread - discourse that Iraq's Shiites have somehow been pawns for Iran or that Iraqi Sunnis provide blanket support for IS militias.

40 See a 2014 statement by Wang Yi, China's Minister of Foreign Affairs, "The Syria Issue can Only Be Resolved Politically", delivered during an interview with Al Jazeera (<http://www.fmprc.gov.cn/ara/zxxx/t1115197.shtml>) (last accessed October 27, 2015).

41 "In October 2012, China's then foreign minister, Yang Jiechi, rolled out a "Four-Point Plan" for Syria that called on all sides to stop fighting, end the crisis, and initiate a political transition. The Associated Press

noted that the plan generated little international interest: Most observers found it "vague, and likely aimed at bolstering China's reputation following criticism of its moves to join Russia in blocking U.N. resolutions aimed at ending Syria's bloodshed." Needless to say, this was a failure." Ilan Goldenberg, and Ely Ratner, "China's Middle East Tightrope," *Foreign Policy*, April 20, 2015 (at <https://foreignpolicy.com/2015/04/20/china-middle-east-saudi-arabia-iran-oil-nuclear-deal/>) (last accessed October 27, 2015).

42 Whether GCC alliance with the US could lead to parity with Israel is, of course, a separate question – and one which the US tends to resist.

43 Dubi ben-Gedalyahu, "China to be Israel's biggest infrastructure partner," *Globes* (April 29, 2015): <http://www.globes.co.il/en/article-china-becoming-israels-biggest-infrastructure-partner-1001031690> (last accessed October 27, 2015).

44 Naser Al-Tamimi, "The uncertain future of China-Israel relations," *Al-Arabiya* (April 4, 2014): <http://english.alarabiya.net/en/views/news/world/2014/04/04/The-uncertain-future-of-China-Israel-relations.html> (last accessed October 27, 2015).

45 Katzman, Kenneth, The United Arab Emirates (UAE): Issues for U.S. Policy, *Congressional Research Service* (September 14, 2015): <http://www.fas.org/sgp/crs/mideast/RS21852.pdf>. See also deal with Lockheed Martin for training <http://www.lockheedmartin.com/us/news/press-releases/2011/february/KnowledgePointLMCPartnership.html> (last accessed October 27, 2015).

46 See a declaration of a Chinese Foreign Ministry Spokesman published by the General Consulate in Chicago: <http://www.chinaconsulatechicago.org/eng/fyrth/t1072338.htm> (last accessed October 27, 2015).

47 It is certainly convenient to China (not so much Russia) that the US provides security from which China benefits in terms of the sea lanes to China. From a Chinese perspective, the Gulf would be a more secure environment if there were an arrangement for collective security including all 8 Gulf states. See Alastair Sloan: China's complex relations with the Gulf states <https://www.middleeastmonitor.com/articles/middle-east/11953-chinas-complex-relations-with-the-gulf-states> (last accessed October 27, 2015).

48 NATO figures prominently in GCC security, and the 2004 Istanbul Cooperation Initiative formalized this relationship, in addition to American and allies' military bases studding the Gulf coast (see <http://www.nato.int/nato_static/assets/pdf/pdf_2014_04/20140331_140401-factsheet-ICI_en.pdf>) (last accessed October 27, 2015).

49 Izzat Shahrour, "Al-Seen wal-Sharq al-Awsat: Malameh Mouqarabah Jadida" (China and the Middle East: Signs of a New Approach) *Al Jazeera Centre for Studies* (June 11, 2012).

50 Andrew Critchlow, "US Says Can't 'Guarantee' Security in Oil-Rich Gulf States as Focus Turns to China," *The Telegraph* (May 15, 2014): <http://www.telegraph.co.uk/finance/newsbysector/industry/defence/10831872/US-says-cant-guarantee-security-in-oil-rich-Gulf-states-as-focus-turns-to-China.html>) (last accessed October 27, 2015).

51 See the interview (<http://elaph.com/Web/News/2015/5/1008309.html>) (last accessed October 27, 2015).

52 For a view of diplomatic ties, see Saudi Arabia's embassy website in China (accessed May 14, 2015: <http://embassies.mofa.gov.sa/sites/China/AR/AboutHostingCountry/HostingCountryInfo/Pages/default.aspx>).

53 Alastair Sloan, "China's Complex Relations with the Gulf States" *Middle East Monitor* (June 8, 2014): <https://www.middleeastmonitor.com/articles/middle-east/11953-chinas-complex-relations-with-the-gulf-states> (last accessed October 27, 2015).

References

Alajmi, Zafer Muhammad, "Gulf Military Cooperation: Tangible Gains or Limited Results?" *AlJazeera Center for Studies* (March 31, 2015).

Al Saud, Turki Al Faisal bin Abdul Aziz, "Saudi Arabia's Foreign Policy," *Middle East Policy* 20, no. 4 (Winter 2013): 37-44.

Al-Tamimi, Naser M., *China-Saudi Arabia Relations, 1990-2012: Marriage of Convenience or Strategic Alliance?* (Oxon, Routledge, 2014).

Cordesman, Anthony H., and Michael Peacock, *Military Spending and Arms Sales in the Gulf: How the Arab Gulf States Now Dominate the Changes in the Military Balance* (International Institute for Strategic Studies, April 2015).

Niblock, Tim, "Strategic Economic Relationships and Strategic Openings in the Gulf", in Hook, Steven W. and Tim Niblock, eds, *The United States and the Gulf: Shifting Pressures, Strategies and Alignments* (Berlin: Gerlach Press, 2015), pp. 5-22.

Sager, Abdulaziz, "GCC-China Relations: Looking Beyond Oil – Risks and Rewards," in Geoffrey Kemp and Abdulaziz Sager, eds., *China's Growing Role in the Middle East: Implications for the Region and Beyond* (Gulf Research Center, and The Nixon Center, 2010).

Sahriatinia, Mohsen, "Iran-China Relations: An Overview of Critical Factors," *Iranian Review of Foreign Affairs* 1, no. 4 (Winter 2011): pp. 57-85.

Weitz, Richard, "Operation Somalia: China's First Expeditionary Force?" *China Security* 5, no. 1 (Winter 2009): 27-42.

11

The GCC and the BRICS in Sub-Saharan Africa Is China the Main Driver?

Gladys Lechini and María Noel Dussort

1. Introduction

The 21st century has unleashed a number of changes in the balance of power of the international system, at political and economic levels, provoking a variety of crises, mostly financial in nature. The unipolarism of the US, dominant after the end of the Cold War, is giving way to multipolarism, mainly in the economic arena. A sign of this transition is the rise of new emerging countries with high growth rates, which in turn has provoked greater demand for natural resources - pushing up their prices to unexpected levels. In addition, a renovated multilateralism is leading to the proliferation of governmental and non-governmental actors in various associations, groups and coalitions around specific areas.

Outside of the powers at the heart of the current global order, principally the US, the European Union and Japan, new poles have arisen in different continents, displacing the traditional axis in "the North" to other latitudes: in Asia (China and a step behind, India), Latin America (Brazil), Sub-Saharan Africa (South Africa, Nigeria, Angola) and the Gulf (Iran, Saudi Arabia, Qatar and the United Arab Emirates). This changing order, from a bipolar and then unipolar world to the present turbulence, does not imply a resounding fall of US power but demands a reconfiguration of forces and even new categories of analysis.

These new actors can be termed "emerging powers", since they are in "a transformation process, from one international position to a higher one"[1] mostly visible in their economic indicators which not only position them as emerging markets but also provide them with a basis for promoting their own international agenda. In this sense, the rise of new states as global players is relevant to understanding the first decade of this century. The countries concerned have been able to emerge thanks to sustained economic growth and a strong state structure backing their international insertion, in a new relationship between economics and politics.

The idea of a new world order shaped by the participation of middle, regional or emerging powers has opened up discussion over a new range of coalitions of states striving for "their place in the world". As a result a new debate has been initiated concerning their role and whether they would be most effective acting individually or collectively.

At the same time, in an international economic context of globalization and 'commoditization'[2], the growing links among emerging countries and other countries from the South offer not only a variety of challenges but also a new era of opportunities to promote their development through the activity of public and private sectors.

To address this phenomenon different terms have been coined for clusters of countries which constitute new coalitions like the BRICS[3], or associations like the Gulf Cooperation Council (GCC)[4], all of them overlapping and acting simultaneously in this new international scenery. In the case under study, BRICS and the GCC are playing an increasing role in the world economy and in global politics. They prioritize different scenarios according to their strategies and issue areas, acting individually or looking for alliances if they need to "add power" to obtain more autonomy of decision-making and wider margins of manoeuvre. They behave according to their own economic and political interests to consolidate a new agenda, but they do not strive for a system change.

One of our assumptions here is that although they constitute groups, these groups are somewhat "elusive" and therefore the commonalities are only important for the juncture, being strategically designed for particular purposes but without a grand strategy. Within these new circumstances, the relations which the GCC states and the BRICS have with Sub-Saharan African countries[5] have potential to flourish and grow exponentially for the years to come. Nevertheless these links could be strained by the strength and extent of China's involvement in the region.

The current engagement of BRICS countries in Africa is not in itself new. On the contrary, the BRIC countries all had an involvement there in the late sixties or early seventies of the last century. Russia and China did so in the context of the Cold War, India as a historic Indian Ocean neighbour, and Brazil in the frame of South-South Cooperation. South Africa was still under white colonial domination. Meanwhile the GCC states went to Africa to seek support for the Palestinian cause, promising oil and loans in exchange, in a context of complex interdependence. The various difficulties most of these countries experienced in the eighties and nineties pushed them out of Africa for almost two decades. Now they are all back. Brazil, Russia, India and China returned in search of raw materials and markets, to fulfil the needs of their capitalist expansion. The GCC countries have also returned with their interest in food and oil.

The purpose of this chapter is to analyze the opportunities and challenges the GCC countries face in their engagement in Africa, taking into consideration their strategic location and their hub capacities. The present scenario has placed them at a crossroads. They could act as a pivot between the Sub-Saharan African countries and Beijing (given that China is the BRICS member with the most substantial interests in both Africa and the Gulf), playing a cooperative role. Or they could suffer from the negative effects of BRICS' influence in the region as a result of China's dominant position. To sum up, they could be a hinge in a triangular relationship, with mutual benefits to the GCC and China or a mere conveyor belt to promote Chinese interests in Africa due to their proximity to the continent and their financial resources.

In order to explain the relations between the three groupings, the chapter will examine the main characteristics of these clusters of countries. It will then analyse the economic relations between GCC countries and Sub-Saharan African states in the light of China's increasing influence in the African continent and assess whether the GCC countries and China have opposing or cooperative interests in Africa. Finally, three possible scenarios which could describe the future relations of these groupings are put forward.

2. The Three Vertices of the Triangle: the BRICS, the GCC and the Sub-Saharan African Countries

2.1. BRICS. From an Acronym to an International Actor

It is widely known that the BRICs (Brazil, Russia, India and China) were first identified in 2001 by the economist Jim O'Neill of Goldman Sachs. He coined the acronym to describe a group of big emerging markets with great potential to absorb inward investments. In other words, they were considered as 'hot spots' in the international economic system. For the first decade of the century, the record of economic growth of the BRIC countries gave substance to this positive assessment. China's growth was particularly impressive. It started the decade as the biggest of the BRICS and has remained so[6]. Trade within the BRICS grouping, and between each BRICS country and every region of the world, was growing fast[7].

Some economists have claimed that O'Neill's assessment of BRIC's growth potential was unjustified, and that the growth which occurred was the product of an unrepeatable set of circumstances: rapid export growth, the commodity boom and unsustainable US demand. Furthermore, they argue that some years after the financial crisis and mainly since 2013-2014, the situation has changed and that all the BRICS and other emerging economies are suffering the results of the spill-over effect of the crisis developed in the central capitalist economies[8].

It was, in any case, not until the 2007-2008 financial crisis that the BRIC countries were motivated to coordinate their policies. The crisis, then, gave them a raison d'être, a window of opportunity to act collectively and benefit from a greater capacity of negotiation[9]. Nevertheless, as emerging actors each of them still had its own particular international strategy, economic performance and political aim according to their national interests and promoting its own international agenda.

What made the BRICS countries self-identify, and then seek to act together as a political and economic grouping, was the realization that they shared "a sense of dissatisfaction with the current system of global governance"[10] and that they could collectively have an impact on the international economy. Consequently, they began meeting at summits[11] to discuss their own visions and possible common actions. Despite the fact that their cooperation is still in its infancy, the creation of the New Development Bank (NDB) in 2014 at the Fortaleza Summit was highly significant because it was the first step towards institutionalising BRICS, fundamentally altering its previous characteristics as a non-binding, informal consultation group[12].

The idea of a new bank, conceived as an alternative to the World Bank and the International Monetary Fund (IMF), can be seen as a response to the lack of democratic procedures in existing international financial institutions. However, it is undeniable that Chinese financial power is crucial in creating the Development Bank, so for the other members there is some danger of them becoming dependent on China. Indeed, the Ufa Declaration, which was the outcome of the 2015 BRICS Summit, stated explicitly that the NDB would cooperate closely with the recently created Asian Investment and Infrastructure Bank (AIIB) - a financing mechanism led by China.

The BRICS grouping can be seen as a platform for Brazil, South Africa and India to obtain international visibility and at the same time push for a significant redistribution of power in global institutions (e.g. as regards the United Nations Security Council). Meanwhile, China "shines for itself" because of the assertive foreign policy it has developed since 2009 and because of its determination to become an economic superpower. For Russia, BRICS could perhaps serve as a path for it to recover its lost glory and relevance.

It is clear that if the BRICS countries were able to articulate and champion common positions on global issues, they could collectively take the role of a global agenda-setter, with the capacity to challenge and disrupt the established powers' control over the world order[13]. This, however, does not currently seem likely to happen. The BRICS, especially China as the most powerful member, have not challenged the present system. They have, in fact, benefited from it.

To sum up, all five BRICS members have global ambitions, some are shared by all of them (the interest in the reorientation of power towards multipolarity, the commitment to state sovereignty, and the need to reform the current system of global governance and achieve equitable representation in the multilateral arena) and some belong to the sphere of competition. Sub-Saharan Africa is a particular area where the BRICS countries seek to achieve individually their economic and political goals.

Africa is in many respects the pearl of China's outward policy. It is for this reason that this chapter focuses on China (as an "example" of BRICS countries) to indicate the possibilities of competition or cooperation with the GCC countries in Sub-Saharan Africa.

2.2 The GCC Countries: Individual Option or Collective Action

The Gulf Cooperation Council was created in 1981 as a response to a regional security problem. It was believed that cooperation among the different gulf monarchies would be a solution to an unsettled regional environment resulting from the Iranian revolution, the Soviet intervention in Afghanistan and the Iran-Iraq war. Hence, Bahrain, Kuwait, Oman, Qatar, Saudi Arabia and the UAE signed the founding Charter on May 25 1981, with the objective of joining forces to face external threats - although this was not made explicit at the time.[14]. The GCC countries have faced considerable difficulties over the years in reaching the goal of having a coordinated military defence (e.g. the experience of the peninsula shield force), and have given more attention to economic issues - although here too they have encountered obstacles[15].

As is well known, the GCC countries are key players in global energy markets in terms of production, exports and the availability of spare capacity. Their role is likely to become even more pivotal in the future as they hold vast oil and gas reserves (about 30% of the global oil reserves[16]) and benefit from relatively low costs in exploiting them[17]. As a consequence of the sheer size of financial petrodollar recycling, GCC countries have emerged as new players in world financial markets[18]. Moreover, they are investing on oil exploration and the development of new oil fields to assure their future production.

In spite of this favourable economic context, the GCC states face challenges related to their own economic structure. They need economic diversification to reduce their dependency on the hydrocarbon sector and to develop the private non-oil sector,[19] as well as solve their dilemma of food insecurity. They need to adapt themselves to changing patterns of trade and create more jobs to respond to a young, rapidly growing national labour force[20].

Recent changes in the global economy, in particular the fall of oil prices since the last quarter of 2014, make it even more important for the GCC states now to reform their economies and widen their links with non-traditional markets. The latter could serve as a means for the GCC to recycle its immense financial capacity, and perhaps as a guaranteed source of food.

The special relations with Western countries, mainly the US, have provided the GCC states with security in exchange for the West gaining stable access to their oil supplies. This trade-off between security and oil has structured the international relations of the Gulf since 1945[21]. The recent development of more fluid economic ties between the GCC states and the Asian emerging powers, mostly China and India, have enabled GCC states to look for new horizons, such as Sub-Saharan Africa. The search for new horizons has been given additional impetus by the US becoming more focused on the Asia-Pacific rather than the Middle East. Nevertheless, the GCC's political and security ties with the United States and Western Europe remain relevant.

The broadening and deepening of their political and economic connections suggests that the GCC countries are combining internationalisation with regionalisation. Moreover, individual GCC states are engaged in intense competition with each other for market share and a central position in the world order. This is the case with Saudi Arabia, which is intensifying its political ties with China and increasing its engagement with the G20, while actively seeking new governance procedures in the World Bank and IMF. Each GCC state is trying to find its place 'in the world', so they display their own strategy in Africa.

2.3. Sub-Saharan Africa as an Economic Target of Emerging Powers

Although Sub-Saharan African states share the same geographical location, each country has its own unique history, where specific political and economic values and goals have evolved[22]. Despite the fact that they are all classified as developing countries, they are at different stages of development according to their particular histories, the possession of natural resources, the type of government and the degree of economic dependence with the former metropolis[23]. Like the GCC countries, Sub-Saharan states are young nations striving for their existence in a changing international scenario.

Africa has for years been considered a continent characterized by hunger, disease, conflict and misgovernment, but in the first decade of the 21st century it has gained global strategic importance. Some African countries have started to display positive indicators and were recording growth rates averaging 5% per annum until the 2008 global financial crisis. The African geo-economic space has been rising in value for the past decade owing to the unexploited natural resources (such as minerals, metals and fertile soil) in their territories. The high prices of, and the increasing demand for, these commodities - due mainly to the economic growth of China, India and Brazil - have changed the international perception of African countries, transforming the region into a good place to do business.

The new role of African countries based on the increase in the value of exports has raised growth rates, increased per capita income, cut the level of poverty, and stoked a rising middle class[24]. Non-African emerging powers have invested heavily in a wide range of sectors.[25]. With the economic "renaissance", devastating civil wars are no longer common, allowing African governments to rebuild their nations. As figures show, during 2001-2010 there were six Sub-Saharan African countries among the world's ten fastest-growing economies in terms of gross domestic product growth: Angola 11%, Nigeria 8.9%, Ethiopia 8.4%, Chad 7.9%, Mozambique 7.9% and Rwanda 7.6%[26]. In terms of nominal GDP, South Africa, which had been the largest economy in the continent over the first decade of the 21st century, was surpassed by Nigeria in 2014, retaining the second place since then just before Egypt, Algeria, Angola and Morocco[27].

The international context is now different from the one in the last decades of the 20th century, when the IMF and the World Bank were the only options for external loans and grants for African countries. Africa has moved from the age of "there is no alternative" to "there are many alternatives",[28] when account is taken of the BRICS and other emerging countries' renewed involvement in African business. African leaders now have much more room to negotiate as they have regained their margins of manoeuvre.

Nevertheless, looking to the future there is an uncertain panorama facing the international economy. It is not clear that economic growth can be maintained. In the last months of 2014 and the first months of 2015, commodity prices decreased dramatically. Using revenues from the sale of commodities to finance development is thrown into question. At the same time, Sub-Saharan African countries lack both economic diversification and sufficient skilled labour to break away from dependency on the exploitation of natural resources.

To conclude, from colonisation to the present, the history of Sub-Saharan African countries has been that of being "objects" of the more developed nations, mainly as raw material providers and as new markets. Nowadays Africa is again "*le continent convoité*"[29], for its precious minerals, oil, crops and markets. They have become targets of this new scramble for Africa. All these considerations make these states more attractive but also more vulnerable in an international economic environment which may be increasingly unfavourable.

3. GCC-Sub-Saharan Africa Economic Relations. China as the Intervening Variable

The revival of relations between GCC countries and Sub-Saharan Africa states will now be examined in the light of China's increasing influence in the African continent. Whether GCC countries and China have opposing or cooperative interests in African countries will be evaluated. Although there is a variety of different issue areas on the GCC-Africa agenda, and despite China's African strategy including security and governance, geopolitics, external aid and South-South cooperation, the focus here is on the remarkable economic bonds which have developed since 2003, mainly in the trade and investments sectors.

3.1. GCC - Sub-Saharan Africa Relations: an Overview on Trade and Investments

Although trade links between GCC and Sub-Saharan Africa are still limited, commercial exchange has increased at an average of 11% per year since 1980. Exports from the GCC to Sub-Saharan Africa reached US$21 billion in 2013, while imports hit US$6 billion, from just US$1 billion in 2003[30]. The main product which the GCC has exported to Africa is fuel, which accounts for about half of all GCC exports to the continent. This is followed by other goods connected to the hydrocarbons sector, such as plastics and fertilizers. The most significant African exports to the GCC are precious stones and metals, followed by electrical equipment, fruit, and iron and steel[31].

At present, just seven Sub-Saharan African countries feature among the GCC's 50 largest trading partners, led by South Africa in the 22nd position and followed by Kenya, Nigeria, Tanzania, Ethiopia, Uganda and Zambia. Africa's most important trade links with GCC countries are with the UAE and Saudi Arabia, which together account for 75% of all this trade[32]. South Africa is responsible for one-third of the trade, receiving just over 40% of GCC exports, 89% of which are oil and related products, indicating that there is still a hydrocarbons-based relationship[33] with almost every African trading partner.

The GCC countries' investments in Africa are growing in scope, both by sector and geographical location. GCC companies, both public and private, are now giving attention to new markets in all parts of Sub-Saharan Africa, investing in three main sectors: infrastructure, communications and agriculture.

Regarding the infrastructure projects, these are mainly focused on energy and power[34]. GCC sources have provided at least US$30 billion of funding for African infrastructure over the past decade, which amounts to between 7% and 10% of total inflows. Telecommunications has been the main field for GCC private sector investment, due to the relatively low risk and high profits compared with other areas.

The GCC investments in agribusiness are related to their high dependence on imported foodstuffs and their rapidly-rising populations. GCC states are trying to create durable new linkages with countries in Africa producing agricultural goods, encouraged by the high food-price inflation in 2007-2008 and the global threat of food security to those net food importers. Qatar's Hassad Foods, the Saudi Company for Agricultural Investment and Animal Production, the Kuwait China Investment Company and the UAE's Minerals Energy Commodities Holding all have been seeking to invest in farmland, mainly in Sudan, Ethiopia, Tanzania, Kenya, Senegal and Mali[35]. In order to diversify markets and reduce vulnerabilities, the GCC states have increased their own food production by outsourcing producing-fields in African states[36].

3.2. China-Africa relations: Is China looking West or is Africa looking East?

The improvements in GCC-African countries' economic relations should be contextualized in a wider spectrum which takes into account the major global players' interests in Africa. China is betting hard on every sector and area. Almost 90% of Chinese imports from Africa are raw materials, especially oil and other minerals. Five countries provide 57% of these imports: Angola 19%, South Africa 17%, Nigeria 7%, Sudan 7% and Egypt 7%. South Africa is China's second biggest African trading partner.

Chinese foreign policy objectives in Africa are to strengthen its economic alliances and promote South-South Cooperation based on the Principles of Peaceful Coexistence. These objectives were laid out at the impressive summit meeting with African leaders in Beijing in 2000 and have been reinforced by the creation of the Forum on China-Africa Cooperation (FOCAC) and by reciprocal head of state visits. As a result of this mutual engagement, China-Africa trade reached US$200 billion in 2014 and Chinese investments stood at US$27.7 billion in that year. In addition, Beijing has committed US$75 billion to aid and development projects in Africa in the past decade[37]. In light of these figures it can be seen that GCC investments and trade efforts with Sub-Saharan Africa are dwarfed by Chinese spending.

4. Possible Scenarios: Separate Actors, Groupings, or Triangular Relationships?

This chapter concerns itself with two emerging groups of international actors, the BRICS and the GCC, which are diverse in nature and constituted by states of quite different status and size. In targeting Sub-Saharan Africa, with its raw materials, arable land and growing markets, the BRICS and the GCC countries could operate in three possible ways: as separate actors, groupings or in triangular relationships.

In the *separate actors* case, each country belonging to the BRICS or the GCC would prioritize its bilateral links in direct relation to its domestic needs. Each of the BRICS countries has its own interests in Africa. China, for example, has actively pursued its interests in terms of FDI and trade with African countries[38] under its "go abroad and buy" policy [39]. In 2000, Chinese President Jiang Zemin invited the African leaders to Beijing to promote China's "African strategy" through the organization of the first FOCAC. This initial meeting has been followed by four more summits, held every three years.[40] The last one was held in December 2015 in Johannesburg.

President Lula Da Silva relaunched Brazil's African policy in 2003. In that year, with the organization in Fortaleza (Brazil) of the "Brazil-Africa Forum", a new era in Brazil-Africa relations was created through an active presidential diplomacy[41]. Under Dilma Rousseff, Africa-related activities have been shared with private actors, such as the Instituto Brasil Africa based in Fortaleza. That approach has involved three summit meetings being organised, in 2012, 2014 and 2015.

A step behind, India's Prime Minister Manmohan Singh met twice with India's African partners, in 2008 and 2011, under the aegis of the India-Africa Forum Summits. In the two latter meetings, the number of African participants was limited to a maximum of 15 heads of state, chosen by the African Union to represent the entire African continent[42]. The third India-Africa Forum Summit was held in October 2015 with the participation of the 54 heads of government of Africa, in a clear attempt to copy China's strategy.

In the case of Russia, despite the fact that in 2002 a Russia-Africa Business Council was created[43] and in 2009 a Coordinating Committee for Economic Cooperation with Sub-Saharan Africa (Afrocom) was organized in 2009, Moscow has lagged behind the other BRICS partners.

South Africa is not only a BRICS member but also a pivotal actor in the African priorities of the other four BRICS partners, with the risk of being used as a hinge in their relationship with the other countries of the continent. With a discourse in which South-South Cooperation is given a privileged place, Pretoria is operating sub-regionally and continentally through policies such as 'Africa Renaissance' and NEPAD (New Partnership for Africa's Development). The country also presents itself as the gateway to the African continent - a hub of the sub-region and the hard core of both at the Southern African Customs Union (SACU) and the Southern African Development Community (SADC)[44].

Each of the GCC countries also has its own new 'enterprises' in Africa. In the case of Kuwait, at the Third Africa-Arab Summit held in 2013, the Amir of Kuwait granted concessionary loans to African countries worth $1 billion. This initiative, for which the Kuwaiti Fund for Arab Economic Development was made responsible, focused on infrastructural projects, which would be implemented in conjunction with the World Bank and other international institutions. It also established an Annual Prize worth $1 million to be awarded by the State of Kuwait for the development of research in Africa conducted under the auspices of a Kuwait scientific development institution[45].

The UAE has also been active, holding the Africa Global Business Forums (AGBF) in Dubai in 2013 and 2014, organized by the Dubai Chamber of Commerce and Industry. The aim of the AGBF in these meetings was to examine five key sectors: agribusiness, trade, logistics, finance and tourism, with a view to growing and expanding cooperation between the UAE and the African continent in these fields. The UAE was projecting itself through this as a gateway to trade and investment flows into and out of the continent[46].

Saudi Arabia has been supporting agricultural partnerships with African countries, notably through the King Abdullah Initiative for Saudi Agricultural Investment Abroad (KAISAIA). Most of the focus has been on Sudan and Ethiopia[47]. Similarly, Qatar's sovereign wealth fund has been investing in East Africa.

At the level of *groupings*, it is contended that this can bring more benefit than an isolated single-country strategy. The BRICS has acted as a grouping in creating the New Development Bank (NDB), conceived as a strategic tool for financing infrastructural and sustainable development projects[48]. The NDB is expected to have a subsidiary in Johannesburg, indicating the attention which would be given to Africa.[49] Yet, BRICS countries clearly operate on the basis of a mixture of competition and collaboration, but it seems that there will be more competition than collaboration here, both with regard to Africa and the GCC.

An example of the GCC acting as a grouping was the signature in 2010 of a memorandum of understanding to enhance commercial and economic cooperation with the Common Market for Eastern and Southern Africa (COMESA)[50]. The GCC member states committed themselves to encouraging their private sector companies to invest in areas such agriculture in Africa[51]. Additionally, the Kuwait Declaration, signed during the Third Africa-Arab Summit in 2013, was framed under the theme "partners in development and investment". Some collaborative mechanisms were initiated by the GCC countries for this, within what they called South-South Cooperation.

The GCC countries are mostly oil exporters, with advanced technology in exploitation and financial capacity. They therefore have the potential to take a lead in creating new cartel formations involving oil-producing African countries to set oil prices, within or outside OPEC.

At the level of *triangular* relationships, BRICS, the GCC and African countries could constitute the three vertices of a cooperative triangle in which the actors (acting individually or in groups) coordinate their bilateral and multilateral strategies so as to complement and support each other's interests. For example, China could act as a hinge and the GCC as platforms of commercial or financial take-off for developing African lands. Or the GCC countries, due to their proximity to Sub-Saharan Africa, could act as hinge to foster China's projects in that continent.

Within this cooperative triangle mutual perceptions and expectations are crucial. China is perceived by Africans as a capital market, a source of investments, a high technology provider and a counterweight to US influence. But China is perceived by the other BRICS differently, as a competitor more than a friendly partner, both in their search for raw materials or in providing manufactured goods. The GCC countries see China as providing opportunities for them to diversify markets for their exports and imports so as to expand their foreign trade. This coheres with the Chinese perspective: the GCC countries are seen as an excellent market to balance its oil dependence, an important financial market, and a platform for Beijing's westward policies to place its multinationals and manufacturing businesses.

The reality for the GCC countries is that they are short on food, but rich in cash. African nations, on the other hand, have fertile land but are short of finance. As ties between the Gulf and Africa strengthen, investment in agriculture is likely to grow. The GCC countries have been investing in African land since 2008 (mainly in Sudan and Ethiopia) with the idea of creating a "reservoir" for their needs in case of food scarcity in the future. Such an approach, however, can pose tough challenges for GCC investors, who mostly lack experience in producing or marketing tropical cash crops and risk finding themselves in direct competition with long-established Sub-Saharan and BRICS players. They need to recruit foreign specialists to establish and run the projects, and the BRICS countries could offer them the 'know how' they need for this.

China's economic expansion, moreover, has an African dimension in its impact on the GCC countries. Beijing considers the Gulf as a linking-point between Asia and Africa. Consequently, some Chinese multinationals are running their African businesses from such GCC cities as Dubai, benefiting from their financial infrastructures and geographical proximity to African countries.

China's largest banks have established offices in the Dubai International Financial Centre, and trading houses use the city as their headquarters for Africa. GCC states have good port and air connections, and it can be easier to fly to African cities from Dubai than from other parts of Africa where air routes are relatively underdeveloped. African air traffic into Dubai's growing city-centre airport grew at 18.2% in 2012 and in 2013 accounted for about 10% of all passengers[52].

Another possible area of cooperation for Sub-Saharan African states and the GCC countries is in the hydrocarbons sector, both in terms of coordination over oil pricing and in GCC technology being used to improve African technological knowledge in the processing of hydrocarbons. Such GCC engagement could also be seen as counterbalancing China's efforts to expand its influence not just in trade but in other areas like infrastructural investment, as has been the case with the telecommunications sector.

BRICS, the GCC and African countries could, therefore, cooperate in a triangular way, taking advantage of the various possibilities offered by this new scenario. Each corner of the triangle would act as part of a transmission belt, enabling the three parties collectively to offer services which would be better than those offered by outsiders.

5. Conclusions

It has to be acknowledged that BRICS and the GCC are in their infancy and it is natural for them to act individually unless they foresee clear benefits from collective action on particular issue areas. Structurally, however, there is no immediate reason why they should be in conflict. The trade and investment patterns that the GCC countries and China have with Sub-Saharan African states are very different. China, as a big emerging power, has the financial capability to sustain a strategic partnership with African nations in multiple forms, as aid projects, loans, grants, FDI, etc. The GCC countries, on the other hand, have only recently re-started their economic engagement in Africa, as a result of the advantageous economic environment they have been experiencing over the past ten years. So, while China has a long-term African strategy, the GCC countries are moved by more short-term impulses.

African countries and China enjoy economic structural complementarities, whereas the GCC and African countries have a competitive economic structure - both are based on natural resources, with hydrocarbons playing a major role. Nonetheless, there remain areas where GCC and African countries can interact positively, as in improving Africa's infrastructure and sharing expertise in the oil industry.

Even though the BRICS and the GCC states have different options it is probable that the "prisoner's dilemma"[53] could be applied here. Despite the possibility of gaining benefits from cooperating, the prisoners - and in this case the groups - will decide to act individually finding it merely difficult or costly to coordinate their activities to achieve consensus.

Assessing the advantages and disadvantages of the three possible scenarios outlined above, the win-win situation for all actors would be a triangular relationship, while the worst option would be for the states to act individually with no group-coordination. Even China, as the major emerging power having the capability to back multiple economic and political strategies in different regions of the world, could benefit from a cooperative context. This is especially relevant in a situation where the forecasts for the second decade of the 21st century are significantly less optimistic on global growth than they were in the first one. An intermediate option for the GCC would be for it to link up with China's African strategy in a new China-Africa-GCC Forum, to benefit from and complement Beijing's activities.

The years to come will show whether these actors are successful in using the present window of opportunity to engage in multiple coalitions, or will behave as "Lone Rangers" – being rivals more than partners.

Notes

1 Susanne Gratius, "The international arena and emerging powers: stabilising or destabilising forces?", *FRIDE* (2008): 4.

2 Maristella Svampa has coined the concept 'Commodities Consensus' opposed to the Washington Consensus to show that it would be a tacit agreement between governments and extractive industries over the persistent extractivist dynamic due to the global increasing demand of raw materials. Under this logic, governments become national guarantors of transnational enterprises assuring better economic conditions in the short-term for the country, which receives them but leaves doubts on when the association will be over. For further information see Maristella Svampa, "El Consenso de los Commodities", *Le Monde Diplomatique* 168 (2013): 5.

3 In recent years, apart from the BRICS (Brazil, Russia, India, China and South Africa), new terms appeared to describe the largest developing countries such as BRICET (BRIC + Eastern Europe and Turkey), BRICM (BRIC + Mexico), BRICK (BRIC + Republic of Korea), Next Eleven (Bangladesh, Egypt, Indonesia, Iran, Mexico, Nigeria, Pakistan, the Philippines, Republic of Korea, Turkey and Vietnam) and CIVETS (Colombia, Indonesia, Vietnam, Egypt, Turkey y South Africa), among others.

4 The GCC is formed by Bahrein, Kuwait, Oman, Qatar, Saudi Arabia and the UAE.

5 We will take into consideration the Sub-Saharan African region which is formed by Angola, Benin, Botswana, Burkina Faso, Burundi, Cape Verde, Cameroon, Central African Republic, Chad, Comoros, Democratic Republic of the Congo, Côte d'Ivoire, Djibouti, Equatorial Guinea, Eritrea, Ethiopia, Gabon, Gambia, Ghana, Guinea, Guinea Bissau, Kenya, Lesotho, Liberia, Madagascar, Malawi, Mali, Mauritania, Mauritius, Mozambique, Namibia, Niger, Nigeria, Republic of the Congo Rwanda, Sao Tome and Principe, Senegal, Sierra Leone, Seychelles, Somalia, South Africa, South Sudan, Sudan, Swaziland, Tanzania, Togo, Uganda, Zambia, Zimbabwe.

6 Jim O'Neill, "Jim O'Neill: BRICs' rapid growth tips the global balance", *The Telegraph*, November 20, 2011. Accessed May 3, 2015. <http://www.telegraph.co.uk/finance/financialcrisis/8902824/Jim-ONeill-BRICs-rapid-growth-tips-the-global-balance.html>.

7 The increasing numbers of exports and imports among the BRICS countries are largely due to Brazil and Russia's supply of the commodities required by China and India. Regarding the impact on the global economy, between 2009 and 2013 BRICS' overall output increased by 60% and during 2014, 20% of global output was generated by the BRICS. Moreover, they have also been piling up foreign exchange reserves. By the middle of 2011, China alone held more than US$3 trillion in foreign exchange reserves, vastly larger than any other country in the world, an increasing factor of concern to the US.

8 Indeed Jim O'Neill has not kept with the concept of emerging markets throughout the years. This is why he has recently stated that the concept of emerging markets could no longer be applied to the BRIC and four of the N-11: Indonesia, Korea, Mexico and Turkey. For him, the term that suits them better is 'Growth markets' because they are "countries with largely sound government debt and deficit positions, robust trading networks and huge numbers of people all moving steadily up the economic ladder".

9 Gladys Lechini, and Clarisa Giaccaglia,"IBSA or BRICS. What is preferable for South Africa and Africa - both or none?" in *Handbook of Africa's International Relations*, ed. Tim Murithi, (London, Routledge, 2013), 389.

10 Karen Smith, "The BRICS Alternative: Implications for Africa and the Global South" (paper presented at the 2014 FLACSO-ISA Joint International Conference, Buenos Aires, July 23-25, 2014).

11 Their first summit was in Yekaterinburg, Russia in June 2009 to discuss economic and financial issues. The second BRICs summit was held in Brasilia in April 2010. By the end of this year [on December 23, 2010], the original acronym was changed by the members' good will when Chinese President Hu Jintao wrote to Jacob Zuma a letter informing him the BRIC's decision to invite South Africa into the group. The third summit was hosted in Sanya in 2011 and the fourth BRICS summit in New Delhi on 29 March 2012, now under the overarching theme of 'BRICS Partnership for Global Stability, Security and Prosperity'. The fifth one took place in Durban in 2013, the sixth one in Fortaleza in 2014 and the latest one in Ufá, Russia, on July 2015, in which was held under the theme "BRICS Partnership – a Powerful Factor of Global Development".

12 Karen Smith, op. cit.

13 Oliver Stuenkel, "Why BRICS matters", *E-International Relations*, March 28, 2012. Accessed May 15, 2015 <http://www.e-ir.info/2012/03/28/why-brics-matters/>.

14 Ornela Fabani, "El Consejo de Cooperación de Estados Árabes del Golfo: un análisis de su evolución a 30 años de su conformación" (paper presented at the V Congreso de Relaciones Internacionales, Octava Jornada de Medio Oriente, La Plata, Buenos Aires, November 24-26, 2010).

15 Despite the good intentions and the fact that economic integration has been on the table of discussions, in the conversations held in 2013 proposing a "Gulf Union", it has not been considered deeply due to individual interests and a limited intra-GCC trade. See more on "Cooperation Council of the Arab States of the Gulf" <http://www.gcc-sg.org/eng/>.

16 "BP Statistical Review of World Energy" (London: BP, 2014), 6-7. Accessed May 22, 2015 <http://www.bp.com/content/dam/bp/pdf/Energy-economics/statistical-review-2014/BP-statistical-review-of-world-energy-2014-full-report.pdf>.

17 Michael Sturm, Jan Strasky, Petra Adolf and Dominik Peschel "The Gulf Cooperation Council Countries Economic Structures, Recent Developments and Role in the Global Economy", *European Central Bank*, Occasional Paper Series 92, (2008): 4. <https://www.ecb.europa.eu/pub/pdf/scpops/ecbocp92.pdf>.

18 Since 2003 the international system has been another commodities prices boom. The GCC members have experienced a dynamic economic development with an annual real GDP growth at around 6-7% on average during the past decade, which enhanced their role in the global economy as investors and trade partners and becoming a hub of global economic growth. See more on Michael Sturm, Jan Strasky, Petra Adolf and Dominik Peschel, op. cit. 6.

19 As it is known, the bulk of GCC countries' exports consist of oil and oil derivatives while their imports are dominated by machinery and mechanical appliances, vehicles and parts, electrical machinery and equipment.

20 Michael Sturm, Jan Strasky, Petra Adolf and Dominik Peschel, op. cit. 6.

21 Kristian Coates Ulrichsen "The Gulf Goes Global: the evolving role of Gulf countries in the Middle East and North Africa and beyond", *Fride and Hivos*, Working Paper 121, (2013): 3. Accessed May 23, 2015 <http://fride.org/descarga/WP_121_The_Gulf_Goes_Global.pdf>.

22 Robert Kappel "Africa: Neither Hopeless Nor Rising", *GIGA Focus*, (2014): 2. Accessed May 16, 2015 <http://www.giga-hamburg.de/de/system/files/publications/gf_international_1401.pdf>.

23 According to the "World Economic Situation and Prospects 2014" report of the United Nations, every Sub-Saharan African countries have been classified as developing nations. At the same time most of them are included in the list of Least Developing Countries (LDC), except Cameroon, Republic of Congo, Gabon, Kenya, Botswana, Mauritius, Namibia, Nigeria, South Africa, Zimbabwe, Cape Verde, Cote d'Ivoire and Ghana. These differences can also be exemplified by the Gross National Income (GNI) per capita of the Southern Sahara richest country which is 83 times than the poorest one. See more on "Africa development indicators 2011", *World Bank*, 2011, 184.

24 The emerging African middle class was defined as those earning between US$2 and US$20 a day in 2010. Africa's middle class is expected to grow from 355 million (34 percent of Africa's population) to 1.1 billion (42 percent of the population) in 2060. At present, about 60% of them – approximately 180 million people – remain barely out of the poor category. Consequently, consumer spending has reached an estimated US$680 billion in 2008, nearly a quarter of Africa's GDP. See more on Mthuli Ncube, "The making of the middle class in Africa", *World Bank*, 2013.

25 Net FDI inflows to Sub-Saharan Africa have increased since 2001 when it was US$15 billion, in 2005 it raised to US$20 billion and in 2011 to US$40 billion, mainly due to China, India and Brazil's FDI. See more on "Africa development indicators 2011", World Bank, 2011.

26 The Economist, "Africa's impressive growth", Daily chart, 2011.

27 World Development Indicators database, World Bank, 18 September 2015, "Gross domestic product 2014".

28 Akyeampong, Emmanuel K. "Africa, the Arabian Gulf and Asia: changing dynamics in contemporary west Africa's political economy", *Journal of African Development* (2011): 11 Accessed July 7, 2015 <http://nrs.harvard.edu/urn-3:HUL.InstRepos:14018060>.

29 Elikia M'Bokolo, Le Continent convoité, **Éd. Études** Vivantes, Paris, 1980, 281.

30 "GCC trade and investment flows", The Economist Insights, *The Economist Intelligence Unit*, 2014. Accessed May 10, 2015 <http://www.economistinsights.com/sites/default/files/GCC%20Trade%20and%20investment%20flows.pdf>.

31 Dominic Dudley, "GCC-Africa trade flows to grow", *MEED*, April 22, 2013. Accessed May 29, 2015 <http://www.meed.com/supplements/2013/africa/gcc-africa-trade-flows-to-grow/3176874.article>.

32 Dominic Dudley, op. cit.

33 The Economist, 2014, op. cit.

34 DP World and Agility of Kuwait are present in ports and terminals; Bin Laden Group (Saudi Arabia) and Kharaf Group (Kuwait) have been building airports and roads; TAQA (Abu Dhabi) is erecting a power plant in Ghana; and Saudi Arabia's ACWA has recently invested in a coal plant in Mozambique, a solar facility in South Africa, and is bidding for plants in Botswana and Namibia. See more on *"GCC trade and investment flows"*, The Economist Insights, The Economist Intelligence Unit, 2014: 16. <http://www.economistinsights.com/sites/default/files/GCC%20Trade%20and%20investment%20flows.pdf>

35 See more on The Economist, 2011, op. cit.

36 Kristian Coates Ulrichsen, "The GCC States and the Shifting Balance of Global Power", *Center for International and Regional Studies*, Georgetown University School of Foreign Service in Qatar, Ocassional Paper N° 6, (2010): 5. Accessed May 4, 2015 <https://repository.library.georgetown.edu/bitstream/handle/10822/558292/CIRSOccasionalPaper6KristianCoatesUlrichsen2010.pdf?sequence=5>.

37 Claire, Provost and Rich Harris, "China commits billions in aid to Africa as part of charm offensive – interactive", *The Guardian*, April 29, 2013. Accessed July 15, 2015 <http://www.theguardian.com/global-development/interactive/2013/apr/29/china-commits-billions-aid-africa-interactive>:

38 BRICS-Africa trade reached US$ 301 billion in 2012 but China-Africa trade reached US$ 169 billion in the same year, accounting for 56% of the BRICS trade with African countries (Standard Bank, "BRICS-Africa trade update, 2013). BRICS countries are significant investors in Africa. Moreover, the BRICS' share in the continent's FDI stock and flows reached 14% and 25%, respectively, in 2010 and China occupied the first place among them in the case of FDI flows (UNCTAD, "The rise of FDI BRICS and Africa", 2011).

39 Such policy also known as "Going Global" explicitly presents China's interest in intensifying its foreign direct investment (FDI). This policy encouraged China's investment projects with potential to 1) enhance natural resources in China; 2) promote exports; 3) ensure the acquisition of specific assets such as technology and management tools; iv) strengthen the competitiveness of Chinese enterprises, as well as their insertion in international markets. See more on UNCTAD, 2006, Agência de Promoção de Exportações, 2012 in Danielly Ramos Beccard, "China diplomacy and trade in Latin America", *Estudos Internacionais*, Vol. 1, N° 2, (2013): 234.

40 More than 80 ministers from China and 44 African countries, representatives of 17 regional and international organizations, people from the business communities of China and Africa were invited to the conference. The conference charted the direction for the development of a new, stable and long-term partnership featuring equality and mutual benefit between China and African countries. The second Ministerial Conference took place in Addis Ababa, Ethiopia, in December 2003, the third one in Beijing, in November 2006, in parallel with a presidential summit, the fourth one was held in November 2009 in Sharm El Sheikh, Egypt and the last one in Beijing in July 2012.

41 President Lula visited the African continent eleven times and twenty eight different African nations.

42 Tim Steinecke, "India's big African opportunity", *The Diplomat,* December 12, 2014. Accessed July 24, 2015 <http://thediplomat.com/2014/12/indias-big-african-opportunity/>:

43 With the participation of 60 businessmen -oil, gas, finance, and tourism-together with high-ranking diplomatic officials and representative agencies.

44 Gladys Lechini and Clarisa Giaccaglia, op. cit. 390.

45 “Kuwait Declaration”, Third Africa-Arab Summit 2013, last modified November 20, 2013. <http://pages.au.int/afroarab/documents/kuwait-declaration>.

46 Hamad Buamim, “Dubai to facilitate African growth”, *MEED*, April 22, 2014. Accessed November 23, 2015 <http://www.meed.com/databank/special-reports/dubai-to-facilitate-african-growth/3176871.article>.

47 Paul Melly, “GCC investors eye African farmland”, *MEED*, April 22, 2013. Accessed November 15, 2015 <http://www.meed.com/databank/special-reports/gcc-investors-eye-african-farmland/3176877.article>.

48 Similar is the case with the Asian Infrastructure Investment Bank (AIIB) created recently as an international financial institution with the initial idea of supporting infrastructure construction in the Asia-Pacific region. This institution will probably turn to Africa too.

49 “Ufa Declaration”, VII BRICS Summit 2015, last modified July 9, 2015. <http://en.brics2015.ru/load/381158>.

50 The member countries of Comesa are Burundi, Comoros, Republic Democratic of Congo, Eritrea, Ethiopia, Kenya, Madagascar, Malawi, Mauritius, Rwanda, Seychelles, Swaziland, Uganda, Zambia and Zimbabwe.

51 “GCC, Comesa sign a MoU on economic cooperation”, *Kuwait news agency,* April 4, 2010. Accessed November 10, 2015. <http://www.kuna.net.kw/ArticlePrintPage.aspx?id=2073386&language=en>.

52 See more on Simeon Kerr, “Dubai becomes centre for Mideast-Africa trade”, *Financial Times,* November 25, 2013. Accessed July 12, 2015 <http://www.ft.com/cms/s/0/30fb31dc-37d6-11e3-8668 00144feab7de.html#axzz3bXHG8r3o>.

53 This model of game theory is often used to illustrate the decisions of two interacting actors under certain conditions. This dilemma presupposes that captives, when faced with the option of cooperating with or squealing one another, will always choose to squeal. In fact, the best option is to cooperate because under these circumstances both of them will be in a win-win situation. Nevertheless, as each prisoner does not know the other’s decision, the best strategy is to “betray” the other. In such a way, if the two captives betray their partner, the result will be worse than if they would have chosen being loyal.

References

Akyeampong, Emmanuel K. “Africa, the Arabian Gulf and Asia: changing dynamics in contemporary west Africa’s political economy”, *Journal of African Development* (2011): 85-115. <http://nrs.harvard.edu/urn-3:HUL.InstRepos:14018060>.

Coates Ulrichsen, Kristian “The Gulf Goes Global: the evolving role of Gulf countries in the Middle East and North Africa and beyond”, *Fride and Hivos*, Working Paper 121, (2013): 1-21. <http://fride.org/descarga/WP_121_The_Gulf_Goes_Global.pdf>.

Coates Ulrichsen, Kristian, “The GCC States and the Shifting Balance of Global Power”, *Center for International and Regional Studies,* Georgetown University School of Foreign Service in Qatar, Occasional Paper N° 6, (2010): 1-27. <https://repository.library.georgetown.edu/bitstream/handle/10822/558292/CIRSOccasionalPaper6KristianCoatesUlrichsen2010.pdf?sequence=5>.

Fabani, Ornela “El Consejo de Cooperación de Estados Árabes del Golfo: un análisis de su evolución a 30 años de su conformación”. Paper presented at the V Congreso de Relaciones Internacionales, Octava Jornada de Medio Oriente, La Plata, Buenos Aires, November 24-26, 2010.

Lechini, Gladys and Giaccaglia, Clarisa, “IBSA or BRICS. What is preferable for South Africa and Africa - both or none?” in *Handbook of Africa’s International Relations*, edited by Tim Murithi, 387-396. London, Routledge, 2013.

M’Bokolo, Elikia, “Le Continent convoité”, **Éd. Études** Vivantes, Paris, 1980: 281.

Sharma, Ruchir, “The ever-emerging markets: why economic forecast fail”, *Foreign Affairs*, January/February (2014). <https://www.foreignaffairs.com/articles/2013-12-06/ever-emerging-markets>.

Smith, Karen, "The BRICS Alternative: Implications for Africa and the Global South". Paper presented at the 2014 FLACSO-ISA Joint International Conference, Buenos Aires, July 23-25, 2014.

Sturm, Michael; Strasky, Jan; Adolf, Petra and Peschel, Dominik "The Gulf Cooperation Council Countries Economic Structures, Recent Developments and Role in the Global Economy", *European Central Bank*, Occasional Paper Series 92, (2008): 1-77 <https://www.ecb.europa.eu/pub/pdf/scpops/ecbocp92.pdf>.

Svampa, Maristella. „El Consenso de los Commodities". *Le Monde Diplomatique* 168 (2013): 4-6.

About the Contributors

Talmiz Ahmad is the former Indian ambassador to Saudi Arabia, Oman and the UAE. He has authored three books: *Reform in the Arab World: External Influences and Regional Debates* (2005); *Children of Abraham at War: The Clash of Messianic Militarisms* (2010), and *The Islamist Challenge In West Asia: Doctrinal and Political Competitions after the Arab Spring* (2013). He writes and lectures frequently on political Islam, the politics and economics of West Asia, and energy security. He is presently based in Dubai as an independent consultant and advises Indian and local companies on business expansion and diversification.

Gafar K. Ahmed is a Sinologist specializing on China's relations with the Middle East and North Africa. He holds a Master's degree from the University of Khartoum, and a Doctorate from Nanjing University. He is a Member of the Institute of Arab-Islamic Cultural Studies of Peking University, and Visiting Scholar at the Middle East Studies Institute of Shanghai International Studies University, and the Institute of Mongolian–Yuan Studies, Nanjing University. He currently works for the Qatar Ministry of Foreign Affairs. He has published extensively on China's policy relations with the Middle East. His most recent work is *Sudan-China Relations 1956–2011* (Centre for Arab Unity Studies, 2016).

Stuti Banerjee is a Research Fellow at the Indian Council of World Affairs, New Delhi. At the Council, she is engaged in research on US and Latin America. Her research interests include nuclear security and risks, Indian foreign policy, US foreign policy, defence and strategic studies. Her articles, such as "The United States and Iran: The Nuclear Deal", "India and the United States: Reinvigorating the 'Energy' Relationship", "United States and Nuclear Pakistan", have appeared in various national journals.

Danielly Silva Ramos Becard is a Fulbright Visiting Scholar at the Sigur Center for Asian Studies at the Elliott School of International Affairs – The George Washington University. She is Associate Professor in the International Relations Institute of the University of Brasilia. She has a major research project on China's Foreign Policy and its political and economic implications for Latin America, with focus on Brazil. Danielly Becard has a Master degree in Political Science - Comparative Politics from Paris 1 University – Panthéon - Sorbonne, France, and a PhD in International Relations from the University of Brasilia, Brazil.

Shanthie Mariet DSouza is President and Founder of Mantraya, Associate Editor for the Journal of Asian Security and International Affairs, expert and contributor to the Middle East-Asia Project at the Middle East Institute, Washington D.C., senior analyst with the Wikistrat Analytic Community, New York, and adviser for Independent Conflict Research and Analysis, London. Her research interests and expertise include: prospects for long term stabilisation of Afghanistan; state building in fragile states; insurgencies and terrorism; regionalism; and India's foreign, aid and security policies. She has also conducted field studies in Pakistan, China, Africa, Jammu and Kashmir and India's North East.

María Noel Dussort is Research Assistant in International Relations at the National University of Rosario, Argentina and a CONICET Phd student. She is a member of the Program on South South Relations and Cooperation (PRECSUR) and responsible for the Indian Studies Group of Rosario (GEIR). She is the author of articles published in various Latin American journals of International Relations concerning issues related to energy security, India, African countries and BRICS.

Nikolay Kozhanov is a Visiting Lecturer in Political Economy of the Middle East at the European University at St. Petersburg (Russia). From 2006 to 2009, he served as an attaché at the political section of the Russian embassy in Tehran where his portfolio included the analysis of the socio-economic situation in the Islamic republic. At the end of his tenure with the Russian Ministry of Foreign Affairs, Dr. Kozhanov continued his research with a special focus on the international relations of modern Iran and the Arab countries of the Gulf. His second book, *Russia's Relations with Iran: Dialogue without Commitments*, was published by the Washington Institute for Near East policy in June 2012. Most recently he published *Russia and the Syrian Conflict: Moscow's Domestic, Regional and Strategic Interests* (Berlin: Gerlach Press, 2016).

Gladys Lechini is Professor of International Relations at the National University of Rosario, Argentina, Senior Researcher at CONICET, Director of the PHD Programme on International Relations and of the Rosario Institute of Studies of the Arab and Islamic World. She is the author of *Argentina and South Africa Facing the Challenges of the XXI Century: Brazil as the Mirror Image* (Rosario, UNR Editora, 2011) and of chapters on Latin America-Africa Cooperation, Brazil as a Case Study (New York, Palgrave Macmillan, 2010); and South Africa's options between IBSA and BRICS. What is preferable for South Africa and Africa- both or none? (Abingdon, Routledge, 2014, with Giaccaglia).

Imad Mansour is Assistant Professor in the Department of International Affairs at Qatar University. His research looks at ideas in governance and foreign policy, regional orders, rivalries and international security relations. His current projects include: theorizing Global South ties from local perspectives and ontologies; and exploring understudied socio-political characteristics of the Middle East, especially societal narratives and tribes. He is the author of *Statecraft in the Middle East: Foreign Policy, Domestic Politics and Security* (London: I.B. Tauris, 2016).

Tim Niblock is Emeritus Professor of Middle East Politics at the University of Exeter, having previous served as Director of the Institute of Arab and Islamic Studies in the University (1999-2005), and Director of the Centre for Middle Eastern and Islamic Studies at the University of Durham (1993-1998). He has also held visiting professorships at Chinese universities. His most recent books (co-edited) are *Asia-Gulf Economic Relations in the 21st Century: the Local in Global Transformation*, (Berlin: Gerlach Press, 2013), *Security Dynamics of East Asia in the Gulf Region* (Berlin: Gerlach Press, 2014), and *The United States and the Gulf: Shifting Pressures, Strategies and Alignments* (Berlin: Gerlach Press, 2015).

Vânia Carvalho Pinto is a tenured Assistant Professor at the Institute of International Relations, in the University of Brasília. She is also an Academic Productivity Fellow (Bolsista de Produtividade) at the Brazilian National Council of Research. She is the author of a number of articles and book chapters focusing particularly on the UAE's nation-building process and foreign policy, as well as on the Gulf more generally. Her current research interests include comparative area studies with a focus on the Gulf and Scandinavian countries' foreign policies, with occasional reference to Latin America; as well as feminism, literature and international relations.

Bibhu Prasad Routray, Director at Mantraya, is a security analyst/ consultant. He previously served as a Deputy Director in India's National Security Council Secretariat, New Delhi and a Visiting Fellow at the South Asia department in the S. Rajaratnam School of International Studies (RSIS), Singapore, where he taught a master's course on India's security policy. Dr. Routray has also worked with various think tanks including the Institute for Conflict Management (ICM), Guwahati, which he headed as Director. He specialises in decision-making, governance, counter-terrorism, force modernisation, intelligence reforms, foreign policy and dissent articulation issues in South and South East Asia.

Degang Sun is Professor in the Middle East Studies Institute, Shanghai International Studies University. His latest articles (with Yahia H. Zoubir) are, "China's Response to the Revolts in the Arab World: A Case of Pragmatic Diplomacy," in *Mediterranean Politics*, and "China's Economic Diplomacy towards the Arab Countries: challenges ahead?" *Journal of Contemporary China*. He is also the co-editor of *Building a New Silk Road: China and the Middle East in the 21st Century* (Beijing: World Affairs Press, 2014).

Tingyi Wang is a PhD candidate of Tsinghua University and currently a Visiting Fellow at the King Faisal Center for Research and Islamic Studies in Riyadh. His research focuses on Sino-Gulf relations, and on political transformations and regional security in the Gulf region. He has been an exchange student at Cairo University and the University of Oxford. Before his work in Saudi Arabia, he was a Visiting Scholar at the University of Cambridge (2013-2014) and the American University of Sharjah (2014-2015).